Software Project Ma....

The management of a software project has been shown to be the number one factor in determining a software development project's success. It has been found that most software projects fail because of poor management. Not surprisingly, most software development managers have not been trained in project management. *Software Project Management: Methods and Techniques* aims to remedy this situation in two ways: familiarizing software developers with the elements of the project management discipline and providing fact-based resources on practicing software project management.

Much like the checklist pilots go through prior to a flight, this book provides a pre-project checklist which enables the software engineering team to review and evaluate an extensive set of technical and sociopolitical risks which will help the software project manager and the team determine the project team's chances of success. This same list and the individual question responses can be used later as part of the project's closeout process helping team members to improve their individual and collective abilities to assess risk.

Intended for both students and software project managers, the book is organized along the lines of the five major functions of a software project manager: planning; scheduling and costing; controlling; staffing; and motivating. The basics of each of these functions are presented in a single chapter. These are followed by a series of narrow topic presentations in the form of appendices that are intended to help solve specific problems that may occur during the conduct of a software project. As in the main portion of the text, the appendices include references that provide an avenue into further detail on the topic. Designed to promote project success, this approach has been taken because software projects are each unique undertakings such that providing a "one size fits all" approach will fail most of the time.

Lawrence J. Peters has a B.S. in Physics, an M.S. in Engineering and in 2002 a Ph.D. in Engineering Management and a CSDP (Certified Software Development Professional). He has applied software engineering technology for more than 50 years in the aerospace, defense, financial, manufacturing and software engineering fields. He authored the first software engineering curriculum published by the ACM and has since developed and implemented software engineering curricula at three universities as well as the syllabus for software project management at three other universities. Throughout his career, he has been a thought leader in the field of software project management and has successfully managed and consulted on dozens of projects as large as $20 million. He currently teaches Software Project Management in English remotely at Universidad Politecnica de Madrid from his office near Seattle, Washington, and has taught that subject at other schools. He has published several papers on the subject.

Software Project Management
Methods and Techniques

Lawrence J. Peters

CRC Press
Taylor & Francis Group
Boca Raton London New York

CRC Press is an imprint of the
Taylor & Francis Group, an **Informa** business

AN AUERBACH BOOK

First edition published 2024
2385 NW Executive Center Drive, Suite 320, Boca Raton FL 33431

and by CRC Press
4 Park Square, Milton Park, Abingdon, Oxon, OX14 4RN

CRC Press is an imprint of Taylor & Francis Group, LLC

ISBN: 978-1-032-77413-8 (hbk)
ISBN: 978-1-032-43057-7 (pbk)
ISBN: 978-1-003-48428-8 (ebk)

DOI: 10.1201/9781003484288

Typeset in Garamond
by SPi Technologies India Pvt Ltd (Straive)

This book is dedicated to the software project managers I have worked for or consulted with whose patience, insights and concerns for the well-being of their team members showed me how success can be achieved in software project management.

Contents

APPENDICES   ADDITIONAL SOFTWARE PROJECT MANAGEMENT RESOURCES

Overview

This book has been developed by incorporating effective project management practices applicable to software engineering without regard to their source. It provides dozens of references throughout. Points made are supported by references in order to provide the reader with a resource with which to do further research. Much like the checklist pilots go through prior to a flight, this book provides a pre-project checklist which enables the software engineering team to review and evaluate an extensive set of technical and sociopolitical risks which will help the software project manager and the team determine the project team's chances of success. This same list and the individual question responses can be used later as part of the project's closeout process helping team members to improve their individual and collective abilities to assess risk. By comparing the responses made before the project began with those made after the project was completed or even cancelled, software engineers and the software project manager can identify risk topics they need to treat more or less critically. This book does not delve into the intricacies of generating source code but instead provides a broad view and many tools to solve specific project management problems rather than a "one size fits all" approach to managing software projects. The title of this text makes a distinction between methods and techniques. A method is a recommended practice based on data, evidence that it is beneficial to the conduct of a software engineering project. A technique is a recommended practice which is beneficial but is not based on data and research. Each method or technique should be viewed as a tool which can be used to address a particular issue(s) rather than a universal solution. Several different types of notations are presented which have been published and have referenced work(s) which can be used to obtain further, more detailed information on their use. A special thank you goes out to those who over the years have contributed in a myriad of ways to the practice of software engineering[1].

Organization of this text

This book is divided into two major sections. The first section is organized according to the five primary functions of software project management (planning; scheduling and costing; controlling; staffing; and motivating) preceded by a risk assessment pre-project checklist.

The final section contains a broad range of methods and techniques associated with the actual conduct and eventual closeout of a software engineering project, maintenance of your software engineering team and other matters related to successfully managing a software engineering effort.

Note

1 Margaret Hamilton, renowned mathematician and computer science pioneer, is credited with having coined the term "software engineering" while developing the guidance and navigation system for the Apollo spacecraft as head of the Software Engineering Division of the MIT Instrumentation Laboratory.

Chapter 1

Introduction to Software Project Management

"Change is the only constant."

–Heraclitus of Ephesus
535 BC–475 BC

1.1 Chapter Overview

The quote that begins this chapter reminds us that as much as software project managers may wish it wasn't true, we have to deal with a continually changing project environment in which nearly everything seems to change in unpredictable, often surprising ways that are not always negative. Software engineering has been in existence for more than 50 years. In that time, there have been incredible developments in computing hardware and a series of software design, programming languages, development methods and environments that, in general, have improved our ability to produce higher quality code and more of it in less time solving ever more complex, challenging problems. One aspect of software development activity that has been seemingly ignored is software project management. For example, there are currently no conferences sponsored by the IEEE Software Engineering Society devoted to the practice of software project management. In fact, the IEEE Software Engineering Society-sponsored annual International Conference on Software Engineering (ICSE) has tracks devoted to many specific topics related to software engineering but not to software project management. This and a lack of available software project management education at the university level have resulted in software project managers having to utilize their own creativity to develop methods and practices which they believe are going to be effective at solving specific problems without the benefit of data to support or refute their assumptions. These practices most often do not benefit from careful measurement of their effectiveness but are utilized anyway. While many software engineers do not recognize the value and benefits of effective software project management, the experience of Google™ [1], studies from IBM [1, 2] and other published material [3] make a compelling case for the recognition and prioritization of the practice of software project management. For example, in the highly acclaimed text "Software Engineering Economics," [4]

DOI: 10.1201/9781003484288-1

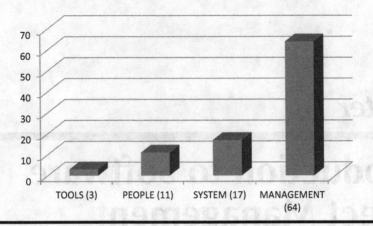

Figure 1.1 Breakdown of factors comprising COCOMO (Constructive Cost Model).

Barry Boehm consciously chose to ignore software project management issues because he assumed "a cadre of competent project managers existed" but later, he found they didn't. Later analysis of Boehm's factors found that those deemed to be related to project management outnumbered all others combined [3] as depicted in Figure 1.1.

This chapter begins by describing the basics of transitioning from software engineer to software project manager. This is a bigger change than many might think. It means moving from a "hard" technology to one that has been described as "soft." This chapter then proceeds to examine software project management starting with a discussion of the nature of software engineers, proceeding to the basic functions of software project management consistent with other models of the practice of project management, a discussion of the role of software development methods and ends with a brief discussion of the reporting that should be done throughout the life of the project and its eventual closeout. Throughout this book, points made are supported by published papers, statistics and/or textbooks both as a reference and a source of further research into the topic for the reader. Conjecture and unsupported statements or advisories are avoided as much as possible.

1.2 Making the Transition from Software Engineer to Software Project Manager

Compared with managing a software project, actually writing the software is relatively straightforward in that there are requirements to be met, programming language syntax and semantics to be observed, tests to pass and so forth. Throughout the development effort, the activities of the software engineer are, in a sense, guided by the stages the software development effort passes through and the software development environment. Software project management activity, except for legal and corporate restrictions, does not have those clear guidelines but relates to a myriad of real and potential issues as evidenced by the large number of single-topic issues listed in the appendices. This can be unsettling for some and can be thought of as being part of the "soft" nature of project management. It is viewed as being "soft" partly because there is no objective measure of whether or not the project manager got anything right until it is too late to correct the misguidance. The remainder of the softness has to do with what most software project managers consider the most difficult and frustrating aspect of their job – personnel issues [5]. Unlike the software engineering role, software project managers are rarely properly prepared for working in this alternative role [6]. This is the result of two factors:

■ Software project management is not a well-defined discipline. The role, activities and senior management's expectations of the software project manager vary from one popular methodology to the next, project to project and company to company and, in most companies, the path from software engineer to software project manager is not clearly spelled out [5]. That may be one of the reasons for the general lack of training in project management among software project managers [5]. Another possible explanation is the widespread lack of knowledge regarding just what it is that software project managers do. For example, advertisements for software project managers often require that the person in this position will be required to contribute to the programming effort. Using the professional sports analogy, it is rare that the manager of a sports team is also a player on that team and the team is successful. Management involves focusing on the five basic functions of project management – Planning, Scheduling, Controlling, Staffing and Motivating [7]. How these are done is an open question in most companies since various authors have proposed a variety of schemes to achieve success in one or more of these areas.

■ If a university software engineering program is offered, training in software project management is most often optional in most graduate and undergraduate programs. A brief survey using repeated Google searches spanning 2016 through 2019 found that worldwide, there are more than 400 software engineering programs at the graduate and undergraduate levels [8]. Of these, less than 10% list software project management as a required course in order to obtain a degree in software engineering while approximately a third do not even offer a course in software project management. This may explain why there is so little understanding among software engineers as to just what software project managers do or should be doing resulting in a broad range of views regarding the value software project managers bring to software projects. Google's experience stands as an impressive, highly successful exception. When the company was founded, the perception on the part of its founders was that managers inhibit innovation so the company started without any managers. Within a short time, the founders realized that management was needed if they were to achieve their goals. They instituted a process for vetting prospective managers, training, performance evaluations and a structure that helped ensure project managers would not micromanage [1].

The fact remains that throughout their career, software engineers are going to be asked management-related questions such as how long an effort will take, how many people may be required and so forth. Without even minimal training in management, they are doomed to failure by relying on what seems reasonable to them with no basis in fact.

1.3 A Change in Perception

"Those who never change their minds never change anything."

–Winston Churchill

There is an adage that "we learn from our mistakes." If that were true, over the last 50 years, software projects should have gotten more and more successful with respect to better cost and schedule predictions, results and quality of deliverables. There have been improvements but not to the extent one would expect through more than a half century of learning. As children and young adults, we recognize that taking an action that results in some form of failure (e.g. not studying for a test) should cause that action or inaction to be called into question and altered. This happens largely because we conclude we are responsible for what happened. But in software project management, a project which fails due to running over budget, delivered late and/or of poor quality can be attributed to many factors (e.g. the schedule was too short, we had to use the Waterfall life cycle, the requirements kept changing and the client was difficult to work with) which enable us to shirk responsibility for failure thereby avoiding learning from the experience [9]. By reviewing the pre-project checklist presented here (Appendix 20), the software project manager and those developing the code get a preview of the kinds of impediments to success that will have to be overcome. The commitment at that point to go forward with the project means that the team is essentially negating the possibility of shirking responsibility for failure because they knew what they were getting into but went ahead with the project anyway.

1.4 Management Styles That Work

Two common hallmarks of management methods that are effective are 1) participation/commitment of the team and 2) the manager is not expected to be the most technologically astute person in the group but, instead, is a remover of obstacles to productivity and success. Examples of these successful styles include [10].

- Manager as "Servant Leader" – a remover of obstacles role, working for the development team as well as leading them.
- *Manager as Negotiator* – communicating between the client and the development team to establish mutually acceptable schedules, task lists and acceptance criteria.
- *Manager as Manager* – The manager is not expected to be the technology expert but does have some knowledge of the domain.

Sometimes, you will inherit a team which contains one or more members whose attitude is "My way or the highway." In other words, they will not compromise or deviate from their own opinion of just what should or should not be done. The most extreme case of this in my consulting practice resulted in the other team members threatening to resign *en masse* if this person was not removed from the project. Fortunately, an independent research position existed in another organization within the firm, a transfer was agreed to by this person and disaster was avoided. When selecting team members, it is advisable to explore their willingness to compromise on technical and procedural issues to avoid situations like this.

1.5 Why Training in Software Project Management Is Important

The lack of training in software project management has resulted in software project managers not seeing the need to review whether or not all the needed elements for a project to be successful are in place prior to project initiation. Again, the pilot analogy comes to mind in that pilots are trained to consider the operational status of all key systems of the aircraft prior to taking flight via a checklist which is executed with the copilot prior to takeoff. The goal of employing such a list is to prevent obvious problems or oversights (e.g. not having the flaps in the takeoff position at takeoff) and to ensure that an unsafe status is not found for a flight critical system. Some of the more obvious undesirable situations that the software project manager should be concerned about include having the development team believe that the project will not be successful, not having the support of senior management [11], having the client prefer a different project manager to conduct this project and others. The point here is that the software project manager is focused on having the project be successful which can result in overlooking one or more important issues which may jeopardize project success.

1.6 Why Teams Don't Learn

Nearly any article or textbook we read these days makes a point that teams need to learn. But they often do not learn very much. We will look at why shortly but first we need to understand the factors that can and do prevent learning. Highly successful companies have striven to become learning organizations and it has rewarded them handsomely. They have also found that learning not only can occur from failure but from success as well. A study of the dynamics of learning in organizations [12] identified four impediments or challenges to organizational learning:

1. Fear of Failure – To some extent, we all fear failure. As a result, we try to avoid situations which we perceive may have a high probability of failure. This fear is often amplified in situations which are highly exposed to colleagues and the upper echelons of the firm. This fear was the cause of a firm I did training at in structured design. A year later, I was hired to do that course again by that firm. I noticed a few of the students had taken the earlier course and I was concerned that I had not done a good job in the previous course. These students told me that their previous manager would not let them use this newer technology. They had since transferred to another group whose manager insisted everyone get trained and use this method. The reason for the suppression of adopting this new method by the first manager was fear of failure. Presumably, that firm had an environment in which failure would penalize a manager but the second manager believed this would work and felt the benefits were worth the risk.

2. A Fixed Mindset – Researchers have found that people's brains react differently to failure. What they found was that the reaction depends on the mindset of a person. They found that there basically are two mindsets which they named "Fixed" and "Growth." People with a fixed mindset believe that intelligence and skills are the result of genetics. You are either born with them or not. People with a growth mindset seek challenges and learning opportunities. They believe that no matter how good one is at performing some tasks, there is always the opportunity to improve.

3. Overreliance on Past Performance – This is a challenge because when hiring, software project managers often put too much emphasis on past performance and not enough on the individual's potential to learn. This often results in performance on the job being less than expected.

4. Attribution Bias – A common phenomenon is for leaders to attribute success to their knowledge, skill and other personal abilities but blame failure on a plethora of factors indicating it wasn't their fault. They fail to recognize that their success may be due to factors that were mere happenstance – luck.

So, how can we best cope with the preceding challenges? Here are some suggested approaches:

■ Destigmatize Failure – Remember, no one seeks to fail. People want to succeed and strive to do so. By making failure what potentially amounts to a career-limiting event, innovation, experimentation and thinking "outside the box" suffer. The environment should be such that failure can be a learning experience which does not penalize the person or the team.

■ Adopt and Teach a Growth Mindset – Researchers have found that software project managers who practice a growth mindset have improved performance in their teams, while the teams led with a fixed mindset do not exhibit this improved performance.

■ Consider Potential when Hiring and Promoting and Making It Known to the Team – A part of the effect of this is to reduce the incidence of the software manager hiring people just like themselves. Experience found that when this is done, greater diversity in terms of race and gender results.

■ Utilize a Data-Driven Approach when Analyzing the Cause(s) of Success or Failure – This is one effective means of combatting the attribution bias cited above [13].

■ Take Time to Think – Plan to take time each day to think about how things went that day or at the start of the day, consider what will be done when and how.

■ Encourage your Team to Reflect upon How Things Went – Whether good, bad or indifferent, encourage the team to freely discuss what could have been done better, what went really well and what changes seem appropriate.

1.7 Is Training Needed?

It is unlikely that persons are born with the skills needed to manage software projects. Hence, training is needed to acquire those skills. The content of that training is discussed throughout this book. However, we do have some data indicating the training that is needed. A study of 2,306 advertisements for project managers [14] provides some insight into what skills companies in various industries are seeking in project managers as well as how desired software project manager skills compare with other industries. Simplified, the results had three relevant findings for software project management:

1. Industry-Specific and Generic Skills – This was the number one requirement. This included knowledge of the technology being used by the prospective project, knowledge of the domain (e.g. computer graphics, gaming and so forth) and knowledge of costing and accounting. It is significant that the software industry was the only one citing a requirement of this type of expertise. This is analogous in the home-building industry to requiring the project manager to be a journeyman carpenter.
2. Communication Skills – This was a close second to industry-specific knowledge. Implying that being able to communicate with stakeholders and others in writing, in person and in meetings was seen as almost as valuable as knowing something about the type of business being engaged in.
3. The Ability to Manage Teams – This one followed numbers 1 and 2 closely indicating recognition by prospective employers that their projects would be complex enough so as to require one or more teams of people to execute them.

People are not born with these skills but, as stated earlier, need to be trained in order to acquire them. Without training, software project managers would be left to their own devices which is were we, as an industry are today. To be fair, other fields such as home construction have existed centuries longer than software engineering. The experience of that industry and others has led to the creation of standardized management practices which, through use over the years, have been continually refined and updated.

1.8 Developing Software Is a "Wicked Problem"

Several decades ago, city planners noted how perplexing it was to try to lay out a new city or reorganize parts of an existing one. Each time they made a change in one area, another area was negatively impacted. On a smaller scale, planners noted that even a single-family home presented the same kind of dilemma. For example, if we are constructing a new home on a fixed budget, we may want to change the plans to accommodate a large window in the living room to take advantage of the view of the surrounding area. This will increase the construction cost requiring us to make one or more other rooms smaller, perhaps to the point where they are not useful. In addition, the cost of heating and/or cooling the home will increase due to the additional heat loss or gain from the window. This may cause us to have to install a larger furnace and air conditioning, at an additional cost. And so, it goes. Each modification causes some other change to accommodate it, resulting in more changes. The class of problems exhibiting this phenomenon has been referred to as, "Wicked" [15]. Software development can also be characterized as a "Wicked" problem. The properties of "Wicked" problems include:

■ They cannot be stated definitively.
■ There is no rule about when one has been solved.
■ They have only good or bad solutions – not "right" or "wrong" ones.
■ They cannot be definitively tested.
■ Solutions to "Wicked" problems are too significant to be experimented with.
■ There is no limit to the number of possible solutions or the means of distinguishing among them.
■ "Wicked" problems are often symptoms of higher-level problems.

Managing the solution to a "Wicked" problem:

■ Changes from one project to the next
■ Requires innovation and patience
■ Can be exasperating at times
■ Often results in "scapegoating" (i.e. blaming others for our inability to solve the problem)

Do any of the preceding sound familiar? Most software project managers have experienced all of the above and more. Yes, software projects are "Wicked" problems! I mention this because I believe it is important for software project managers to realize these seemingly intractable problems encountered in the course of a software project are normal and that the manager is not encountering them because they have failed. A commitment to completing the project as best we can under these circumstances is all we can do but as described above, solving a wicked problem remains beyond our reach.

1.9 Software Project Management as a Process – From Concept to Testing and Release

"If you don't see everything you do as a process, you don't know what you are doing."

– **W. Edwards Deming**

While the preceding statement may seem harsh to some, it is never the less true. And that statement is particularly true in the practice of software project management. In Appendix 20 we will present a list of statements that constitute a checklist of potential risks to be considered before the software project begins and used as part of the project closeout when it ends with the goal of comparing what we foresaw at the start with what we actually experienced during the project. That practice executed on each software project should result in improvement in the software engineering team's risk-assessment capabilities over time. But before we get to that list, we will examine the nature of the people, the software engineers, who will actually be doing the software development. It should be noted that the software project manager will not be doing any of the actual source code development but will be collaborating with the software engineers to plan and schedule what will be coded. As you will see throughout this book, the software project manager has too much to do to be able to devote any significant time to coding. Besides, managing the software engineering effort is a very different mindset from writing code. A high-level overview of the process of managing a software project is presented in Figure 1.1.

The notation used in Figure 1.2 will be used elsewhere in this text and requires some explanation. Moving from left to right, the major stages in the project management process go from the start of the project to its end or closeout. The left edge of the figure lists the primary participants in the project with lanes (sometimes referred to as "swim lanes") containing the activity the participant is responsible for. For example, in the Requirements Definition phase, the team members and analysts are responsible for generating the measurable objectives, use cases, and so forth. It should be noted that the figure may not correlate well with the software development life cycle you or your firm currently use as a standard as well as the participant list and content of each phase. The figure is presented to provide an example of what you can do to portray just one software development process leaving you free to portray some other as you may wish.

1.10 The Nature of Software Engineers

More than 50 years ago, most software engineers were people who had started their collegiate and/or professional studies in fields other than software development. Many came from fields not related to science, technology, engineering or mathematics. This apparent anomaly attracted the attention of two psychologists [16] who wondered just what was it that caused people from so many diverse career paths to switch to software development. In my career alone, I have worked with software developers who started their careers in musicology, library science, engineering, psychology, theoretical nuclear physics and others as well as some who taught themselves how to program. In fact, one of these self-taught individuals is one of the best five software engineers I have ever worked with in more than 50 years. In order to identify what it was about software development that attracted so many different professionals, the psychologists put together a study which examined 60 different professions. What they found was that software people were unique among the professions studied. They had two characteristics which distinguished them:

- High Growth Needs Strength (GNS) – The need to solve difficult or challenging problems
- Low Social Needs Strength (SNS) – The preference to work to solve these problems alone

These characteristics hardly seem to describe someone who would be easy to manage since many software engineering projects require multiple software engineers to work as a mutually supportive team to bring it to a successful conclusion. As we shall see later in this text, there are ways we can overcome this reluctance to work in a collegial manner to ensure an effective team effort and how some well-meaning management practices intended to mold a group of software engineers into a

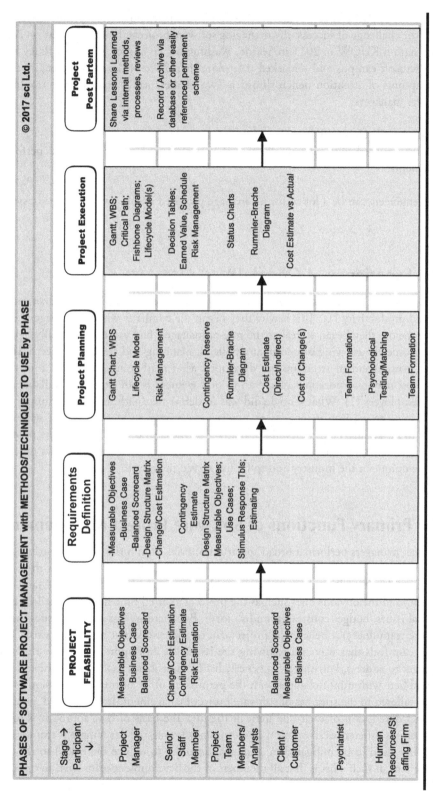

Figure 1.2   A simplified model of software project management.

team can have the opposite effect. There are other characteristics possessed by software engineers which add to the challenge of successfully managing software projects. In an interview on National Public Radio station KUOW in 2011 in Seattle, Washington, co-author [17] John Ratey had just visited the Microsoft campus and remarked that more than 70% of the software engineers there exhibited symptoms of attention deficit disorder. Two of these can be particularly troubling for software project managers:

■ They continually change their code to improve it.
■ Not being satisfied with their code even if it passed all required tests and performance requirements.

Yes, software engineers can be a lot of fun to manage provided we are aware of the idiosyncrasies they possess.

1.11 The Experience at Google™

Some years ago, when Google was founded, its founders were convinced that managers would stifle innovation and productivity [1]. This is why they began the company without managers. It didn't take very long before they began to realize the role of managers had value and actually helped the company to prosper by carrying out company policies, planning and steering projects. They not only installed a management structure but developed what may be unique in the industry. For example, in most major corporations, the path to management is not explicitly available to non-management employees [1]. What Google did was to define that path, create a training program for people wanting to get into management, a screening process to identify people who had the qualifications to be a manager and establish a policy that those who went through the process and into management but then decided it wasn't for them would not be penalized. This process and system may be unique in the industry and so far has served them well.

1.12 The Primary Functions of Software Project Management

Software project managers perform a broad spectrum of tasks from hiring and evaluating software engineers to presenting project status to clients and much, much more. Throughout the course of the project, they identify risks and strategize to avoid or eliminate them altogether. Many of these risks go well beyond the obvious ones such as the project's allotted time flow, the needed technical skills, technical issues, budget constraints and so forth. But there are less-obvious issues they must consider. If the team does not believe the project can be successful, that represents a risk. Finding out why the team feels that way and resolving the issue(s) is an important task for the software project manager to address. Fortunately, a generic list of these issues has been published [18] and is being reused here with minor changes with the permission of its authors. The version presented here has been tailored to the specifics of software project management. It is presented in Appendix 20 with a brief description of each line item in the list. The basis of that approach is to ensure there are no serious differences in opinion or viewpoints among the development team members. If there are, they need to be mitigated in some way in order to reduce the risk(s) to the project. One big advantage of such a list is that all members of the development team have an opportunity to contribute what they see as a risk. Those multiple viewpoints will most certainly identify more issues than the single viewpoint of the software project manager. If we look at what software project managers do, we can break their responsibilities and actions down into five broad categories, as described below.

1.12.1 Planning

This occurs once we have agreed to a set of requirements. In fact, it often occurs while the requirements are still evolving because requirements' definition is truly a discovery process because we "discover" what a statement means while our understanding of it evolves over the course of the project. The plan lists what needs to be done. That is, the tasks and subtasks that must be successfully completed in order for the project to be completed. This is done in collaboration with the client and the team. Some have claimed that planning and scheduling are the same [19] – they are not. Planning delineates what will be done while scheduling details how it will be done. Although it is closely related to the scheduling of the project, planning and scheduling are not the same activity [7].

1.12.2 Scheduling (and Costing)

This activity estimates the amount of time each task and subtask will take to complete, when it should start and when it needs to be finished. It is also done in collaboration with the team since they will be doing the work. It includes identifying the critical path. It is referred to as the critical path because any delay in the start or completion of tasks on the critical path will cause the project to finish late. If you are using project management software (e.g. Microsoft Project™), then that software will identify the critical path for you. The associated cost of each task is estimated to arrive at a total.

1.12.3 Controlling

A tracking method is used to determine project status. Whatever method is used must be objective since we are often biased to believe the project is in a better state than it really is. Earned Value Management (EVM) is employed in this text as it enables us to objectively compare what we planned to do with what we actually did and are doing at any point in time [20]. It also has an additional benefit whereby, based on our rate of spending and completing tasks, it projects forward in time estimating our final costs and completion date.

1.12.4 Staffing

It may not always be the case that we can select our team. Often, the team already exists and we are tasked with managing it for a specific project. Building a team from nothing or revising an existing one is a challenging task. What we are looking to create is a group of people who can work together as a mutually supportive group. Together, they effectively constitute a virtual "super software engineer" capable of solving software issues a single software engineer is unlikely to resolve. Throughout the staffing activity, it is vital to keep in mind that the quality of results is free [21]. Yes, free. This is because psychologically high-technology people want to produce results they can be proud of. This is a particularly strong motivation among software engineering professionals because the results of their work may be more closely related to them as an extension of themselves than any other profession [22]. That relationship is particularly strong because the software engineer is, essentially, the sole creator of the content and quality of the software they are responsible for. Psychologically, if the code is flawed, since it is an extension of the software engineer, then the software engineer is flawed [23]. This may also explain the difficulty many software engineers have in finding and correcting their own programming errors. They subconsciously believe they and what they produce are unflawed. When a software bug occurs, they can have difficulty seeing the problem. A symptom of this is when a colleague looks at the troublesome code, they spot the problem quickly. Why? Because the code is not theirs and does not represent evidence that the colleague is flawed. In the early days of computing, the software engineer was lucky to get one submission and result per day. As a result, they carefully examined their code before submitting it to prevent delays in getting their assigned work done. Today's high-speed remote entry means the software engineer can get several submissions in a day and, in a sense, let the computer do the debugging. Whether this is an improvement over the previous program entry scheme depends on the care with which the code is examined before it is submitted – a case of self-discipline.

1.12.5 Motivating

Anecdotally, I have observed that unmotivated software teams tend not to be as proficient as motivated ones. The problem for the software project manager is that not everyone is motivated by the same management actions. However, we now know enough about software engineers that a small set of actions by the software project manager will work for everyone on the team [11].

1.13 Summary

Much of what is presented throughout this book may challenge many of your beliefs, what you may have heard from others and conclusions about software engineering and software project management. That is why points made have references to published studies by others and are explored in much more detail in the chapters that follow. This provides you with an opportunity to research a topic further to confirm if the researchers involved did their work correctly and if their findings are applicable to your situation. Read on – new and fact-based information on software project management awaits you.

1.14 Additional Resources

The appendices listed in Table 1.1 provide additional, narrow-focus, single-topic material you may need in managing a software project. For the most part, the topics are discussed briefly but each appendix provides references where more detailed discussions can be accessed. There are a broad range of topics because unlike coding, software project management issues are somewhat unbounded with a wide range of topics from how software engineer's brains react to various situations to managing risk. A list of these appendices with a brief description of what each contains from a software project management viewpoint is presented in Table 1.1.

Table 1.1 Additional Resources

Appendix	Title	Content
1	A Word from Our Sponsor – The Brain	Discussion of studies on how the brain impacts the quality and productivity of software engineers' work
2	Basics of Negotiation	Nearly every aspect of a software project must be negotiated – here are some pointers on how to
3	Brainstorming	How to get the best results when the team tries to use their collective knowledge to solve a problem
4	Characteristics of Successful High-Technology Teams	A study of successful high-technology teams provides data on forming them to be successful
5	Computing the Cost of a Change	Changes are inevitable but estimating their cost may make a huge difference in budgeting & success
6	Developing a Business Case	Almost nothing happens in the industry without a business case to justify it – the basics are here
7	Developing a Project Closeout Plan	Planning how to close down a project can have long term multiple benefits for the firm
8	The Effect of Cultural Differences (on Software Development Teams)	Today's software teams are composed of multiple cultures offering unique challenges and benefits
9	Emotional Intelligence	The effectiveness of management can be eroded by immature behavior
10	Environmental Factors Affecting Productivity	Studies found the workspace in which code is developed impacts the quality and quantity of results
11	How Software Project Managers Are Evaluated	Knowing the balancing act needed to be successful is one key to surviving as a software project manager
12	How to Run Effective Meetings	Meetings are conducted all the time during the project – how to keep them from being wasteful
13	Ishikawa (Fishbone) Diagrams	This highly effective diagramming technique helps to pinpoint the source of errors
14	Knowing When it Is Time to Cancel a Project	Not all projects remain viable from start to finish and can reach a point where continuing is impossible

(Continued)

Table 1.1 (Continued)   Additional Resources

Appendix	Title	Content
15	Lying and Software Projects	For many reasons, some managers assumed lying would save the day but it doesn't
16	Managing Multiple Generations	Perhaps for the first time in modern history, multiple generations working together creates issues/benefits
17	Outsourcing (Offshoring)	Originally, this practice provided both promise and savings but it should be engaged in carefully
18	PERT [Program Evaluation Review Technique]	PERT is a method developed for the first nuclear submarine program with great success
19	Planning using Integrated Cost and Schedule Work Packages	This method integrates cost and schedule into a notation making project status clearer
20	Pre-Project Launch Checklist	Much like a pilot's pre-flight checklist, this list elicits feedback from team members to ensure readiness
21	Putting Pressure on the Team Can Reduce Productivity	Some managers believe that pressuring the team will increase productivity but the opposite occurs
22	Reducing Affinity Bias	Although it is natural to hire team members who are just like us, it does not result in a productive team
23	Risk Management Methods	Managing risk must be a high priority. Multiple methods to do this are explored
24	Software Project Management Antipatterns	Some actions taken by the manager are intended to help matters but don't – they are antipatterns
25	Software Project Managers	The nature and characteristics of software project managers are examined with their effectiveness
26	Software Engineering Ethics	Unknown to many in the software profession, a code of ethical behavior was developed decades ago
27	Technical Debt – The Ultimate Productivity Killer	This may be the ultimate productivity killer and a prime example of an antipattern
28	Transitioning from Software Engineer to Software Project Manager	Moving from software engineer to software project manager involves much more than a new job title

(*Continued*)

Table 1.1 (Continued)   Additional Resources

Appendix	Title	Content
29	Why Smart People Make Dumb Decisions	The reasons for this phenomenon vary but one key pattern is consistent which you can overcome
30	Why Software Engineering Teams Should Be Kept Intact	Only if a software team is kept intact do they form what amounts to a collective knowledge base
31	Why We Don't Learn from Success	While we should learn from success – we don't. Here is how to avoid that phenomenon
32	Stoplight Charts	Developed by one of the most successful managers in the world, this method helps control issues
33	The Theory of Constraints	This method is based on the notion that there exists one or more impediments to maximizing productivity
34	Documenting the Undocumented	Many legacy systems are undocumented and being maintained by people who will be retiring soon
35	Making Documentation Transparent	Documenting code has always been an issue. This discussion shows how it can be made part of coding
36	Capability Maturity Model (CMM)	While beneficial, what level of CMM represents the most cost effective?
37	Motivation Basics	Unmotivated teams perform 40% below motivated ones – here is how to motivate your team

Chapter 1 Review Questions

1 Is the subject and practice of software project management, and its development actively supported by the IEEE Software Engineering Society? Explain your answer.

2 Name at least two of the cost-factor categories which comprise the COCOMO methodology.

3 How does the management of software projects differ from that of writing code?

4 In what way does one's viewpoint in moving from being a software engineer to a software project manager?

5 When Barry Boehm developed COCOMO and later its successor, he assumed he did not have to consider software project management because he assumed a cadre of competent software project managers existed. What did a later analysis of COCOMO variables show?

6 How could the transition from software engineer to software project manager be best conveyed?

7 What is the most effective leadership style and how does it work?

8 Do software project managers need to be trained for their leadership role?
9 What keeps teams from learning if they have been successful?
10 In what way can software development and its management be characterized as "wicked?"
11 Name two personality characteristics that make software engineers unique among professionals and a challenge to manage.
12 What was unique about the experience at Google? What can we learn from it?
13 Name the five primary functions of software project management.

References

[1] Garvin, D.A., "How Google Sold Its Engineers on Management," *Harvard Business Review*, December, 2013.
[2] Gulla, J., "Seven Reasons Why IT Projects Fail," *IBM Systems Magazine*, February, 2012.
[3] Weinberg, G., *Quality Software Management*, Volume 3: Congruent Action, Dorset House Publishing, New York, 1984, pp. 15–16.
[4] Boehm, B., *Software Engineering Economics*, Prentice-Hall, Englewood Cliffs, NJ, 1984, pp. 486–487.
[5] Katz, R., "Motivating Technical Professionals Today," *IEEE Engineering Management Review*, Vol. 41, No. 1, March, 2013, pp. 28–37.
[6] Tarim, T., "Making a Transition from Technical Professional to …," *IEEE Engineering Management Review*, Vol. 10, No. 3, September, 2012, pp. 3–4.
[7] Peters, L. and Moreno, A., "Enriching Traditional Software Engineering Curricula with Software Project Management Knowledge," co-author, *International Conference on Software Engineering, Conference on Software Engineering Education and Training (CSEET)*, May, 2016, Austin, TX.
[8] Peters, L., unpublished results of Google searches worldwide of universities offering software engineering degrees, 2020–2022.
[9] Myers, C.G., Staats, B.R. and Gino, F., "My Bad! How Internal Attribution and Ambiguity of Responsibility Affect Learning from Failure," Harvard Business School Working Paper 14-104, April 18, 2014.
[10] Linger, K.R., "Job Satisfaction among Software Developers," Doctoral Dissertation, Walden University, May, 1999.
[11] Thamhain, H., "Team Leadership Effectiveness in Technology-Based Project Environments," *IEEE Engineering Management Review*, Vol. 36, No. 1, 2008, pp. 165–180. College, Cambridge, UK.
[12] Gino, F. and Staats, B., "Why Organizations Don't Learn," *Harvard Business Review*, November, 2015.
[13] Catmull, E., "How Pixar Fosters Collective Creativity," *Harvard Business Review*, September, 2008.
[14] Chipulu, M., Neoh, J.G., Udechukwu, O. and Williams, T., "A Multidimensional Analysis of Project Manager Competencies," *IEEE Transactions on Engineering Management*, Vol. 60, No. 3, August, 2013, pp. 496–505.
[15] Rittel, H.W.J. and Weber, M.M., "Dilemmas in a General Theory of Planning," Institute of Urban and Regional Development, Working Paper No. 194, Berkeley, CA, University of California, November 1972.
[16] Couger, D.J. and Zawacki, R.A., *Motivating and Managing Computer Personnel*, Wiley-Interscience, New York, NY, 1980.
[17] Hallowell, E. and Ratey, J., *Driven to Distraction: Recognizing and Coping with Attention Deficit Disorder*, Anchor Publishing, 2011.
[18] Maylor, H.R., Turner, N.W. and Murray-Webster, R., "How Hard Can It Be? – Actively Managing Complexity in Technology Projects" Research-Technology Management, July-August, 2013, pp. 45–50. [Used here with the permission of the authors].
[19] McConnell, S., "The Software Manager's Toolkit," *IEEE Software*, July/August, 2000.
[20] Fleming, Q.W. and Koppelman, J.M., *Earned Value Project Management*, 4th edition, Project Management Institute, Newtown Square, Pennsylvania, 2010.
[21] Cosby, P., *Quality Is Free – The Art of Making Quality Certain*, Mentor Books, New York, NY, 1980.
[22] Weinberg, G.M., *The Psychology of Computer Programming*, Van Nostrand Reinhold, New York, NY, 1971.

Chapter 2

Planning Software Projects

"People don't like to plan – planning is unnatural – it is far more fun to just do. And the nice thing about just doing is that failure comes as a complete surprise. Whereas, if you have planned, the failure is preceded by a long period of despair and worry."

–Sir John Harvey Jones

"Plans are nothing, planning is everything."

–Dwight D. Eisenhower

2.1 Chapter Overview

Planning is needed in any significant activity in order to better ensure success. This chapter presents several life cycle models which have been used as part of the planning process. It also presents the means by which your plan can be refined to minimize flow time and reduce unanticipated negative side effects. Some software tools which can provide automated assistance with the many changes that will occur over the course of the project are also discussed. The planning activity involves much more than planning the programming effort. It includes laying out how we plan to establish and maintain effective communication between ourselves and our clients. This aspect is also presented.

2.2 The Nature of Planning

From the very start of the planning process, the initial plan and subsequent revisions must be done as a team – the software engineering manager together with the software engineers. In this way, it becomes the team's plan and not just yours resulting in a commitment to see that it works. This is vitally important to the success of the project as changes will be ongoing throughout the lifespan of the project. The quote by Eisenhower that begins this chapter needs some explanation. General Eisenhower is not suggesting that we do not plan. What he is stating emphatically is that planning is an ongoing, continual activity. During software projects, there will be events which occur that were not planned for, but which impact the project negatively or positively. This requires

DOI: 10.1201/9781003484288-2

replanning in order to meet the project's schedule, satisfy new or modified requirements, adjust the delivery schedule due to a particularly troublesome bug that took an inordinate amount of time to track down and correct as well as other events. In a very real way, the project plan is a work in progress throughout the life of the project. This is why it is vital that open, honest and effective communication be established and maintained throughout the life of the project. This includes keeping and maintaining an *extemporaneous* log during the project for later review and to identify lessons learned for use in future projects. This chapter discusses project planning for the tasks that the project entails, the communication plan and the best management style with which to manage software projects in that order.

2.3 Blaming and Software Development Life Cycles

If the aphorism, "We learn from our failures" was true, the software engineering community should be quite knowledgeable regarding how to be successful but failures continue. In order to learn from a failure, two conditions must be present:

- We accept that it is a failure and do not deny that a failure has occurred.
- We accept responsibility for the failure.

Unfortunately, some software project managers have blamed the failure of their projects on a broad range of factors [1] including:

- The client was difficult to work with.
- The requirements kept changing.
- We did not have enough people on the team.
- We did not have the skills on the team to be successful.
- We were required to use the Waterfall life cycle.

And on and on it goes. There is a litany of reasons for failure none of which included mismanaging the effort [1]. It should be noted that a study by IBM [2] of failed projects found that 53% failed due to "poor management" while 3% failed due to "technical challenges." None of the failures were attributed to using the wrong life cycle – specifically, the Waterfall life cycle. As far as I have been able to determine, the role of the software development life cycle (SDLC) in the success or failure of a software project has not been subjected to scientific scrutiny. There are as many SDLCs as there have been software projects because there is no "standard" life cycle used in software projects. This lack of standardization is not, necessarily, a negative because of the frequent uniqueness of each software development effort. The most common aspect of all SDLCs is that they begin with figuring out what needs to be done (e.g. requirements definition) and end with code development and project closeout. It might be appropriate for us to briefly discuss what an SDLC is before reviewing some of those available.

2.4 A Typical Software Development Life Cycle

As noted above, there is no one "standard" SDLC but several have been published. There are many reasons for this. One major one is the differences that exist between software projects combined with the independent nature of software engineers. The software projects that will employ a life cycle range from brand new ventures to major upgrades to existing, working systems, simple to complex and so forth. In spite of the broad spectrum of project types, they all have some features in common. They all start with an idea of what the software project will produce that gets refined into some functionality which then gets turned into source code is tested and finally gets put into use. A search on the internet will yield many different SDLC models each of which is purported to be the best. One thing many of the life cycle models agree on is the number of stages or phases – each consists of four to seven. Although the names of these phases differ from author to author, the typical phase list looks like:

- Planning – Laying out a high-level view of the tasks and subtasks required to bring the system into existence. Excellent guidance on this has been published free by the National Aeronautics and Space Administration (NASA) [3].
- Scheduling (and Costing) – Detailing how long each task and subtask will take and its estimated cost in terms of labor and other resources.
- Designing – Developing a detailed blueprint of the system to be built.
- Implementing – Turning the design into code.
- Testing – Applying software testing principles to detect and remove coding errors.
- Deploying – Releasing the software for use.
- And over the longer term, support and maintenance.

Beyond the preceding, there may be many upgrades to accommodate unforeseen usage issues as well as to correct errors that were not found during testing. Some changes that need to be made are due to changes in user behavior patterns, laws and other circumstances which we cannot predict.

2.5 The Planning Fallacy

Most software project managers are well aware of the poor record of software projects with respect to projects' overrunning schedules and budgets. The estimates on projects of all kinds reflect over optimism resulting in flow time estimates being overly optimistic. Similar comments apply to cost estimates. The reasons for this were not well understood until research work by two psychologists, Kahneman and Tversky [4], over a 20-year period revealed the forces at work. The question they sought to answer was, "Mankind has been building roads and bridges for more than 2,000 years, why can't we estimate their cost and development time more accurately?" What they found is that humans are not able to predict accurately. This is discussed in more detail in the work of Kahneman and Tversky [4]. Being aware of Brooks' observation that adding people to a late project makes it later, some software project managers increase their allocation of personnel beyond what they reasonably expect they will need in order to decrease their chances of the project running late. This seems reasonable but as it often happens, reality is not what seems reasonable. The fact is that there is a law of diminishing returns when it comes to building an overly large project team on a high-technology project in order to shorten execution time [5]. The advantage of keeping the team size down to what is reasonable reduces cost. This can be particularly true if the people comprising the team are people you have worked with before so the team members are confident they can work with each other and get the job done in the time allocated. But this still may not result in an on-time delivery. Much of this failure to deliver on time within budget lies not in the technology employed but in the software project manager's relationship with the team. We know that open, honest communication and a collegial atmosphere work toward success [6] but given the belief held by many software engineers that the software project manager must be the most technically astute person on the team, establishing such an environment can be a monumental task. Solving this problem requires that software engineers be educated in at least the basics of what software project managers do and their importance to a project's success. For example, how many software engineers and software engineering educators are aware that a study of failed software projects by IBM found that 53% of the failures could be attributed to "poor management" while 3% could be attributed to "technical issues?" The fact is developing software is a human endeavor requiring "soft" (i.e. nontechnical) skills to guide the work to success. Few firms have recognized this and acted on it but those that have (e.g. Google) have benefitted greatly [7].

2.6 Estimating Tools and Methods

Over the history of software engineering, dozens of methods for estimating software projects have been developed and published. Their authors seem to presume that their method works better than others or why publish it in the first place? The ironic part of all of this is that nearly two decades of research has shown that human beings are incapable of estimating accurately [4]. The research was prompted by the curiosity of two psychologists as to why major projects like rail lines, tunnels and highways overran their estimates by significant amounts when mankind has been building roads, bridges and tunnels for millennia. Their research took place over nearly 20 years and resulted in a Nobel Prize in Economics in 2002.

What they found was that two factors are at work when humans make estimates on complex efforts:

- Overconfidence – When we estimate, we project our skills or our team's skills with respect to solving the problems we are likely to encounter. Inevitably, we perceive our abilities to be better than they really are to the extent that we will be able to successfully complete the task(s) at hand in a reasonable amount of time.
- Overoptimism – While estimating, we foresee the benefits of the completed project to be so great that we are blinded to the risks involved which may jeopardize the project. While this positive attitude is necessary, its effects set us up for failure.

Apparently, these findings, as surprising as they may seem, have been ignored by many in the software engineering community as books and papers continue to be published regarding how to do a better, more accurate job of estimating the cost and duration of software projects. However, there is a method for correcting these erroneous estimates. It is called Reference Class Forecasting [8] and is presented in Chapter 3. I present other estimating methods as well in this text because you may not have collected the data needed to use Reference Class Forecasting and need that data to arrive at an estimate for a project. These additional estimating methods are presented in Chapter 3.

2.7 Some Alternative Software Development Life Cycles

Since there is no "standard" SDLC, this has led to a plethora of life cycle models being published with each implying it is the best. In a very real sense, each software development project is unique in significant ways resulting in a life cycle that is unique. Here are five examples which are neither the best nor worst but are in use in various sectors of the software engineering industry.

2.7.1 The "Waterfall" Life Cycle

It was somewhere between 1910 and 1915 that Henry Gantt created the first bar charts to show a project schedule. It was the beginning of Gantt charts, but it definitely wasn't the end. The first precursor to these charts actually occurred back in 1896, with Karol Adamiecki, who called them harmonograms. The Gantt chart has been used on a broad range of project applications, including Agile [10] and methodologies. Keep in mind that the intent of the Gantt chart is to visualize the tasks, timing and hierarchy that comprise our project, it is not a methodology. It is listed here because it is so widely used and because it has proven itself to be a means of documenting our project plans at whatever level of detail we wish to convey. Here are some useful guidelines for generating Gantt charts keeping in mind the project plan will undergo nearly continuous change over the course of the project:

- Breakdown the project into major phases or stages at a high level in coordination with the contractual obligations of the project utilizing the decomposition guidelines described in [3]. This includes both the overall project schedules and the planned release schedule.
- Identify critical points which could impact the overall project schedule. These are referred to as the "critical path" and incorporate how these will be tracked and communicated to the various stakeholders. If you are using project management software (e.g. Microsoft Project), these systems will identify and report on the critical path for you.
- At least initially, provide date ranges rather than fixed dates because the various dates will change not only as the project proceeds but as our understanding of the amount of work involved becomes more accurate.

An example of a Gantt chart generated using Microsoft Project™ is presented in Figure 2.1.

Figure 2.1 was created using Microsoft Project with some enhanced features. These include the status or "stoplights" in the left-hand column indicating red, yellow or green corresponding to behind schedule, in danger of falling behind or on time, respectively. Unlike some simple Gantt drawing tools, Project provides an extensive suite of features enabling you to build in automatic increases in various costs, automatic computation of Earned Value management parameters and many other features which enable your plan to more accurately reflect project status.

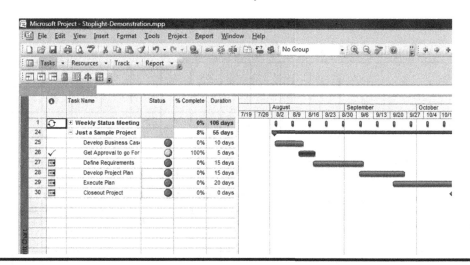

Figure 2.1   Example of a Gantt chart.

2.7.2 *The Agile Life Cycle*

The concept upon which Agile is based [9] was predated by an experiment conducted at IBM's Thomas J. Watson Research Center in the early 1980s [10]. The experiment involved applying a simple concept, "code a little, test a little." In that experiment, some features were developed, users were invited to use the partially developed system and provide feedback regarding errors and needed refinements. The development team proceeded to make the indicated corrections and added more features going through this process repeatedly. The team found that this early, continuous testing resulted in a final result that was quite stable, contained few bugs and reflected user preferences better than their previous approaches. Today, the Agile approach to software development has been refined as original concept and, to some extent, codified it. Classes, papers, textbooks and workshops exist which promote the use of this method. In it, the development team commits to implementing specific "stories" (features) over the next period (typically 2 weeks). Two weeks is typical because that is the longest period that people can confidently know what it is they will be doing. This is much more reliable than predictions involving months or years into the future. The team reviews what they did achieve and if they did not complete all the stories originally planned try to identify why and reschedule them. Table 2.1 shows a simplified chart of projected story counts. This can be an effective means of reducing the overestimation of capabilities Kahneman and Tversky [4] cited because team members begin to learn how to prevent overestimating their possible achievements. Regardless, by having testing throughout the development effort the number of errors delivered in the final product is reduced and since the users were involved from the start, they psychologically identify with the system as theirs contributing to the acceptance of the final system. There are some precautions that should be taken when using this life cycle and accompanying methodology:

- It requires a mature development team. Otherwise, it can result in early-on (runaway) coding.
- There is a learning curve involved as people discover how to more accurately they can commit to versus what they can actually accomplish.
- Independent verification of the benefits of this methodology by those not involved in its promotion may not have occurred.

Table 2.1 A Simplified Agile Stories Completion Table

Analysis												
Design												
Implementation												
Time Period	1	2	3	4	5	6	7	8	9	10	11	12
No. of Stories Proposed	50	40	40	60	70	45	65	50				
Number of Stories Done	50	35	30	43	54	39	65	50				
Number of Stories Remaining	0	5	10	17	16	6	0	0				
End Date in Period												

A simplified version of a chart of stories described and scheduled is presented in Table 2.1.

I have left the dates of the periods out in order to focus attention on the stories. This is a very simplified example. Dates have been left out as well as the identification of each of the stories. In actual practice, the order in which the stories would be addressed would be an important part of the overall project plan so that the features are developed in an order such that the functionality that is needed is present when it is needed instead of an uncoordinated development of stories in a chaotic manner. In speaking to those who have or are currently using Agile, it appears the way of estimating it in terms of cost and flow time is to break the system down into manageable pieces, estimate each piece and combine these estimates to get a total cost and flowtime. The estimates of each portion become *de facto* budgets.

2.7.3 The Spiral Life Cycle

This life cycle was developed in response to the failures and issues in the United States Department of Defense software projects. It has been refined and promoted by Barry Boehm and is the result of research done at the University of Southern California Information Sciences Institute. Their website has additional details on its use [11]. It is called spiral because the phases or stages that the project goes through are arranged in a spiral rather than a linear arrangement.

2.7.4 The Synchronization and Stabilization Model

This is the strategy used by a major software production company in preparing their systems for release. Although the exact details are company proprietary, this is an approximation of their process:

- Build a skeletal system.
- Add features on a regular schedule with testing via a cadre of test suites/reviews.
- Schedule intermediate release candidates.
- Reduce changes with each successive candidate based on the severity of fixes/importance of features to release.

A graphic representation of this strategy is shown in Figure 2.2.

2.7.5 The Stage-Gate Life Cycle

This life cycle [12] has been applied to a broad range of systems from construction to the energy grid and more. The concept is to employ a series of time-ordered stages with the requirement that the project can only move from one stage to the next when all the requirements for the subsequent stage to proceed have been met. In manufacturing of aircraft, for example, this concept has been successfully applied and is really a necessity since some parts of the aircraft will no longer be accessible at certain points. So, it is important that the complete installation of parts, fasteners and so

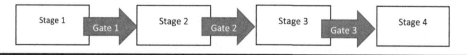

Figure 2.2 A simple generic stage-gate process flow.

forth be complete before proceeding to close off that part of the airframe permanently. In a situation where we had previously experienced runaway coding wherein the software engineers generated a lot of code in an unsynchronized manner in order to meet the schedule with the predictable disastrous results involving reworking much of the code and overrunning the schedule. We weren't trying to discourage the software engineers from developing code. What we were encouraging was that at each defined stage, the required tests were conducted, the code quality requirements met and so forth. This was the first time we had used this method and used it because we were, in a sense, desperate to get control of this highly talented but not very disciplined software engineering team. This team had earned a reputation for poor quality, late finish and extensive rework. This first experience was an overwhelming success. The project was delivered nearly on time with little rework. Compared with previous projects, it was considered a success. It was first used at least in one case to dissuade runaway programming wherein software engineers had pushed forward in developing one part of the system when other parts that were needed for everything to work had not been developed. The key to controlling runaway development cannot proceed through a gate unless all the requirements to proceed through that gate (e.g. until a checklist of all items needed by the next stage have been completed). Graphically, a simple stage-gate might look like Figure 2.2.

In Figure 2.2, the stages or software projects, phases, are separated by gates. Since each gate would specify a different set of criteria, each has a unique identifier. Table 2.2 presents this information in table format.

Some things to keep in mind about the stage-gate approach:

■ The stages can be decomposed or represented in more detail at another, more detailed level and some of those stages decomposed further to whatever level of detail is deemed appropriate.
■ A stage-gate model for a real project will be quite a bit more complex than the trivial model presented above.
■ You need to establish who will have the authority to declare that the needed items to clear the gate have been achieved. Will this be a single person or a team?
■ A different person or team may be used for different gates depending on the circumstances.
■ How will the checklist of needed items for each gate be developed?
■ What process is applied when the software engineering team thinks it is ready to proceed to the next stage but they are declined?
■ Can unfulfilled items in a gate be deferred to a later time (i.e. gate)? What would be an allowable justification for that?

Stage gating has the effect of keeping the software engineering team focused on makeable short-term accomplishments which has been shown to increase productivity due to an increase in oxytocin [13].

Table 2.2 Stage-Gate Description

Stage	Gate
1. Define requirements	Obtain client approval
2. Create design	Ensure design conforms to requirements
3. Implement design & test	Ensure code consistent with client feedback
4. Deliver system	

2.8 Life Cycles – Summary

Each software engineering project will have its own life cycle either by design or by serendipity. The life cycles presented here for the most part really represent categories of life cycles. None of them may suit your project perfectly but at least one should be close enough to be used perhaps with some alterations. When subscribing to a life cycle or a methodology, it is best to remember an aphorism attributed to the Swiss Army, "When the map and the terrain disagree, trust the terrain." In a very real sense, your project is the terrain while the methodology is the map. Postmortems of failed projects have shown some common flaws:

- A significant lack of planning on the part of management, especially for contingencies.
- Management's reluctance to accept realistic but negative observations.
- Management was motivated by something other than what was good for the company.

2.9 Strategies for Controlling Project Flow Time

Due to many factors, at some point, you may need to reduce the flow time of your project. There are several strategies for doing this, but we will look at just a few. The one that may be best for your project is a judgment call on your part and you may have to use more than one:

- Reduce Features – Delaying or eliminating certain features can reduce the flow time to completion but there are some important issues to be considered. This needs to be closely coordinated with the client so that we don't eliminate a feature the client must have, perhaps due to some legal regulation. Also, this can be demoralizing to the team member(s) who were developing the feature being eliminated. If several features are involved, the morale of the team could be impacted. This sometimes results in people transferring or quitting the company.
- Rough-in for Future Implementation – In this case, we are only delaying certain features and building the structures needed to support them at a later time.
- Task "Chunking" and Restructuring – The term "chunking" refers to the grouping of related tasks and subtasks together and rearranging the order in which these "chunks" are implemented. This technique saved one automobile company millions of dollars annually by merely changing the order in which some subassemblies were installed. The design structure matrix (DSM) [14] is an excellent tool for identifying "chunks" that can be reordered. This method is described in the Section 2.9.1.
- Parallelism – Scrutinize the Gantt chart to identify tasks that can be done in parallel (at the same time) rather than sequentially.

2.9.1 The Design Structure Matrix

The DSM has been applied to a broad range of engineering system problems, often with surprisingly positive results [14]. It is a two-dimensional view of requirements, policy and other factors. The DSM is a rigorous method of analyzing, sequencing and sorting out dependency(s) among project elements but simple enough to be used on simple projects while powerful enough to be used on a large scale. Major corporations (e.g. Ford Motor Company) have saved millions of dollars by using it to revise the order in which tasks are done. The two dimensions the DSM employs are labeled "Provides" and "Depends" (see Figure 2.3).

			P R O V I D E			
D E P E N D		**Item A**	**Item B**	**Item C**	**Item D**	**Item E**
	Item A		●	●	●	
	Item B				●	●
	Item C	●			●	
	Item D		●			
	Item E	●	●	●		

Figure 2.3   A generic model of a DSM.

To interpret the matrix, we need to make some observations and apply a few simple rules:

- Off diagonal elements indicate a dependency between two elements (one row, one column element).
- Reading across a row identifies elements that element provides to.
- Reading down a column reveals what elements that element depends upon.
- Alternatively, reading down a column reveals input sources and reading across a row identifies output sinks.

Using the preceding rules, we can interpret the earlier matrix (i.e. Figure 2.3)

- Item B provides something to elements A, D and E.
- Item B depends on something from item D and item E.

Now let's reexamine our shoes and socks process in DSM form (Table 2.3).
    Some observations regarding Table 2.3:

- Inspecting the shoes at the end creates the possibility for recycling.
- "Inspect shoes" is not a "provider."
- Therefore, "Inspect shoes" could be moved to a point earlier in the process resulting in the matrix shown in Table 2.4.

2.9.1.1 A Software Project Application of DSM

A software project to replace an existing system, upgrade it to faster hardware and improve the quality of the code had a challenging schedule (impossible) using DSM as shown on the following

Table 2.3   Our Socks and Shoes Model

	Get Socks	*Get Shoes*	*Put on Socks*	*Put on Shoes*	*Inspect Shoes*
Get Socks					
Get Shoes					●
Put on Socks	●				
Put on Shoes		●	●		
Inspect Shoes		●			

Table 2.4   Our Revised DSM for the Shoe Process

	Get Socks	*Get Shoes*	*Inspect Shoes*	*Put on Shoes*	*Put on Shoes*
Get Socks					
Get Shoes					●
Inspect Shoes	●				
Put on Socks		●	●		
Put on Shoes		●			

slides I was able to foreshorten the process flow time – it sensitized me to the fact that test case development could occur in parallel with other work so that as new code was developed, the test cases were ready and waiting (the new system was intended to do everything the old one did only better, faster and more reliably and with some new features). Initially, we had a seven-phase life cycle as shown in Table 2.5. It was modified to identify the task "Generate Test Cases" resulting in Table 2.6. An analysis of Table 2.6 showed that the "Generate Test Cases" task could be moved to occur in parallel with other tasks. Doing that resulted in Table 2.7. Making that change resulted in flow time savings which helped the project finish within the allotted schedule.

2.9.2 DSM Summary

The concept is a simple one – Identify parts of the project that are independent and move them earlier in the project's timeline as practical. The role of the matrix tool is to make the independence characteristic more easily identified. I have used the DSM to communicate to a client the ramifications of a change they wanted to make to a requirement(s) since the DSM graphically shows what the proposed change will impact causing rework, increased cost and delays. Sometimes the client will want to go forward with the change anyway due to business and/or competitive reasons. Keep in mind that due to the size and complexity of many software systems, a fair amount of abstraction may be necessary to keep the size and complexity of the DSM from overwhelming our ability to comprehend just what is going on with respect to the relationships and how they impact each other. The text cited in the references to this Appendix provides many examples of the application of the DSM to various industries plus a large number of published papers from which you can obtain additional insights into the application of this valuable method.

Table 2.5 Initial Seven-Phase Life Cycle

	Define Reqts.	Reqts. Analysis	Prelim Design	Detail Design	Coding	Conduct Tests	Install
Define Reqts.							
Reqts. Analysis	•						
Prelim. Design	•	•					
Detail Design	•		•				
Coding				•		•	
Conduct Tests	•	•		•	•		
Install						•	

Table 2.6 Revised Seven-Phase Life Cycle to Eight Phases

	Define Reqts.	Reqts. Analysis	Prelim Design	Detail Design	Coding	Generate Test Cases	Conduct Tests	Install
Define Reqts.								
Reqts. Analysis	•							
Prelim. Design	•	•						
Detail Design	•		•					
Coding				•		•		
Generate Test Cases	•	•		•				
Conduct Tests				•	•	•		
Install							•	

Table 2.7   Revised Order of Generating Test Cases per DSM Analysis

	Define Reqts.	*Reqts. Analysis*	*Prelim Design*	*Detail Design*	*Generate Test Cases*	*Coding*	*Conduct Tests*	*Install*
Define Reqts.								
Reqts. Analysis	●							
Prelim. Design	●	●						
Detail Design	●		●					
Generate Test Cases	●	●		●				
Coding					●		●	
Conduct Tests				●	●	●		
Install							●	

To see how this works, we will use a trivial example. Most mornings we engage in a simple activity (process):

■ Get socks
■ Get shoes
■ Put on socks
■ Put on shoes
■ Inspect shoes

What if the shoes are a mess? If so, we will have to redo (cycle) some steps. In an industrial setting, a redo costs time and money.

2.10 The Work Breakdown Structure

A strategy attributed to the Roman army in ancient times is "Divide et Vince" or "Divide and Conquer." That strategy forms the basis for the Work Breakdown Structure (WBS). As its name indicates, what we are trying to do is break the problem of building a system down into manageable pieces small enough that we can estimate the resources needed to successfully complete them, estimate how long each piece will take to complete and schedule the order in which the pieces need to be completed as well as which ones could be accomplished in parallel. As one might expect, relatively simple projects are much easier to build a WBS for, while more complex ones, such as

Table 2.8 Work Breakdown Structure for Preparing the Yard for Sale of a Home

What	How	Notes
Prepare yard for home sale	Pick up toys, etc. in yard	
	Mow lawn	
	Trim trees and shrubs	
	Replace dead plants with living ones	Get flowering plants
Pick up toys, etc. in yard	Offer kids a reward for cleaning up the yard	

the development of a new passenger aircraft, present significant challenges. What this strategy does is develop a decomposition of the project. The Project Management Institute (PMI) recommends that we stop decomposing a task when its pieces are small enough that they could be completed in eight hours or whatever the standard day length is in your country. According to the PMI, decomposing any further amounts to micromanaging which is ill advised [15]. Let's look at how to generate a WBS using a "what-how" approach. In this approach to developing a WBS, we create a series of statements describing what we are trying to do and how we are going to do it. Then, in the next cycle, letting the previous statement of "how" become the "what" of the next cycle, and so forth. A simple example is presented in Table 2.8. Only the first few items are shown but the method should be obvious.

As you may have guessed, the WBS is only the beginning. It is only a high-level description which must undergo the development of many details to eventually arrive at enough detail that we can begin designing and eventually developing the actual code. To do this, we have to estab-lish high-quality communication with our client. In some cases, particularly government projects, the client (the governmental agency involved) has included a statement of requirements with the published request for proposal. Even so, we will need to communicate with the client in order to confirm our understanding of the requirements they provided. That is going to require a plan to establish and maintain communication with the client from the beginning of the project through project closeout – that is referred to as a communication plan.

2.11 A Natural Communication Gap – Between Project Manager and Software Engineer

There exists what amounts to a natural communication gap between managers and the people they manage [16]. This is due to the way each sees the world, the project situation and their value system(s). While this may not seem important to some, it can result in managers and software engineers each inadvertently acting in ways which demotivate the members of their team(s) result-ing in reduced productivity, missed delivery dates and higher costs due to turnover in personnel. This last item (turnover) has been shown to increase development costs by as much as 60% [17]. Table 2.9 lists the parameters which constitute this communication gap demonstrating once again that money is not the highest, most important factor in non-managers' work relationship.

Table 2.9   Value System Rankings (from [18], 10 = highest)

Value System Factor	Manager's Importance Rank	Non-Manager's Importance Rank
Salary	1	5
Job Security	2	4
Promotion/Growth Opportunities	3	7
Working Conditions	4	9
Interesting/Challenging Work	5	6
Personal Loyalty to Workers	6	8
Tactful Discipline	7	10
Appreciation for Work Done	8	1
Help with Personnel Problems	9	3
Being in on Things	10	2

A quick review of Table 2.9 will probably produce some disagreements with some published results. Just about everyone will disagree with one or more of these findings but once again, we have facts and data challenging what we may believe. Let's look at some examples:

■ Salary – One thing we can probably all agree on is that we need money to purchase the goods and services we need to just survive. As indicated in Table 2.9, managers rank its value at the top of their list. There can be many reasons for this including status among their peers. Regardless of the reason(s), with salary being their highest value, they see increasing a software engineer's salary by a meaningful amount as the most effective form of motivation improvement. Unfortunately, while the engineer may welcome the increased pay, it is not as important to them as the software project manager assumes it is. Note that salary is not as high on the software engineer's list as it is on the software project manager's list. So, the increase in salary is not nearly as effective as an item further up the list – appreciation for work done. This difference can lead to some puzzling situations for software project managers in that they go out of their way to get a salary increase for one of their engineers only to have that person resign from the company or voluntarily transfer to another project. If this has happened to you, ask yourself when was the last time you thanked that person for their work? Conversely, when was the last time your manager thanked you for your efforts? How did that make you feel?

■ Working conditions – As DeMarco and Lister found [19], working conditions (e.g. office space, noise level) can provide an environment where people can perform at their highest or keep them from doing their best. Their findings are summarized in Table 2.10.

Looking at the environmental factors listed in Table 2.10, we can see why the highest performing software engineers perform better than the lowest performers. Interruptions, crowded work space and other factors all contribute to preventing a software engineer from focusing on the problem at

Table 2.10 Impact of Environmental Factors on Productivity [19]

Environmental Factor	Highest Performers [% Yes]	Lowest Performers [% Yes]
Amount of dedicated workspace	78 square feet (7.2 square meters)	46 square feet (4.3 square meters)
Work area is acceptably quiet	57%	29%
Work area is acceptably private	62%	19%
Phone can be silenced	52%	10%
Phone can be diverted	76%	19%
People interrupt you needlessly	38%	76%

hand and finding a solution. Some firms still have not taken the results of [19] to heart failing to recognize that the cost(s) of improving the work environment will be realized by improved productivity. Instead, some are still engaging the World War II model of having hundreds of engineers in open bays with high noise levels and little or no private space.

2.12 Developing a Communication Plan

One of the most important aspects of successfully managing a software engineering project is establishing and maintaining effective communication with everyone involved in the project [20]. Why? Because there will be events during the project which were not planned for which could jeopardize the success of the effort. If everyone involved (i.e. the software team, the clients team and management in both organizations) is aware of how the project has proceeded to date, there is less likelihood that delays will be mistakenly attributed to incompetence on the part of your team. Establishing effective communication involves more than just emails and meetings but a relationship in which open and honest communication occur throughout the project. Lying is really worthless [21] because the truth will come out eventually and that could make matters worse over the long term. One glaring example of this occurred a few years ago in a United States Department of Defense project. For legal reasons, the company involved cannot be named. The project was scheduled to be 24 months long. The software development company was required to report the status, including the various Earned Value parameters each month. They reported everything as nominal until the 22nd month when they reported the project would be six months late. Under these circumstances, it is highly unlikely that the contract monitors in the Department of Defense would award another contract to that firm let alone believe anything they reported regarding status. Without effective open communication, even if you fulfill all requirements in a timely manner, your client may view the effort as a failure. Here is how this can happen:

■ The client does not view the system as being theirs – More recently the Agile method has helped remedy this by involving the client throughout the development process. The feedback the client provides results in changes to the user interface and other system properties resulting in identification of the resulting system as psychologically being theirs. This can result in some forgiveness on the part of the client when things don't go exactly as planned.

■ The client does not feel that your team was being open and honest with them particularly when things did not go well. Keeping the client in the dark about problems that could delay final delivery is not a good idea. They will find out later anyway. Besides, knowing early that the software is going to be late enables the client to prepare for this. Also, finding out late that the project is going to be late means they may have already made commitments that will now be broken thereby damaging their credibility within their company and/or their clients.

■ A key element in dealing with late delivery is finding out which functionality is most important to the client. That way, if the full system can't be delivered in a timely manner, at least these most important features will be. These could be high priority due to some legal or regulatory requirement. Put these at the top of the priority list and work with the client to develop a schedule to incorporate lower priority features.

2.13 Communication Plan Basics

The communication plan is a document intended to ensure that the relationship between the client and the contractor is a good one in that it ensures that both parties maintain an open and honest information flow beneficial to both. Some software project managers prefer to keep the client unaware of problems encountered assuming that they will be overcome and the client does not need to know about them. In my experience, this is simply wrong headed. If we specify date and so forth, we can avoid serious negative consequences. For example, if the client plans to launch an advertising campaign regarding the new services they will provide their customers by a certain date, those services depend on the successful completion of this project and they are unaware of the potential for a delay, there will be serious consequences such that the client may cease doing business with your firm. Based on experience in exactly this situation, a strategy we employed was to have the client identify the most important features that would be needed on time while deprioritizing the rest. As it turned out, they were able to run their advertisements, gain competitive advantage and introduce the lower priority features over time.

2.14 Example of a Communication Plan

As a matter of personal preference, I prefer a chart or table rather than a multipage document. As stated elsewhere, the communication plan should include all participants who have a vested interest in the project either as a beneficiary of its results, a member of the team creating it or the management team of either group. The value systems and goals of the various members of the groups differ greatly. For example, the software engineers want to create a system that is technically advanced, something they can be proud of and relate to their colleagues [22] while the users of the system don't really care about technical superiority but want something that is easy to use, makes their job easier and is stable. The management of the company receiving the system wants a system their software engineers can maintain and adapt to new and unforeseen business and security issues. A typical communication plan must include:

■ Name of Meeting – Depending on the organization that is the client, some of these may be built into the contract to do the work. For example, the United States Department of Defense had a progression of meetings starting with the preliminary design review. At each of these meetings, they had their own personnel and outside consultants who reviewed progress, critiqued content and checked to see if the project had proceeded as directed to correct the situation by a specified date.

■ The Participants for Each Meeting – Who will be invited and expected to be at each meeting either by name or role.

■ The Purpose of the Meeting – A statement of why this meeting will be held. If we can't state why the meeting should be held, then why have it?

■ The Frequency of the Meeting – Some meetings, such as the software bug review, should be held on a regular basis so as to prevent a build-up or backlog of work which may jeopardize the schedule. Weekly bug reviews also enable us to prioritize what will be fixed and when. This prevents the most critical items from being delayed.

■ The Differences between Planning and Scheduling.

■ Risk Management Methods.

Chapter 2 Review Questions

1. What did Dwight Eisenhower mean by "Plans are nothing, planning is everything?"
2. Has the software life cycle used ever been documented as the cause of the failure of a software project?
3. What is the overwhelming cause of software project failure?
4. Approximately, how many different software development life cycles are there?
5. List at least four stages in a software project life cycle.
6. What is the planning fallacy? Explain.
7. List the two primary reasons why humans can't estimate accurately.
8. What was the primary goal of the Gantt chart?
9. Is the Agile life cycle unique? If yes, how? If not, why?
10. Name two concerns about using and managing Agile. Explain/describe each.
11. What are "gates" in the stage-gate life cycle? Detail/describe.
12. List and describe the pros and cons of each of the three ways to shorten a software project's flow time.
13. What is the design structure matrix? What can it be used for?
14. What is a work breakdown structure?
15. What are the primary causes of a communication gap between software engineers and software project managers?
16. Why should we develop a communication plan to foster communications between our team and our client?

References

[1] Myers, C.G., Staats, B.R. and Gino, F., "'My Bad!' How Internal Attribution and Ambiguity of Responsibility Affect Learning from Failure," Harvard Business School Working Paper 14-104, April 18, 2014.

[2] Gulla, J., "Seven Reasons Why IT Projects Fail," *IBM Systems Magazine*, February, 2012.

[3] National Aeronautics and Space Administration (NASA), Work Breakdown Structure (WBS) Handbook, NASA/SP-2016-3404/REV1, January, 2018.

[4] Kahneman, D. and Tversky, A. "Judgment under Uncertainty: Heuristics and Biases," *Science*, New Series, Vol. 185, No. 4157, September 27, 1974, pp. 1124–1131.

[5] Staats, B.R., Milkman, K.L. and Fox, C.R., "The Team Scaling Fallacy: Underestimating the Declining Efficiency of Larger Teams," *Organizational Behavior and Human Decision Processes*, Vol. 118, No. 2, 2012, pp. 132–142.

[6] Chen, J. and Lin, L., "Modeling Team Member Characteristics for the Formation of a Multifunctional Team in Concurrent Engineering," *IEEE Transactions on Engineering Management*, Vol. 15, No. 2, 2004, pp. 111–124.

[7] Garvin, D.A., "How Google Sold Its Engineers on Management," *Harvard Business Review*, December, 2013.

[8] Flyvberg, B., "From Nobel Prize to Project Management: Getting Risks Right," *Project Management Journal*, August 2006, Vol. 37, No. 3, pp. 5–15.

[9] Dyba, T. and Dingsoyr, T., "Empirical Studies of Agile Software Development: A Systematic Review," *Information and Software Technology*, Vol. 50, No. 9, pp. 833–859, 2008.

[10] Private communications with Laszlo Belady regarding software development strategies, May 1983.

[11] Boehm, B., "A Spiral Model of Software Development and Enhancement," *Computer*, V. 21, No. 5, May pp. 61–72, 1988.

[12] U.S. Department of Energy, Industrial Technologies Program, "Stage-Gate Innovation Guidelines: Managing Risk through Structured Project Decision-Making," February 2007.

[13] Zak, P.J., "The Neuroscience of Trust," from "Management Behaviors That Foster Employee Engagement", *Harvard Business Review*, January-February, 2017.

[14] Eppinger, S.D. and Browning, T.R., *Design Structure Matrix Methods and Applications (Engineering Systems)*, MIT Press, February 12, 2016.

[15] Project Management Institute, *Guide to the Project Management Body of Knowledge*, 5th Edition, 2013.

[16] Lindahl, L., "What Makes a Good Job," *Personnel*, January 25, 1949.

[17] Cone, E., "Managing that Churning Sensation," *Information Week*, May 1998, No. 680, pp. 50–67.

[18] Thamhain, H., "Team Leadership Effectiveness in Technology-Based Project Environments," *IEEE Engineering Management Review*, Vol. 36, No. 1, 2008, pp. 165–180. College, Cambridge, UK.

[19] DeMarco, T. and Lister, T., *Peopleware*, Dorset House, New York, NY, 1999.

[20] Dow, W. and Taylor, B., *Project Management Communications Bible*, Wiley Publishing, 2008.

[21] Glass, R.L. Rost, J. and Matook, M.S., "Lying on Software Projects," *IEEE Software*, Vol. 25, No. 6, Nov.–Dec. 2008, pp. 90–95. doi: 10.1109/MS.2008.150

[22] Katz, R., "Motivating Technical Professionals Today," *IEEE Engineering Management Review*, Vol. 41, No. 1, March 2013, pp. 28–38.

Chapter 3

Estimating Cost and Schedule of Software Projects

3.1 Chapter Overview

Scheduling is an activity where our everyday experience can mislead us. As in the planning activity, what seems reasonable does not work because our everyday experience is mostly not applicable. For example, throughout our lives, we frequently have to deal with situations where adding people to a task will make completion occur sooner. By now you should realize that developing software does not work like that. Why? Because it is not a deterministic (outcome determined by cause and effect) process and controlling it until it is complete is an evolving activity. But schedule we must. There have been dozens of papers and books on the topic of project planning and scheduling. The two activities are related but not the same [1]. Our project plan lays out what we are going to do while the schedule spells out how (and when) we are going to do it. It prescribes what activities will occur, in what order as well as which tasks can occur in parallel. Since we are estimating how many person-hours and how much flow time will be required to do each task, we can compute the cost of labor related to the project plus any other costs such as hardware purchases, the use of professional services (e.g. lawyer, accountant), cost to access the internet, other costs and our profit. The planning and scheduling of even relatively simple software projects have rarely been successful. By that I mean the estimated flow time and person-hours at the start of the project were most often exceeded. In hindsight, our estimates were overly optimistic. That optimism resulted in a project that was late and over budget. Although some see this as unique to software projects, it is not. Complex construction projects and even some relatively simple ones have also run late and over budget often in spectacular fashion. As we shall see in this chapter, a 20-year study [2] that resulted in a Nobel Prize in Economics in 2003 showed that human beings are incapable of accurately estimating. But other published work [3] showed how we can correct for this as we shall describe.

DOI: 10.1201/9781003484288-3

3.2 Scheduling versus Planning

Why are we discussing planning and scheduling together? Contrary to what you may have read [1], they are not the same. They are closely related but not the same activity. Some software professionals believe that planning and scheduling are the same activity, but they are not. A schedule is just a list of events together with the dates on which they are expected to start and end. For example, the schedule for a commuter train lists the arrival and departure times for each train and station. It provides no insight into how this schedule will be accomplished on time. On the other hand, a plan details how the events listed in the schedule will be accomplished. For example, the schedule may call for "Project Kickoff Meeting" to occur on March 1 and "Status Review 01" to occur on April 15 while the plan lists the tasks and subtasks that must be accomplished to prepare for and deliver the status review. In most cases, it will also identify the person(s) responsible for each task and subtask. Yes, by name and not just by labor category. As Brooks [4] pointed out, assigning a task to a labor category (e.g. senior software engineer(s)) leads to misestimates because we are, in fact, thinking of a specific person, including their expertise and our experience with them, not a "generic" person.

Planning depends heavily on dividing the work that needs to be done into small enough pieces that they are manageable and comprehensible. In other words, into small enough tasks that those who will be doing the work feel confident that they can predict how long it will take using the human and other resources at hand. Although the history of software engineering has shown we are not very skilled at making these estimates, other engineering activities have also experienced difficulties of this type. We will come back to this seemingly common inability for people to estimate accurately, present one of its primary causes and demonstrate how that factor can be corrected [3].

3.3 The Basics of Costing

Whether we are refining an existing project schedule or creating a new one, the elements of the engineering model of a project [5] will need to be satisfied. The format and content for project plans vary from one company and industry to another. For example, in the United States, the HIPAA (The Health Insurance Portability and Accountability Act) requires the privacy of patient health information be maintained and not distributed without the patient's permission. This requirement makes security, control and limited access to such information a prominent element of any software project plan in the health industry in the United States. Other industries (e.g. Financial Services) have their own unique requirements and these also vary from country to country. The most common elements of a project plan and its justification (the justification is often called a "business case"), regardless of location (note that titles for these elements may vary internationally but the content remains the same), include:

- The Business Case – This is the economic justification for doing the project. In general, if you cannot make a business case for an effort, it isn't going to go forward. In simple terms, the business case states the problem this project intends to solve, if the project is successful, what the savings will be, what the return on investment (ROI) will be (this describes how long it will take the firm or customer to recover the funds expended, the assumptions made in this analysis and so forth), an overall strategy that will be applied (frequently, this is one that has worked before), the staff to be used, equipment needed and so forth.

■ Risk Analysis – The concept of risk is discussed in more detail in Appendix 20. But a simple definition is a statement of the likelihood of the success of the project where the measurable goals of the project are clearly stated and of the highest priority.

3.4 The Business Case

There are many different definitions of just what constitutes a business case. According to the United States General Accounting Office (USGAO) [6], a business case is:

A structured method for organizing and presenting a business improvement proposal.

In this text, we use the term "business case" to be broader than the preceding definition. We use it to include what might best be termed a proposal. That is, the justification for an altogether new product or service. In keeping with the definition provided by the USGAO, organizational decision-makers typically compare business cases when deciding to expend resources. A business case typically includes an analysis of business process performance and associated needs or problems, proposed alternative solutions, assumptions, constraints and a risk-adjusted cost/benefit analysis.

There is no fixed format for business cases, so they vary from organization to organization. They are a vital part of go–no go decisions on projects and assist greatly in helping to prevent the project from expanding into a different project than originally envisioned (scope creep, again).

The four key elements that a business case should contain?

It should include:

■ The problem and business need – why you are putting forward your Business Case.
■ Benefits and risks of the options – solutions to the problem.
■ Return on investment – what the overall gain will be to the business.
■ Final recommendation – based on the information presented.

Generally, there are five categories of issues that need to be considered:

■ The problem to be solved or (business) opportunity.
■ Changes that must be made.
■ Benefits of the changes.
■ Costs and risks associated with the changes.
■ Measure(s) of success.

Although profitability is the most common criterion used in evaluating a business case, it is not the only one. Social responsibility, corporate image, community welfare and other criteria not related to profit may be the driving factors. There are many other business case models presented in the literature, but we have enough here to demonstrate the application of the concept from a project I consulted on.

3.5 Computing Project Costs

What many entrepreneurs do not understand is how to compute the pricing of their labor, services and products. The basic principle to keep in mind is that in setting a price, that price must help reimburse us for our costs as well as make a profit. Stated another way, our client who may be paying us hourly to develop some software should be paying us enough to cover our costs plus a profit. If we are paying a software engineer $50 per hour, that is not our true cost. That is because, in the United States and other countries, there are payroll taxes part of which the employer must pay. As a company, we have several business taxes; if we have a facility, even if we are operating out of our garage, we have heating and cooling, electricity, the cost of internet hookup, plus rent, office furniture, a server, licenses to various software systems we are using, legal fees and more. If we do not know what all of our costs are and build their recovery into our pricing structure, we are likely to be out of business quickly. All of this is elaborated on in this chapter. These so-called indirect costs are why that $50-per-hour software engineer actually costs us $75 or even more per hour. Not accounting for the indirect costs in our pricing structure deteriorates our profit margin and amounts to subsidizing our clients.

3.6 Cost Estimating Methods

Over the years, there have been literally hundreds of different methods for estimating the cost of a software project. At this point in time, none of them have proven themselves to be consistently accurate. Part of the problem is that, in estimating, we are trying to predict the future and that is always a risky business. But estimate we must in order to both inform our client and to set a target for ourselves. The basic approach for most software cost estimating methods is to utilize the strategy of the Roman army from ancient times and divide and conquer. That is, to break the entire software system down into pieces small enough that we can estimate their cost and flow time and then put everything together to get a total cost. The resources we have to help us create an estimate are more than a bit "sloppy." Some make no distinction between the number of lines of source code that end up being in the build and the number of lines of source code including those that are thrown away. In addition to this conundrum, there are widely varying assumptions about how many lines of code a software engineer can create in an hour or some other time unit. For example, the Dzone Agile Zone website estimates that the average software engineer generates about 50 source lines per day while other sites estimate the number lies somewhere between 300 and 1,000 lines per day. Again, some sites do not clearly distinguish between what gets shipped and what gets tossed out. To get an estimate of the size of the "typical" software project, we can turn to data published by the biggest purchaser of software in the world, the United States Department of Defense [7]. Some facts they have published regarding software productivity and costs are presented in Tables 3.1 and 3.2.

Table 3.1 Productivity Rates by System Type

System Type	Production Rate (KLOC = 1,000 Lines of Code)
Real-Time Software	1.5 months per KLOC
Engineering Software	1.3 months per KLOC
Mission Support Software	1.3 months per KLOC
Automated Information Systems	1.1 months per KLOC

Table 3.2 Burdened Costs

System Type	# of Software Engineers & Monthly Cost
Real-Time Software	8.1 people = $101,250
Engineering Software	6.7 people = $83,750
Mission Support Software	3.9 people = $48,750
Automated Information Systems	2.5 people = $31,250

The above is based on an average size of 25 KLOC and Burdened Labor at $150,000 per staff member per year or $12,500 per month – burdened figures include wages, payroll taxes, workman's compensation insurance, vacation, sick leave and other benefits or ~50% more than wages alone.

They found that the average size of a software project was about 25,000 lines of source code for the projects they studied. Typically, the estimating formulae which have been published take the form:

$$COST = SLOC^*Cost \text{ per Line}$$

where

COST = the total cost.
SLOC = the number of source lines of code.
Cost per Line = the average cost of a source line of code.

There have been a lot of criticisms of this style of estimating. One I have is that, in my experience, when I have asked a software engineer how long a software change will take, no one ever replied with a flow time based on the number of lines of code but after they have studied the problem sufficiently, they reply in terms of a number of days or hours. The number of lines of code will vary due to the fact that some efforts may involve the reuse of existing code and other factors. Boehm [8, 9] has suggested the concept of "Equivalent Source Lines of Code" (ESLOC), which is the homogeneous sum of the different code sources that may be involved in the effort. The components of ESLOC are:

$$AAF\left(0.4\times\%DM\right)+\left(0.3\times\%CM\right)+\left(0.3\times\%IM\right)$$

where

%DM = % Design Modified
%CM = % Code & Unit Test Modified
%IM = % Integration & Test Modified

Therefore, our total ESLOC is given by:

$$ESLOC = New\ SLOC + AAF_{DM}\ X\ Modified\ SLOC + AAF_R\ X\ Reused\ SLOC$$
$$+ AAF_{AG}\ X\ Auto - Generated\ SLOC$$

Here is just a small sample of the estimating methods available today. They are provided in order to let you decide what does or may work best in your circumstance:

■ COCOMO and COCOMOII (as described above)
■ IBM Federal Systems Method
■ Function Points

3.7 IBM Federal Systems Estimating Method

This method of estimating was developed by IBM based on a study of 60 software projects [10]. It estimates the amount of effort based on the number of source lines of code and a productivity factor. The following formula is used to make the computed estimate:

$$Effort = 5.2L^{0.91}$$

where

L = size in KLOC
KLOC = thousand lines of code
5.2 is a scaling factor related to productivity

The pros of using this method include that it is simple to use and based on real-world data.

The cons of using this method include the inverse relationship between the size of a project and the economy of scale [8] which this method does not address.

3.8 Function Points

This may be the most well-thought-out and refined approach available [9]. The concept is to estimate the complexity of the future software system and use that together with some established weighting factors to obtain the required estimate. The details of this method together with examples and user experiences are available in books and published papers as well as via searches on the internet. Also, this method is used worldwide and is supported by a society devoted to its use and refinement. At its heart is the estimation of the complexity of each function point as being simple, average or complex. This is based on the opinion of the estimator(s) who must rely on their experience, opinions and guidelines provided in published materials. Table 3.3 depicts a simplified view of an automated patient drug administration and monitoring system. The details of the system are not necessary for this discussion.

There are free software applications which will use information like those in Table 3.3 to apply programming language adjustments (e.g. the "Center for Systems and Software") and arrive at a coding estimate. What is done is to use the contents of something like those listed in Table 3.3 for your project with simple, average and complex as weighting factors to obtain the resulting coding estimate. There are several sites which have the computational functionality you will need. What is done to estimate the number of application elements of each complexity level is to multiply the value of the weighting level of that complexity level by the number of

Table 3.3 Example of a Simple Function Points Table

Function Point Type	Characterized As		
	S – Simple	A – Average	C – Complex
External Inputs	3	4	6
External Outputs	4	6	7
Queries	3	4	6
External Files	5	7	10
Internal Files	7	10	15

applications classified at that level and then compute the sum of all of the computed values to arrive at the total number of function points. Next, multiply the number of function points by the number of hours estimated per function point (e.g. 8 hours per function point) to obtain the total number of hours estimated. It should be noted that this method adjusts the estimate to take into account the simplicity or complexity of the code to be developed. The underlying assumption of this method is the more complex the code to be developed, the longer it will take and conversely.

3.9 Business Case Example

A few years ago, a kindergarten through high school educational facility was being built by a Native American tribe. Their goal was to provide their children and young adults with a state-of-the-art educational facility while at the same time demonstrating the tribe's commitment to core values that included respect for the environment. The school would be utilizing more than 400 personal computers. The era in which this development occurred was such that personal computers (PCs) consumed much more electricity than they do today, generating heat which caused the HVAC (heating, ventilation and air conditioning) systems to remove heat during warm weather. A second factor associated with the use of these PCs was the fact that electric rates from the company serving the area where the school was located were going up. The simple, obvious solution was to have teachers and students turn off their PCs before leaving for the day. This could not be guaranteed in all cases. Besides, teachers and students complained about boot-up times since many of them were rushing to complete an assignment late. A vendor was identified that sold software that would put a PC central processor into a state which drew very little current from which it could be awakened quickly into an operational state. It could install itself via push technology and allow each user to set a schedule for their PC to "go to sleep" or defer to the default. Without getting into all the cost and savings details, Table 3.4 shows the results of our analysis.

Some of the elements comprising the table are listed below. Also, projects may not always be justified based on profit. Many projects are justified based on their benefit to society or the community in general or a segment of the population (e.g. those with disabilities, reducing our impact on the environment).

Table 3.4 Data Developed for Our Business Case

	Year 0	Year 1	Year 2	Year 3	Year 4	Total
Energy Savings	€ 3.968	€ 4.167	€ 4.375	€ 4.593	€ 4.823	€ 21.926
HVAC Savings	€ 595	€ 625	€ 656	€ 689	€ 726	€ 3.291
Product Cost	(€ 8.000)	€ 0	€ 0	€ 0	€ 0	(€ 8.000)
To Date Totals	(€ 3.437)	€ 1.355	€ 6.386	€ 11.668	€ 17.217	€ 17.217
ROI @ 5%	€ 8.000	€ 8.400	€ 8.820	€ 9.261	€ 9.724	€ 9.724
ROI @ 10%	€ 8.000	€ 8.800	€ 9.680	€10.648	€ 11.713	€ 11.713

Explanation of notation

■ Amounts are in Euros.
■ An amount surrounded by parentheses is a negative amount.
■ A period is used instead of a coma consistent with European conventions.
■ ROI represents Return On Investment if the original purchase price was invested at 5% or 10% compounded.

In the preceding example, the total positive cash flow of €17.217 being greater than what would have been received via a simple investment at 5% or 10% means the business case is a viable one both from a financial and an environmental standpoint.

Project Charter – The Project Charter legitimizes the project in that it authorizes the expenditure of company funds to specific ends. It bounds the project and attempts to reduce "scope creep." It states what the project will and will not do. It is necessitated by the fact that software often touches so many other aspects of the enterprise. Not bounding the project in some way almost guarantees that the scope of the project will expand to include some of the systems it interfaces with perhaps resulting in the budget and/or schedule exceeding the plan. Most importantly, the project's charter gets everyone related to this effort to think about what will and will not be addressed by this project. There have been many formats published for project charters. Most software companies will have their own, possibly unique, format. Regardless, the project charter should contain at least the following elements:

Project Name – This is how this project will be referenced.

Owner(s) – Who, in the organization, is responsible for maintaining this document (it will be under change control).

Executive Summary – This section lists the measurable objectives of this project, proposed start and end dates, estimated costs, assumptions, risks, project overview, scope and any other factors senior management may need to know in order to make an informed decision about approving this effort.

Approvals List – This is a list of the people, by job title, who are approving this effort as signified by their signature. Typically, this list would include the Project Manager (who usually prepares this document), Project Sponsor, Senior Manager (the Executive) who is sponsoring this effort and the Client Representative.

Stated another way, the Project Charter is a high-level view of the proposed project – the project described without all the details

- Measures of Success – This item is one of great importance and often overlooked. It states clearly and (hopefully) simply what the resulting system must do in order for the project to be deemed successful. These must be stated in a measurable way, including the current baseline from which we may be measuring improvement. For example, "With all hardware and operating system software in working order, the system shall prompt the user for a password within 60 seconds after a 'Power On' event has been detected." Certainly, there is a lot more to that one, but the essence of this item is there. The conditions under which this acceptability requirement must be met are stated together with acceptable performance under those conditions.
- Risk Analysis – What are the risks associated with developing this system, its use and so forth? How are or will these risks be mitigated? For example, if we are developing a system to automatically park an automobile, how will the driver regain control in the event of a failure of the software? How will the driver know the system has failed? How many different ways could the system fail and how can we prevent them from occurring?
- A Multidimensional View – The best policy to have regarding business case development is to consider all the various dimensions a new or revised system can impact. The best system for this right now is "The Balanced Scorecard." [10]. It considers the entire spectrum of impacts organized into four dimensions or viewpoints:

   Financial: What will this cost versus what will it save the company? What confidence level can we attribute to this estimate?

   Customer: How will this impact the customer? Is it likely to be well received by our customers? What are the acceptance criteria?

   Internal: Are we organized or structured in such a way that will support this change? If not, what changes will we need to put in place?

   Learning: Will we have to train some of our people in this new technique(s)? If so, who will be trained and what will this cost?

Anyone who has called a company's technical support team with a problem that needs some explanation only to encounter an automated answering system that requests you to press a number for this type of problem or that then requests another selection and so forth none of which seem to match your issue has experienced what can happen when a company only considers profit and loss issues. These systems can be frustrating, particularly if they do not have the option of pressing zero in order to speak to a human being to explain the nature of the problem you are calling about. To summarize, the point of the Balanced Scorecard method [11] is when making a decision, we consider all four dimensions of that decision, not just profit or some other single factor.

3.10 Success and Differences in Value Systems

"Success is the ability to go from one failure to another with no loss of enthusiasm."
–Winston Churchill

In the early days of software development, a project manager's goals were threefold: Bring the project in on time, on budget, and meeting requirements. Since then, we have become aware that today, these are the absolute minimum and not the complete requirements needed in order to be successful. For example, meeting those three criteria but delivering a system the users find difficult to use is unreliable or cannot be modified to meet changing needs is just the start of an extended list of what makes a system a success. Our more up-to-date view is that success is a multifaceted phenomenon. The development team wants to develop something technically elegant but the client does not care if the resulting system is technically superior, only that it meets users' needs in a responsive, reliable and secure way. Thus, our development team may deliver results that they consider great only to have the client see them as inadequate. This dichotomy became apparent to me some years ago while working on software for an international telephone company. The operating company used measurements (counts) of various types of calls as a means of balancing the phone network in real time. The development team saw collecting, storing and reporting these counts as drudgery which would needlessly slow call processing. So, the developers set the priority for data collection to the lowest level. What that meant was that when the phone switching center was the busiest, the data would not be collected but when it was not very busy it would be. It turned out that it was of utmost importance to the client to obtain this data when the phone office was the busiest in order to ensure the network could continue providing service to the company's subscribers. When these facts became known to the operating company, there were angry exchanges, directives for immediate modification, hurried rework and considerable expense over and above the original budget. All of this resulted from the development team putting their need for "technical excellence" ahead of what the sponsor needed. To the sponsor, the initial version of this system was not a success. Over the years, I have seen this scenario repeat itself like some kind of syndrome or habit which is difficult if not impossible to break. This is paradoxical in that job satisfaction is a key element in achieving high productivity and to software developers, contributing to a technically superior product is equated to job satisfaction.

The challenge for you as the software project manager is to maintain a balance between delivering what the sponsor sees as a successful product while maintaining a sense of technical excellence within the software development team.

3.11 Cost Categories

In computing the cost of our project, we need to keep in mind the goal of establishing our pricing. What we are trying to do is recover the costs that we incur by building them into our pricing system. Without maintaining that viewpoint, we end up subsidizing our client, not profiting sufficiently and going out of business. How can we achieve a survivable pricing structure? Without being trained in the basics of cost allocation and recovery, a software project manager may only be sensitive to the direct costs associated with the project. For example, if we estimate a client requested change to require 100 hours of labor by a software engineer whom we are paying $50 per hour, we see the cost as $5,000 ($50 per hour times 100 hours), plus profit. But $50 per hour is not the total hourly cost of the software engineer. In the United States as well as many other countries, there are payroll taxes similar to Social Security and Medicare which the employer must pay which increases the hourly cost of the software engineer. In addition to those costs, there may be other taxes which vary from country to country – office space, heating and cooling, connection to the internet, various types of insurance, fringe benefits and others. So, some small businesses try to avoid many of these costs by hiring people as contractors who will provide their own workspace, internet connection and so forth but the small business still incurs expenses just to stay in business such as a business license, errors and omissions insurance, legal fees for creating contracts, advertising

Project Planning Process

Steps in Process	ESTABLISH SUCCESS CRITERIA	BUILD WORK BREAKDOWN STRUCTURE	Estimate Resources / Schedule	Identify Risk & Develop Mitigation Plan	Develop Project Control Plan	Conduct Overall Review of Plan	Finalize Plan
Project Manager	1] Establish Initial Budget, Schedule, Requirements 2] Identify Fixed versus Flexible Requirements 3] Separate Distinguish Project requirements from Product requirements 4] Establish Earned Value reporting process	Select Lifecycle / Assemble WBS Model	Apply Estimation Methods, Identify Needed Skills / Poll All Team Members for Their Input	Assess Critical Issues / Explore Jeopardizing Scenarios / Develop Mitigation Plan	Identify Metrics, Data Collection and Analysis Scheme	Develop Presentation and Documentation of Plan	Review/Revise Success Criteria & communicate to Stakeholders
Senior Staff Member							
Software Team Members		Detail Major/ Minor Tasks					
Senior Management Team		Review WBS	Review Resource Estimate	Review Resource Risk Approach	Review Project Controls	Review Project Plan / Make Go / No Go Decisions	Confirm Final Plan Content
Client / Customer							

and promotion, telephone service, internet access and on and on it goes. In each country, there exists accounting standards setup by some central authority which establish what are valid business expenses. In addition, governmental agencies also have rules they set forth for companies doing business with that agency. In the United States, the federal government agencies require businesses that provide material and/or services to comply with the Federal Acquisition Regulations (FAR). These amount to "hidden" costs which, if not incorporated into our pricing, eat away at our profitability invisibly. Overall, there are three cost categories. Each cost that the company incurs can be allocated to one of these categories. Remember, the main reason for categorizing and tracking all three cost categories is to better incorporate our operating costs into what we charge our client(s) for our services. If we do not capture our operating costs in this way, they will be paid for out of our apparent profits resulting in our company going out of business. Two broad categories of cost are direct costs and indirect costs as detailed below.

3.11.1 Direct Costs

Direct costs can best be described as expenses we can "see." Examples include the cost of our computers, electricity, heating and cooling of our office area, rent for our office space, business license fees and many others.

3.11.2 Indirect Costs

In many respects, these costs are not obvious. Some would say these costs are hidden. They can be broken down into two categories as described below.

3.11.2.1 Overhead Costs

These costs are the costs that the business incurs just to keep its doors open. They are incurred even if we have no customers. Different companies compute overhead (OH) in their own way. No matter how they are computed, keeping OH cost low is one of the ways by which managers in large corporations are evaluated. Since OH cost comes directly out of profit (remember, these costs occur even if we have no business), keeping OH low is desirable because there will be times when we have little or no business.

3.11.2.2 General and Administrative Costs

These are costs that are incurred only as a result of conducting business (i.e. we are developing code under contract for a client). Examples of general and administrative (G&A) costs include telephone service, shipping costs, export licenses, reproduction fees, fees to services (e.g. CD copying services, fees paid to consultants, accountants, lawyer fees) and others.

3.11.3 How to Compute Overhead

The way OH is computed is to add up all the costs associated with this category, divide it by the number of working hours in the year (nominally 2,000 hours in the United States and some other countries) and that gives you your hourly rate for OH. If you have ever wondered why it is so difficult to get a job as a consultant, you can see why right here. Consulting costs are most often allocated to the OH category. Paying a consultant or contractor to do some work thereby increases OH across the board. In most companies and government agencies, management's goal is to reduce or minimize OH and managers are evaluated in large part on how well they keep OH cost under control (i.e. low).

3.11.4 How to Compute General and Administrative Expense

This is computed in a slightly different manner. Here, the total cost for the year is added up and the percentage of the total operating cost of the company is computed using the formula

$$[GA]/[OH+GA]^* 100\%.$$

where

   GA = General and Administrative Expense
   OH = Overhead Expense

3.11.5 The Chart of Accounts

The chart of accounts is a categorized list of all the company's expenses and income. For the purposes of this discussion, we will only be listing the expenses. An example of a simple chart of accounts is presented in Table 3.5. Remember, if you do not know what your costs are, you won't be able to correctly price your services. This creates a bit of a quandary. You may know that a competitor charges less for their services and you are tempted to lower your fees to be more competitive. This is not advisable unless you can find a way to reduce your costs and still make a profit. Although the chart of accounts shown in the example only lists expenses, a typical chart of accounts would also list income categories, assets and other nonexpense items. The advice of an accountant in your locale would be well worth the cost. However, in the United States, the SCORE program provides such advisory services free. Some other countries have similar programs all intended to help small businesses and start-up businesses survive and grow.

3.11.6 Example of a Simple Chart of Accounts Listing OH & G&A

Some of you may be wondering what is a Chart of Accounts? In simple terms, it is a list of all the expenses in a given accounting period (often a calendar year) that the company has incurred organized by categories. For example, the money spent on computing hardware may constitute a cost category. Most of the terms in the table are self-explanatory but a few may need further explanation:

■ Depreciation – Devices do wear out. The number of years that we can expect them to work properly is commonly referred to as its "useful life." There are standards for what the useful life of an object or system is as well as criteria for whether or not an object can be depreciated or expensed. These are established by a governing accounting body in each country. For example, if a $5,000 computer is listed as having a five-year useful life, then we can claim a $1,000 per year depreciation expense for five years. Alternatively, if that $5,000 expense is less than the expense limit (e.g. $10,000), we can claim the entire $5,000 expense in the year the purchase was made provided it was made at the start of the year. Otherwise, we must prorate it based on when the purchase was made. In such a circumstance, it is often better to expense

Table 3.5   Example of a Simple Chart of Accounts

Overhead Expenses	Amount	Budget	Variance
Depreciation on equipment	8,421	2,200	6,221
Insurance expense	6,306	3,055	3,250
Rentals	10,258	4,500	5,758
Salary expense	50,675	18,900	31,775
Taxes — payroll	7,025	3,350	3,675
TOTAL OVERHEAD EXPENSES	**82,685**	**32,005**	**50,680**
GENERAL AND ADMINISTRATIVE EXPENSES			
Answering service	559	180	379
Auto mileage reimbursement	1,433	0	1,433
Bank Charges	218	50	168
Communications (e.g. cell phone, landline)	2,530	1,200	1,330
Directors fees	4,000	4,000	0
Dues and subscriptions	199	50	149
Depreciation	666	500	166
Insurance expense	4,577	0	4,577
Miscellaneous	101	20	81
Professional activities	375	150	225
Professional services	1,900	500	1,400
Royalties	0	0	0
Repairs	105	0	105
Reproduction expenses	5,110	1,200	3,910
Salary for bids and proposals	12,192	0	12,192
Shipping expenses	4,978	800	4,178
Supplies expense	2,399	2,400	-1
Taxes payroll	0	0	0
Taxes business	3,400	1,200	2,200
TOTAL GENERAL AND ADMINISTRATIVE EXPENSE	**45,037**	**12,275**	**32,762**

Note: Companies who have been doing business for some time will budget values for various costs and then track how much the actual cost has deviated from the budgeted amount (the "Variance") to help them make more accurate estimates in the future. Some costs (e.g. airfare) may vary between the time a proposal is submitted and the contract award occurs due to circumstances beyond our control. For example, in the table above, the Depreciation category has a large variance due to an unexpected change in accounting rules.

the entire purchase rather than to depreciate it provided the amount does not exceed the limits imposed within the jurisdiction but issues like this should be referred to an accounting professional.

3.11.7 Explanation of Items on the Chart of Accounts

Again, it is advisable to consult with an accounting professional in your area who is cognizant of the accounting rules and practices used in your locale. To do so otherwise risks being in violation of some rule or law. Be sure that your chart of accounts contains only direct costs and not burdened ones because the burdened cost factor(s) are computed from these direct cost amounts. Some of the items on the preceding chart of accounts may not be self-explanatory. They are listed here together with a brief explanation:

- Depreciation on equipment – This accounting concept involves the observation that after a period of time, a hardware item becomes out of date. The Oxford Dictionary defines the accounting concept of depreciation as, "a reduction in the value of an asset with the passage of time, due in particular to wear and tear." Although the concept is based on experience with hardware (e.g. factory equipment), it is just as applicable to computing hardware since it can be unable to operate at the new high-speed communications, employ the latest operating system and so forth. Although accounting standards vary from country to country, depreciation can be computed according to accounting standards agreed to within a country. For example, in the United States, the useful life of a laptop computer may be five years. There are different formulae for computing its depreciation, but "straight line" is a common one. This means that if that laptop had a direct cost of $2,000, its depreciation per year would be $400 (i.e. $2,000/5). There are also rules about what must be depreciated versus charging off the total amount. As you may have observed, if you spent $2,000 it would be better if you could charge the full amount off in the tax year in which the purchase was made to reduce your taxes versus spreading it out over five years.
- Insurance expense – your business owns computers, desks and other physical objects which could be lost due to a fire, flood, earthquake, theft and other disasters. Insuring them is more than just advisable, it is absolutely necessary. In addition, you will need to take out insurance for what are referred to as "errors and omissions." This protects your firm from liability from claims that you advised your client, they took the advice and it caused them to lose money. It is generally not overly expensive.
- Rentals – you may find it necessary to rent rather than buy office furniture, rent office space and so forth. Remember, even if you are running your business out of your home, you need to charge yourself office rent at the rate that is common in your geographic area. Otherwise, you will be creating a false sense of profitability.
- Salary expense – This is the direct cost of what you pay employees including yourself.
- Taxes – These vary from country to country and locale to locale within countries.

3.11.8 Computing the Project's Estimated Total Cost

Let's use an example to put all the costs together and find out what the contract is really going to cost the client. The effort we will be involved in is estimated to take 1,000 person-hours. Assume the hourly rate is $50 per hour. Our G&A expense rate is 25% (some government auditors will balk at this but even higher rates occur in small businesses – a general rule – the smaller the business, the higher the G&A rate), our OH is $20 per hour and we want a profit margin of 8% (again the government will try to drive this one down). Also, there will be three trips involved. One trip will kick off the project, another will occur at the mid-term of the project and the third will occur when the final delivery is made. We have established that our out-of-pocket cost for each trip will be $1,500. The numbers involved in the computation are presented in Table 3.6. Also, if you are not dealing with a government agency, you should not have to reveal your OH, G&A expense and profit. In some countries, these values are considered trade secrets and are not openly available to clients otherwise larger firms like Airbus, Embraer Air, Boeing and others would bid projects showing lower profit in order to gain greater market share.

Table 3.6 OH versus G&A Expenses

Overhead Expenses	*Description [Amounts Are for the Contract Term]*
Depreciation on equipment	The amount incurred during the project
Insurance expense	Amount paid for fire and theft insurance
Rentals	Amount paid for rental of equipment
Salary expense	Total salaries of those working on the project
Taxes – payroll	Amount paid to the government
TOTAL OVERHEAD EXPENSES	**The sum of the preceding five items**
General and Administrative Expenses	
Answering service	Amount paid if you have a service
Auto mileage reimbursement	Contract-related automobile travel mileage
Bank Charges	What the bank charges for your account
Communications	Telephone landline and/or mobile phone
Directors fees	Amount paid to owners of your firm
Dues and subscriptions	Professional memberships and subscriptions
Depreciation	Cost due to expending useful life of item
Insurance expense	Business insurance
Miscellaneous	Business expenses not categorized
Professional activities	Attendance at professional conferences
Professional services	Lawyer fees, consultant fees, contractor fees
Royalties	Amount paid for use of software
Repairs	Expense for repairing broken printers, etc.
Reproduction expenses	Cost of having documents copied, bound, etc.
Salary for bids and proposals	Cost of generating proposals

(Continued)

Table 3.6 (Continued)   OH versus G&A Expenses

Overhead Expenses	Description [Amounts Are for the Contract Term]
Shipping expenses	Cost of shipping final report, etc.
Supplies expense	Printer paper, laser printer cartridges, etc.
Taxes payroll	Payments to government
Taxes business	Local and regional taxes and business licenses
TOTAL GENERAL AND ADMINISTRATIVE EXPENSE	**Sum of the preceding items**

3.11.9 Project Cost Computation Example

At this point, we have what we need to compute what the total project, including our profit, will cost the client. The details are presented in Table 3.7.

What that 1,000-hour project is really going to cost your client is more than $100 per hour. If it was being done for a group within your company, the cost would be a little less because there

Table 3.7   Computing the Project's Cost

Cost Element	Item Description	Amount
Labor:		
	1,000 hours at $50/hour	$ 50,000
	Overhead at $20/hour	$ 20,000
Travel:		
	3 trips at $1,500/trip	$4,500
Sub Total		**$74,500**
General and Administrative Expense	At 25%	**$ 18,625**
Grand Total (our cost)		$ 93,125
Profit @ 8%		**$7,450**
Grand Total (Cost to the client)		**$100,575**

Note: The client is only privy to the final project cost. It is important that they do not see the actual cost, G&A, OH or profit. Throughout the world, these figures are considered trade secrets. The only exception to this is when working with some government agencies. In those cases, the agency has a policy of "non-disclosure." That is, as part of pursuing the lowest cost for work done for the public, they will try to negotiate the profit percentage lower and will have the right to audit your accounting records if they suspect some of the costs being claimed are being exaggerated. The adage that "honesty is the best policy" applies here because falsifying values to increase the fees you will be paid by the government is, in most countries, a serious crime punishable by a fine and/or a possible prison sentence.

would be no profit. Also, in some companies, they have an internal (intra-company) rate which may lower the OH a bit.

In our example, if we only considered direct costs, we would have thought the cost would be $50,000 plus the $4,500 out of pocket for travel for a total of $54,500 plus profit. It was just this kind of misconception and the lack of accounting advice that has led to the demise of many small start-up software companies.

3.11.10 Total Cost Computation

Again, you will need to confirm what the financial accounting standards are in your locale, but the following formula is compliant with many if not most countries:

$$\text{Total Cost} = \left[(\text{DLC} + \text{OVH}) + (\text{DOC}) \right]^* (1 + \text{G \& A})$$

where
 DLC = Direct Labor Cost
 OVH = Overhead
 DOC = Direct Other Costs
 G&A = General and Administrative cost as a decimal
 For example, 25% = .25

3.11.11 Risk Reduction via Bias Removal

Mankind has been building roads, tunnels and bridges for thousands of years but getting costs right still eludes us as shown in Table 3.8 [3]. The reason why we can't seem to accurately estimate such projects and, in fact, all projects, was researched resulting in a Nobel Prize in Economics. Those findings resulted in a method that has worked so well that the American Planning Association has recommended that its members use it together with traditional planning methods [3]. What the prize-winning work showed was that "Human judgment" is generally optimistic due to overconfidence and insufficient regard to distributional information. Thus, people will underestimate cost, completion times and risks of planned actions, whereas they will overestimate the benefits of the same actions [2]. Even though hundreds of roads, bridges and tunnels have been developed over the centuries, we still have trouble accurately estimating their costs (Table 3.8).

The method which adjusts estimates to account for our human biases is called Reference Class Forecasting. In simplified terms, it amounts to basing our estimates of the new project on how we did estimate previous, similar projects constituting our Reference Class. The more projects we have recorded information on, the more statically significant and accurate our results.

Table 3.8 Examples of Project Cost Misestimating (from [3])

Type of Project World Wide	Average % Overrun	Overrun % Range
Railways	45	7 to 83
Bridges and Tunnels	34	−28 to 96
Roads	20	−10 to 50

Table 3.9 Percentile Range and Aggregate Percentages

Percentile Range	Aggregate Percentage
–30% to –20%	06%
–20% to –10%	17%
0% to 10%	33%
10% to 20%	44%
20% to 30%	72%
30% to 40%	89%
90% to 100%	94%
100% to 170%	100%

Note that this approach does not result in a single cost number but rather, a cost estimate and a contingency amount based on the degree of confidence we desire for finishing within that combined cost (i.e. cost estimate + contingency). To use this method, for previous, similar software projects, we need:

■ The original cost estimate for each project
■ The actual final cost of each project

Be careful to avoid mixing different types of projects together. Reduce the data to percentiles and form a plot (in this example, a least squares fit) of Acceptable Chance of Cost Overrun (x-axis) versus Required Increase in Estimate/Contingency (y-axis). For this example, I was only able to locate one company with 18 similar projects that had collected the required data. The percentile range and aggregate percentages are shown in Table 3.9.

Reducing this data to a plot results in Figure 3.1. What the plot tells us is if we want approximately a 70% confidence level, we need to increase our estimate by approximately 50%. Note that since this plot is in terms of percentages, it is not dependent on the actual amount of the initial estimate we arrived at by whatever other means we may have used. Furthermore, this inherent bias is in all humans and hence affects any method we use (e.g. [8–10, 12, 13]). If we were to estimate our project at €100,000 and want to have a 70% confidence that it will finish at or below that amount, using this chart as our experience guide, we would have to increase our estimate by €50,000 or simply hope for the best. The problem for most software companies is that competitive bids tend to cause firms to keep bids low in hopes of winning the contract by engaging in the overly optimistic pursuit of new business to the extent that the risks are ignored or significantly downplayed.

3.11.12 Estimating the Cost of Change(s) during the Project

Well before the software profession "discovered" it, project managers had probably known since before the Roman Empire that changes made to a project increased in cost later in the project that they occurred. But throughout the course of software projects, changes will be made. While some are inevitable (e.g. to correct programming errors – bugs, miscommunication regarding user interface preferences, changes due to revisions in applicable laws and others), some could best be described as customer-directed changes. For example, modifications of the user interface requested

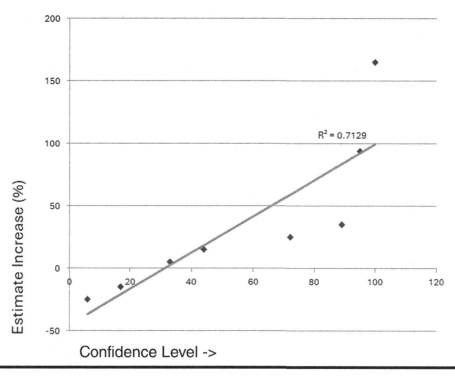

Figure 3.1   Confidence level versus set aside or cost estimate increase.

by the customer, changes in how taxes or interest rates are computed due to changes in tax law, privacy and security changes and so on. These changes tend to increase development costs. A study of several thousand projects in the construction industry [14] provides us with some much-needed insights into what the total cost of a project will be when we include the cost(s) associated with making changes. The mathematical relationships developed in that study are not specific to the type of project and are applicable to software. A side effect of the formulation that the study developed gives us the opportunity to provide our customers with some semblance of control over the total cost of the project. This result is formulated along two lines. One is the average cost of a change. The other is the relative cost of a change with respect to the total cost of the project. For example, if the burdened cost (this includes all direct and indirect costs) of a software engineer is €50/hour based on a 2000-hour work year, the cost for an average change which we estimate to be 8 hours (development, debugging, testing and so forth) gives us an average change cost of € 400. The formula for estimating the impact of the changes that may occur over the life of a project would be:

$$CV = \left(n^2 \, f_c^2 \, u_c^2\right)\Big/C^2$$

where

n = our estimate of the number of changes which will occur during the project
f_c = coefficient of variation of cost change
u_c = average cost of a change expressed as a decimal – it is the ratio of the cost of the change to
    the estimated total project cost
C = original project cost estimate

If we originally estimated the total project cost to be € 100,000 and estimate there will be 100 changes, each costing € 1,000 then

$$C = 100,000, n = 1000, f_c = 1,000, u_c = .01 \text{ substituting into our formula}$$

$$CV = \left[1,000^2 \ 2000^2 \ 0.01^2 \right] / 100,000^2 = 0.04$$

104,000. Again, the cost estimate is not an exact number but a value or range within the realm of possibility.

The obvious but incorrect answer would be to simply multiply the 100 changes by the cost per change and add it to our original estimate. But the research work showed that would be fallacious because changes occur while development is occurring so some economies can be wrought.

3.12 Outsourcing

Over the last three decades, major corporations have chosen to contract with firms in parts of the world which have software engineering talent and lower wages than where the corporation is located. Many of these arrangements appear to be quite beneficial for both parties. They are frequently fixed-price contracts meaning that the work will be done for a certain, unchanging price. Many of the early off-shore software development efforts turned out quite well. The quality was high, changes due to errors or alteration of requirements were made in a timely manner and customers were pleased with the results. But in more recent years, clients have told me that delivery dates were missed, response to requested changes (even when accompanied by bonus payments) was slow and sometimes non-existent and the quality of the deliverables is not what it used to be. Upon further investigation, it was determined that in some cases key people in the contractor organization had left it to form their own company and lacked the business knowledge, managerial skills, experience and organizational skills to deliver on commitments. These factors plus cultural differences between organizations have greatly reduced the advantages of outsourcing that were experienced in its early years.

3.13 Summary

The only possible way to avoid all risks is to do nothing. No matter what action(s) we take, there will be some associated risk(s). Some of these we can predict with a fair amount of certainty while others will occur without us foreseeing them. Regardless, ignoring risk leaves the project at the mercy of the whims of fortune. Being open and forthright about the possibility that risks may fire puts us in a position to ask two very positive questions:

1. If it does happen, what should we do about it?
2. What can we do to prevent the risk or make it less likely to fire?
3. What can we do now to ensure the project can survive a risk if it fires?

Either way, addressing risk is a healthy discussion and it causes us to shift our mentality from, "Everything is going to go well," to "Everything might go well but there may be some negative events along the way that we should be prepared to deal with." That change may be difficult for some teams to accomplish without the software project manager's leadership to ask the difficult, unpopular questions challenging the assumptions made by the team but no one said that managing a software project would be easy and popular.

Chapter 3 Review Questions

1. What is the difference between planning and scheduling?
2. What is the problem with using a "generic" software engineer as the basis for estimating?
3. What is the business case?
4. What is the role of the business case in the development of a software project?
5. Name the four viewpoints of the Balanced Scorecard.
6. What is meant by the term "Burdened Cost?"
7. What is the purpose of using the Burdened Cost when estimating a software project?
8. Why aren't there any accurate software project estimating methods?
9. Why are software project cost estimates based on lines of code?
10. What is the difference between Direct and Indirect costs?
11. What is the difference between Overhead (OH) and General and Administrative (G&A) costs?
12. When outsourcing, what are some of the forms of "Due Diligence" that are needed?

References

[1] McConnell, S., "The Software Manager's Toolkit," *IEEE Software*, Vol. 17, No. 4, pp. 5–7, July/August, 2000.

[2] Kahneman, D., Sibony, O. and Sunstein, D.R., *Noise: A Flaw in Human Judgement*, Little, Brown and Company, Boston, Massachusetts, Reprint edition, May 31, 2022.

[3] Flyvberg, B., "From Nobel Prize to Project Management: Getting Risks Right," *Project Management Journal*, August, 2006, Vol. 37, No. 3, pp. 5–15.

[4] Brooks, F., *The Mythical Man-Month: Essays on Software Engineering*, 20th Anniversary edition, Addison-Wesley, Reading, MA, 1995.

[5] Peters, L.J., *Getting Results from Software Development Teams*, Microsoft Press Best Practices Series, Redmond, WA, May, 2008.

[6] United States General Accounting Office May, 2000.

[7] Software Technology Support Center Cost Analysis Group, October 2010, 239 pages, *Software Development Cost Estimating Guidebook* download at no cost from this site: http://stsc.hill.af.mil/consulting/sw_estimation/softwareguidebook2010.pdf

[8] Boehm, B., et al., "An Overview of the COCOMO 2.0 Software Cost Model," *Software Technology Conference*, Salt Lake City, Utah, April 1995.

[9] Boehm, B., *Software Cost Estimation with COCOMO II*, Prentice Hall, Saddle River, New Jersey, August, 2011.

[10] Walston, C. and Felix, C., "A Method of Programming Measurement Estimation," *IBM Systems Journal*, Vol. 16, No. 1, 1977, pp. 54–73.

[11] Kaplan, R.S. and Norton, D.P., *The Balanced Scorecard*, Harvard Business School Press, Boston, MA, 1996.

[12] Kemerer, C.F., "An Empirical Validation of Software Cost Estimation Models," *Communications of the ACM*, Vol. 36, No. 2, 1993, pp. 416–429.

[13] Abran, A. and Robillard, P.N., "Function Point Analysis: An Empirical Study of Its Measurement Processes," *IEEE Transactions on Software Engineering*, January Vol. 22, No. 12, 1997, pp. 895–910.

[14] Touran, A., "Calculation of Contingency in Construction Projects," *IEEE Transactions on Engineering Management*, Vol. 50, No. 2, May 2003, pp. 135–140.

Chapter 4

Controlling

"You can't control what you don't measure."

—Tom DeMarco

4.1 Chapter Overview

Although the quote that starts this chapter seems logical enough, it is only partly true. For example, we can measure various aspects of the weather, but we can't control it. Anyone who has been the manager of anything but the simplest software project will agree that control is something of a myth. Events take place over which we have no forewarning and no control. As a result, we are not only constantly replanning but sometimes seem to be scrambling from one scheduled event to the next while responding to unscheduled events that have occurred. This happens even if our plan and schedule had what we thought was sufficient extra flow time built in to prevent failure to hit key milestones. This is a form of chaos within which we are trying to conduct our project. We do not have to be totally passive about our attempts at control and can incorporate actions to preemptively keep us from overrunning schedule, budget and so forth. But total control is just not going to happen.

Inherent in the notion of control is the need to measure. If you are driving an automobile and want to keep your speed at or slightly under the posted speed limit, you have to know how fast you are going. Similarly, in managing a software project, one needs to know how the project team is doing with respect to the project plan. Remember, the plan and schedule go together. Completing the planned tasks in the order set forth in the plan and consistent with the schedule is only part of the issue of control and measurement. Another equally important part involves our expenditure of funds and the consumption of other resources (e.g. use of contracted labor also a cost). Since the project undergoes nearly continual change, we need to measure the project's status frequently. If we restrict our evaluation(s) to our expenditure of funds, we can stay at or below our planned "burn rate" (the rate at which we spend money) possibly at the expense of getting the work done consistent with the agreed-upon schedule. Conversely, if we ignore the "burn rate," we can drive the project to completion, possibly on time, but exceed the budget. What is needed is a means of objectively

DOI: 10.1201/9781003484288-4

evaluating project status that combines the measurement of both the value we are creating (work done) and its cost. Faced with a similar dilemma, industrial engineers developed such an evaluation method more than 100 years ago. That method is called Earned Value Management (EVM).

4.2 Background of Earned Value Management (EVM)

In the late 19th century, industrial engineers were grappling with the problem of computing the total cost of products produced by a production line. Adding up the total annual cost of the building, labor, materials, and other costs and then dividing this by the number of parts produced just did not seem to be sufficient. For example, there were some products that were of such poor quality that they could not be shipped and others that could be shipped provided some rework was performed. There were other complications as well. Before long, the concept of "value" was developed. It involved more than just time and money. It focused on the notion that the work performed imbued the product with "value." As an example of value, consider two situations. We make a purchase at one store and purchase the same item at another store for 25% less. The second store represents a better value than the first. A beneficial side effect incorporated into the value concept is the ability to measure the efficiency with which resources were being expended. Project engineers began seeing the benefits of these measurements as they became aware that just because half the funds were spent and/or half the schedule elapsed did not mean that the project should be considered half complete. Over the more than 100 years since EVM came into existence, many refinements have been added to enhance its benefits to project managers.

4.3 Using EVM

Throughout the description of EVM, keep in mind that its measurements are mostly ratios of what we planned to do or planned to spend to what we actually occurred. The reason for this approach is to obtain an objective measure of various aspects of our project plan's execution. The importance of the "objective" perspective should be obvious to anyone who has attended a software project status meeting. During the meeting, software engineers who are members of one team or another report on the status of their portion of the project. This is where objectivity suffers because one cannot truly be objective in judging one's own work. In addition, there is peer pressure that can defeat objectivity. No one wants to be reporting that their work is not going well – it reflects badly on their abilities. This lack of objectivity defeats the purpose and value of the status meeting. Remember, what we are trying to do is get an accurate picture of the status of the project in order to take remedial action if needed. This is one of the most critical activities a software project manager engages in. EVM can act as an early warning system of sorts enabling the software project manager to be aware that a problem(s) is developing and take remedial action before it is too late to correct it. Leaving the determination of the status of individual tasks up to the person(s) responsible for completing them is not a good idea. Software engineers have often been described as the "most optimistic" people in the world. I have often seen software engineers report that a task is almost complete at the weekly status meeting with only a couple of minor issues to clean up only to have the task run late and not be completed until several weeks later. Part of this is due to peer group pressure. Nobody wants to admit in front of their colleagues that their work is falling behind schedule which may impact other parts of the project. Another factor is that the software engineer involved can conceptualize how the issues in his/her code could be resolved but ignoring details that can lengthen the time to resolve them and complete the task. Remember, no one is intentionally trying to put the project behind schedule. However, seriously troublesome software issues can cause delays the length of which we cannot reliably predict. Some coding errors I have observed took months to clear, having a serious impact on our schedule. The best way to reduce the impact of over-optimism is to apply the either/or approach. The code is either ready to incorporate in the next build or it isn't.

EVM tracks the project from a "Value" standpoint where value is seen as how efficiently time and money are expended. In a way, it is similar to a measure of efficiency or "value." It is applicable to any type of project. Its focus is on tasks completed for money and calendar time spent. There are several equations involved in using EVM broken down into categories such as time/schedule and cost. The naming conventions used to refer to these factors were changed a few years ago. In the discussion below, both naming schemes are used because many textbooks exist which still use the older conventions. Also, keep in mind that these factors are evaluated at a point in time and should be reevaluated on a regular basis. My preference was for weekly evaluations of these factors. A term you may encounter regarding value is "Planned Value." This is a key element of EVM. It is referred to in the literature as "Budgeted Cost of Work Scheduled" or BCWS. It is the portion of the budget we planned to spend at this point in the project. It is discussed below together with other EVM components.

All of the factors that comprise EVM have some formulation. The values generated by these formulae all have the desired or best results and not achieving them can reveal problems in the project. Knowing about problems in an objective format like EVM can be invaluable to the software project manager. This focuses our energy and analysis on finding the source of the problem(s) and taking action which, hopefully, will remedy the situation before it becomes impossible to correct.

4.4 What Is Needed to Use EVM

The requirements for using EVM are straightforward and are found in most project plans:

- A Work Breakdown Structure (WBS) listing tasks, subtasks and sub-subtasks.
- A baseline schedule showing when each task will start, finish and a budget for each.
- A measurement for the work listing completion criteria for each WBS item.

An EVM factoid:

- A study of more than 700 projects found that if a project is 15% complete and over budget and/or behind schedule, its chances of finishing on time and/or within budget are nil – that is, it won't happen [1].

The previous statement emphasizes the importance of tracking and staying on plan right from the start in order to avoid getting so far from the plan that correction is not possible. It is unlikely that very many software project managers are aware of this.

4.5 Cost-Related EVM Variables

Unless otherwise stated, the term "cost" as used here refers to the burdened cost, not the direct cost (refer to Chapter 3 for details on computing "burdened costs"). When we refer to cost in this discussion, we are referring to the true or "burdened" cost because that is what the task actually costs us. Using just the direct or "unburdened" cost makes the expenses appear deceptively low. Also, burdened cost does not include profit. EVM's cost-related factors are described below.

4.5.1 ACWP – Actual Cost of Work Performed

This is the sum of the actual costs incurred in performing the work. ACWP is also referred to as "Actual Cost."

4.5.2 BAC – Budget at Completion

The sum of all costs approved for the project (the budget) at evaluation time. BAC is also referred to as the "Performance Measurement Baseline" (PMB).

4.5.3 BCWP – Budgeted Cost of Work Performed

This is the amount budgeted for the work actually performed – now referred to as "Earned Value."

4.5.4 BCWS – Budgeted Cost of Work Scheduled

This is the sum of the budgeted amounts of work scheduled – now referred to as "Planned Value."

4.5.5 CPI – Cost Performance Index

A measure of how efficiently money is used on the project – one of the most important metrics included in EVM. Its formula is:

$$CPI = BCWP / ACWP$$

Interpretation:
   = 1, the project is right on track.
   1, ahead of plan, cost underrun possible.
   < 1, behind plan, cost overrun possible.

4.5.6 CV – Cost Variance

This is a measure of the difference between budgeted and actual costs.

$$CV = \left[\left(BCWP - ACWP \right) / BCWP \right] \times 100\%$$

Interpretation:
   = 0%, right on track.
   0%, actual is less than budgeted amount.
   < 0%, cost is overrunning budgeted amount.

4.5.7 EAC – Estimate at Completion

This is a projection forward in time of the total cost when the project ends. There is nothing "magic" here since this metric is basically a measure of the efficiency of the project's use of money over time – this may be the metric most closely watched by the customer.

$$EAC = BAC / CPI$$

Interpretation:
    = BAC (i.e. CPI = 1), on track.
    < BAC (i.e. CPI > 1), under budget.
    BAC (i.e. CPI < 1), over budget.

4.5.8 ETC – Estimate to Complete

This is an estimate of the cost that will be incurred from this point in the project to complete the project.

$$ETC = EAC - ACWP$$

Interpretation:
    = remaining budget, project is on track.
    project will overrun the remaining budget.
    < project will underrun the remaining budget.

4.6 Schedule Performance factors

These factors all relate to the project schedule. They are.

4.6.1 SPI – Schedule Performance Index

This is a measure of the efficiency with which the project performs to the project's schedule.

Interpretation:
    = 1, project is on track, likely to finish on time.
    1, project will likely finish ahead of schedule.
    < 1, project will likely finish late.

4.6.2 SV – Schedule Variance

This is a measure of the difference between the value of the work actually performed and the budgeted value of the work planned.

$$SV = \left[(BCWP - BCWS)/BCWS\right] \times 100\%$$

Interpretation:
    = 0, exactly on track.
    0, % ahead of schedule.
    < 0, % behind schedule.

4.6.3 TSPI – To Complete Schedule Performance Index

This is an estimate of the efficiency the project must perform in order to finish on time (i.e. consistent with the schedule)

$$TSPI = (Total\ Budget - EV)/Total\ Budget - PV)$$

Interpretation:
- = 1, the project team is on track.
- 1, the project team at high efficiency.
- < 1, the project team must increase efficiency.

4.7 Work and Content-Related Parameters

4.7.1 TCPIB – To Complete Performance Index within Budget

This is a measure of the budget-related efficiency with respect to work done. In other words, the rate at which we are getting useful work for the money spent.

$$TCPIB = (BAC - BCWP)/(BAC - ACWP)$$

Interpretation:
- = 1, money remaining (budget at completion) and work remaining are consistent.
- 1, the efficiency (in %) needed to complete on budget.
- < 1, high efficiency, likely to finish under budget.

4.7.2 TCPIP – Another, a Work to Money Ratio

$$TCPIP = (BAC - BCWP)/(EAC - ACWP)$$

Interpretation:
- = 1, on track to finish within EAC.
- 1, work left < work current efficiency will finish.
- < 1, work left >

4.8 An Example of the Application of Earned Value Management

To demonstrate the use of EVM, I will use an example based on a real software project. The numbers and circumstances have been altered to avoid revealing the client or nature of the software project. The length of the project was 17 months. Due to several ancillary issues, the project was fixed price and fixed term – that is, it had to be completed within a predetermined flow time and completed within the budgeted amount ($500,000+).

The flow times by phase are shown in Table 4.1 and burdened labor costs in Table 4.2.

The cash flow by month is shown in Table 4.3.

Table 4.1 Project Flow Times by Phase

Phase	Duration (Months)	Person-Load
Plans and Requirements Definition	2.7	1.9
Product Design	3.6	3.4
Programming	7.2	6.0
Integration and Test	3.5	4.8

Table 4.2 Labor Costs (People Names Withheld)

Category	Rate/Hour	Hours/Month	Hours/Year
Project Manager	$45	167	2,000
Sr. Software Engineer	$40	167	2,000
Software Engineer	$35	167	2,000
Software Tester	$30	167	2,000

Table 4.3 Cash Flow by Month

Level of Effort/# Persons	Project Manager	Sr. Software Engineer	Software Engineer	Software Tester	Total Cost per Month
Plans and Requirements	0.9/1	1/1			$13,444
Product Design	0.4/1	1/1	½		$21.376
Programming	0.4/1	1/1	1/4.6		$37,573
Integration and Test	0.4/1	1/1		1/3.4	$26,720

According to the project plan, expenses would occur as shown in Figure 4.1. Note that expenses were computed at fully burdened rates.

In examining Figure 4.1, we note that the actual expenses are consistent with the planned expenses for the first five months. Then, starting in the sixth month the actual expenses exceed the plan by a small amount. Applying EVM to the figures in the first seven months, we get Table 4.4.

In examining Table 4.4, we note that early on, overruns appear to be slight. The CPI is perfect (1.0) until months 6 and 7 when it trends toward trouble. The CV is about –17% meaning we are going to overrun by about 17%. By month 7, TCPIB needs to be 1.15 in order to hit our cost and schedule targets. In other words, we need to be 15% more efficient or productive than we have been to that point which is highly unlikely. So, what are our "target" EVM values that will keep us on track with our plan? Table 4.5 lists the ideal or "target" values to use as guidelines.

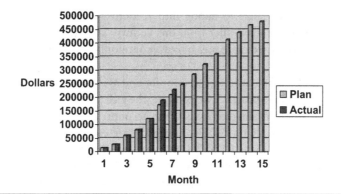

Figure 4.1 **Planned expense rate versus actual expenses.**

Table 4.4 **EVM Variables for the First Seven Months of Example**

Month->	1	2	3	4	5	6	7
ACWP	OK	OK	OK	OK	$121,903	$190,301	$245,874
BCWP	OK	OK	OK	OK	$109,713	$155,071	$209,874
CPI	1.00	1.00	1.00	1.00	0.90	0.81	0.85
CV	0.00%	0.00%	0.00%	0.00%	-11.11%	-22.72%	-17.15%
SPI	1	1	1	1	0.9	0.9	1
SV	0.00%	0.00%	0.00%	0.00%	-10.00%	-10.00%	0.00%
TCPIB	1	1	1	1	1.03	1.12	1.15
TCPIP	1	1	1	1	0.9	0.81	0.85

Table 4.5 **Ideal EVM Variable Values by Types**

Coefficient	Related to	Desirable	Nominal	Undesirable
CPI	Cost	>1	=1	<1
CV	Cost	<0%	0%	>0%
EAC	Cost	>1	=1	<1
ETC	Cost	<Remaining Budget	=Remaining Budget	>Remaining Budget
SPI	Schedule	>1	=1	<1
SV	Schedule	>0%	=0%	<0%
TCPIB	Work	<1	=1	>1
TCPIP	Work	>1	=1	<1

The term "burdened rate" refers to taking into account all of the costs associated with the project. Although the language may differ from one country and system of accounting from one country to another, there are three categories of costs commonly considered:

■ Direct Costs – These are the easiest to account for and as the name implies are what we generally will see the easiest on a project. For example, the €40 per hour we pay a software engineer is a direct cost. If we only take direct costs into account, we will be losing money at a rapid rate. You may have heard that a €40 per hour software engineer earns €80,000 per year but may actually cost the company €120,000 per year, possibly much more. That bit of hearsay happens to be true. Here is how. As a company, we need to provide working space for the software engineer, heating and cooling, pay various social services taxes, business licenses, liability insurance, health insurance premiums, various other benefits, administrative support, legal fees for the company and so on. Not accounting for and incorporating those indirect costs into our estimates for doing work for our clients can and will put us out of business.
■ Indirect Costs – These relate to just keeping the doors of the business open and running our software engineering firm. These break down into two categories:
  – Overhead Costs
  – General and Administrative Costs

Perhaps the best way to explain the role and content of these various costs is through an explanatory example but first a few basics. The term "Chart of Accounts" refers to a listing of the various expenses and sources of income of a company. Different countries have different rules about what must be listed in a chart of accounts and how each item should be categorized so what is depicted here may be different from what an accounting firm in your locale would consider standard accounting practice in your country. Table 4.1 presents a generic example from which you could begin to develop a chart of accounts for your startup firm. If you work for an established company, they have already created a chart of accounts. In general, the actual numbers are not publicly available because they reveal the pricing structure of the firm.

Chapter 4 Review Questions

1. In EVM, what is the concept of "value?"
2. What information is needed to use EVM?
3. If a project is 15% complete and over budget and/or behind schedule, without changing budget, schedule or requirements, what are its chances of eventually getting back on schedule and/or within budget?
4. What underlying assumptions comprise EVM?

References

[1] Fleming, Q.W. and Koppelman, J.M., *Earned Value Project Management*, 4th edition, Project Management Institute, Newtown Square, PA, 2010.

Chapter 5

Staffing

5.1 Chapter Overview

Although the software project manager has been found to be the most important factor in the success of a software project, having a software engineering team with the knowledge and skills necessary to be successful is also a vital factor. Picking that team is not a simple task. But even as we are selecting the team, we are mindful of what role each team member will play. Although people can play different roles in software development efforts, there are some they will be better at than others most often due to their preferences. As we discuss in this chapter, there are many mistakes that can be made in putting the team together that can jeopardize the team's chances of success. This chapter presents an approach which has been used successfully to assemble and maintain a team that performs to its full potential. It also provides guidance and examples of how to resolve unusual situations.

5.2 Acquiring and Developing the Software Development Team

Putting together a software development team and maintaining it may be the most important responsibility a software project manager has. It is hard work; it may take a lot of your time and it never ends. It never ends because the team is continually evolving as its members work together, learn more about each other and strive to achieve a successful project. As you read this section, think about a time when you were a member of a software development team that is or was effective. It did not have to be an ideal situation but it worked. If it didn't work, the remainder of this chapter may reveal why and what could be done in a future project effort to prevent problems and better ensure success by carefully assigning software engineers to tasks for which they are best suited and prefer to do. This chapter also explores ways to ensure that remote teams work together across cultural, geographic and time zone differences that often endanger success.

As in sports, having a productive software development team requires much more than simply selecting talented people. While selecting people with knowledge, experience and some level of talent is important, selecting people who can work together and support each other is also important but motivating the team may be the most important factor. If you have been part of more than a few projects at different companies, you have probably seen some projects with talented people run into serious difficulties. Some of these situations may have been puzzling in that the people were

DOI: 10.1201/9781003484288-5

talented and experienced, the requirements were well understood and the schedule was not impossible, so what was the problem? In my professional career, consulting practice and elsewhere, I have seen this many times. Some people simply attribute the difficulties to "The management" but the source of problems goes much deeper than this.

5.3 Software Engineering Is a People Activity

No matter what kind of software is being developed, or how skilled or challenged a software development team is, software is built by people. That fact brings into play all the various foibles and idiosyncrasies that constitute a person including their psychological makeup, value systems, education and work preferences – what they prefer to work on. Technology will not solve the "People Problem" because it is focused on definable issues with what amount to closed-form solutions. The term "People Problem" refers to the challenges the software project manager is faced with when putting a project team together, keeping them together and motivating them to get along and be productive. Just to be clear, the issues involved include the pace at which some folks work, interpersonal skills (or the lack of them), attention to detail, reliability (i.e. showing up for work every day), on-time delivery, meeting commitments, mutual respect (or the lack of it), a shared sense of urgency and others. What a messy challenge. However, there are a variety of ways to meet these challenges as we shall see in this chapter. A key factor to keep in mind is that there is no formula or defined process by which you can be successful at team building and management because each situation is different based on many factors which are discussed here. Being a people activity, we need to be aware of the differences in how people deal with the world, how they go about solving problems and more.

5.4 What Does a Successful Software Project Team Look Like?

Many software project managers have wondered just what do they have to do in order to build a software engineering team most likely to be at least minimally successful. That is, the team brings the project in on-time, meeting requirements and within budget. Fortunately, we have some guidance in this regard. A study of successful high-technology projects and multidisciplinary teams [1] described the fundamental properties a team needs to have in order for them to potentially be successful. All of these "winning" teams were composed of people who shared these three characteristics:

1. Tacit Knowledge – They had some knowledge of the technology involved. They were not experts in this technical field but had some experience with it or knowledge of it.
2. Team Experience – They had worked as part of a team before – not necessarily with these team members but had experienced the give and take of negotiating what happens when teams make decisions. More recent work [2] found that the ideal situation occurs when the team members have worked together as a team before.
3. Team Member Compatibility – The team members had psychological profiles which were compatible. Using the Myers-Briggs Type Inventory (MBTI) or some other personality type/inventory system, the personalities of the team members were deemed to range from reasonably compatible to incompatible. We have all experienced instances in work situations where some people we worked with seemed easier to work with than others. It turns out that at least part of the nature of this was the personality profile of the individuals involved.

5.5 Psychological Compatibility

No matter what line of work you are in or have been in, there are people you have worked with easily and others you simply had a difficult time working with but could not always explain why. One team of researchers studied dozens of successful and failed technology projects in an attempt to find what made teams work or not work [1]. They found, as stated above, that psychological compatibility was one of three primary factors present in successful technology projects. As a software project manager, you have probably figured out ways to establish whether or not a prospective team member possesses the training, technical knowledge and experience your team will need on a given project but what about compatibility with other team members? It turns out that for more than 2000 years various people have been trying to understand human personality well enough to do just that. One of the most widely used is MBTI [3]. It views personality as having four dimensions with each dimension having two opposing factors. The dimensions and their opposing factors in this model of human personality are:

- **Focus of Attention** – The two opposing forms this dimension can take are:
  - Extravert (E) – These are people who are at ease talking to and sharing with others. They gain energy from working with groups.
  - Introvert (I) – These people relate best to their inner self. Their energy is drained from working with groups.
- **Seeking Information** – The two opposing forms this dimension can take are:
  - Sensing (S) – These people rely on facts, reality and are no-nonsense individuals. When they review documents, they are most likely to find typographical errors and misspellings.
  - Intuitive (N) – These are people who use/rely on their intuition, speculation and imagination. When they review a document and they are most likely to find problems in how the document was developed.
- **Decision-Making** – The two opposing forms this dimension can take are:
  - Thinking (T) – These people make decisions based primarily on sound principles, laws and so forth. Thinkers are analytical, logical and objective.
  - Feeling (F) – These people make decisions based on values, devotion, sympathy and harmony. Feelers will take the emotions and opinions of others into consideration. They strive to maintain harmony in the group.
- **Relationship with the World** – The two opposing forms this dimension can take are:
  - Judging (J) – These people are outcome-oriented, regulated and decisive. They make decisions quickly, drive toward getting closure of issues and settlement.
  - Perceiving (P) – Process-oriented, flexible, open-minded and make decisions slowly. They like to get new information or consider other possibilities.

Each person is a combination of one of the two possibilities in each of the four categories (e.g. INTJ) giving us 16 possibilities. Table 5.1 contains the distributions in percentage of each type for the population of the United States. It is presented here in order to demonstrate the broad range of personality types that exist in the United States and likely similarly in other developed nations.

The reason for presenting Table 5.1 is to demonstrate the wide variety of personality types present in the general population and as we shall see, the types that are concentrated in the software engineering profession. One study [5] found results shown in Table 5.2 with subsequent researchers finding similar results.

Table 5.1   Distribution of Personality Types in the United States using the MBTI Model [4]

ISTJ: 11.6%	ISFJ: 13.8%	INFJ: 1.5%	INTJ: 2.1%
ISTP: 5.4%	ISFP: 8.8%	INFP: 4.4%	INTP: 3.3%
ESTP: 4.3%	ESFP: 8.5%	ENFP: 8.1%	ENTP: 3.2%
ESTJ: 8.7%	ESFJ: 12.3%	ENFJ: 2.5%	ENTJ: 1.8%

Table 5.2   Combined Population of Personality Types among Software Engineers [5]

ISTJ: 25%	ISFJ: 13.8%	INFJ: 1.5%	INTJ: 16%
ISTP: 5.4%	ISFP: 0%	INFP: 4.4%	INTP: 15%
ESTP: 4.3%	ESFP: 8.5%	ENFP: 8.1%	ENTP: 0%
ESTJ: 8.7%	ESFJ: 0%	ENFJ: 2.5%	ENTJ: 1.8%

What the various studies of software engineers' MBTI profiles conducted over the years have consistently shown over the years is an evolution with introverts, thinking and judging prevalent with sensing and intuitive types nearly equal. Part of this shift in MBTI type population in software engineering is changes in the nature of the work. Initially, highly mathematical and scientific to today with heavy emphasis on communication, ease of use and human interfaces.

5.6 Teams Need Compatibility

Some possible types work better together or are more compatible with others as shown in Table 5.3. To use the table, select are type on the vertical that corresponds to one person then move to the right to the column representing a second person's type. The higher the compatibility index, the more compatible the type is with another type. For example, an INTJ type would be very compatible with an ESFJ type (0.83) but not very compatible with an ENTP (0.17).

Some advisories are in order here. Regardless of the model used (MBTI is only one of several available), personality type should not be the only factor used to select team members. Besides, work rules in some countries and organizations may preclude the administering of the MBTI or some other typing instrument, even if it is put forward as a condition of employment. Also, this information must be retained in the strictest confidence unless the team member explicitly gives permission to share it. There are other factors as well so it would be wise to check your local laws and organization's rules.

Interviewing prospective members of the development team should involve all current members – if they do not believe they can work with the interviewee, then find someone else who can.

Table 5.3 Normalized Personality Compatibility using the MBTI

	ESTJ	ESTP	ESFJ	ESFP	ENTJ	ENTP	ENFJ	ENFP	ISTJ	ISTP	ISFJ	ISFP	INTJ	INTP	INFJ	INFP
ESTJ	0.67															
ESTP	0.33	0.67														
ESFJ	0.83	0.50	0.67													
ESFP	0.50	0.83	0.33	0.67												
ENTJ	0.83	0.50	1.00	0.67	0.67											
ENTP	0.50	0.83	0.67	1.00	0.33	0.67										
ENFJ	1.00	0.67	0.83	0.50	0.83	0.50	0.67									
ENFP	0.67	1.00	0.50	0.83	0.50	0.83	0.33	0.67								
ISTJ	0.50	0.17	0.67	0.33	0.67	0.33	0.83	0.50	0.33							
ISTP	0.17	0.50	0.33	0.67	0.33	0.67	0.50	0.83	0.00	0.33						
ISFJ	0.67	0.33	0.50	0.17	0.83	0.50	0.67	0.33	0.50	0.17	0.33					
ISFP	0.33	0.67	0.17	0.50	0.50	0.83	0.33	0.67	0.17	0.50	0.00	0.33				
INTJ	0.67	0.33	0.83	0.50	0.50	0.17	0.67	0.33	0.50	0.17	0.67	0.33	0.33			
INTP	0.33	0.67	0.50	0.83	0.17	0.50	0.33	0.67	0.17	0.50	0.33	0.67	0.00	0.33		
INFJ	0.83	0.50	0.67	0.33	0.67	0.33	0.50	0.17	0.67	0.33	0.50	0.17	0.50	0.17	0.33	
INFP	0.50	0.83	0.33	0.67	0.33	0.67	0.17	0.50	0.33	0.67	0.17	0.50	0.17	0.50	0.00	0.33

For a variety of reasons, you may end up having to manage a team with members who are incompatible. There are several things you can do to mitigate the situation:

Try working with the individuals involved directly, privately and together. The key issue here is whether or not they are willing to set aside their differences for the good of the project.

Do not single anybody out as a troublemaker. The rest of the team probably already knows who this person(s) is.

Make sure everyone on the team puts the success of the project ahead of their personal agendas. A gentle reminder on the merit or annual performance review may help in some circumstances.

If you have tried everything you can think of, enlist the help of a psychology professional who specializes in team development. I had this exact situation before and the cost was money well spent.

The most common software types are ISTJ and INTJ. To use the table, go to the intersection of two types. For example, ESTP and INTJ have a compatibility index of 0.33. Recalling that the higher the compatibility index the more compatible the personalities, 0.33 is not highly compatible.

Using the compatibility table:

1. Determine the MBTI personality type for each individual on the team.
2. Select the appropriate column for one of the individual's MBTI types.
3. Find the horizontal row for the second person's MBTI type.
4. Find where the column and row selected above intersect. That is the estimated compatibility index.

5.7 An Advisory about the Compatibility Index

While the compatibility of team members is important, it should not be the only or primary factor in determining whether or not to extend an invitation to an individual to join the team. Other factors should be considered as well. These include but are not limited to whether or not the job candidate possesses the knowledge and skills needed by the team, whether or not the members of the team believe they can work with this person and how strongly the candidate wants to be a member of this team working on this particular project.

5.8 Software Engineer Task Preferences and the MBTI

We have seen how compatibility between/among members of the software development team can impact project success but interpersonal compatibility is only part of the software project manager's team formation and deployment problem. Another part is the assignment of each team member to tasks that are part of the project. Thinking about your own career, there were tasks you were assigned that you found you preferred over others. It turns out that from a productivity standpoint, like other people, software engineers are less productive when they are performing tasks which they dislike versus ones they prefer [6]. Studies have demonstrated a correlation between certain MBTI types and software engineering tasks [7] as well as the most-and least-represented MBTI types in software engineering [4]:

- Most-represented MBTI types
  ISTJ
  INTP
  ESTJ

- Least-represented MBTI Types
  ENFJ
  INFJ

The actual data for all 16 MBTI-type categories are shown in Table 5.4.

It should be kept in mind that your project will need software engineers doing more than writing code (programming). Analysts, designers and testers will be needed as well as some software engineer(s) to maintain the code. In smaller projects and company settings, software engineers might be required to perform in more than one role. This raises the issue of which MBTI types are better suited to one or more of these roles than others based on their task preferences. The work has been [5] done to help us make these assignment decisions. Of course, the individual software engineer must agree to the assignment but at least we have some guidance as to what roles are most likely to be acceptable or preferred by the software engineer. The findings regarding task preferences in Carpretz [7] are structured according to MBTI temperament categories (i.e. SP, SJ, NT and NF) as shown in Table 5.5.

The preferences in Table 5.5 are just that, preferences. It does not mean that software engineers should only be assigned to their preferred tasks. They could very well be effective at working on other tasks as well. This largely depends on the individual's value system and work ethic. Although MBTI or some other personality type indicator should not be used exclusively to make the decision to hire or assign a software engineer, the temperament profile of the software engineers that were hired provides a strong indication of which role(s) each individual would prefer and likely perform well at.

Table 5.4   Frequency of Occurrence (%) of MBTI Types among Software Engineers [4, 7]

Type>	ISTJ	ISFJ	INFJ	INTJ	ISTP	ISFP	INFP	INTP	ESTP	ESFP	ENFP	ENTP	ESTJ	ESFJ	ENFJ	ENTJ
	17.3	3.6	2.2	9.0	8.1	1.6	3.9	11.5	4.7	2.0	3.8	9.7	12.7	2.1	2.0	6.0

Table 5.5   Task Preferences of Software Engineers by MBTI Temperament Type [7, 8]

Task Type ->	Analyst	Designer	Programmer	Tester	Maintainer
SP	85%	59%	74%	11%	22%
SJ	84%	66%	64%	25%	25%
NT	65%	85%	60%	20%	15%
NF	75%	63%	63%	13%	13%

Chapter 5 Review Questions

1. Name the three attributes common to successful high-technology project teams.
2. What does psychological compatibility mean?
3. What should you do if you have one or more team members who are incompatible with each other or other team members?
4. What role should the compatibility index play in the hiring process?
5. In making team member task assignments, what role should the MBTI or other profiles you may be using play?

References

[1] Chen, J. and Lin, L., "Modeling Team Member Characteristics for the Formation of a Multifunctional Team in Concurrent Engineering," *IEEE Transactions on Engineering Management*, Vol. 15, No. 2, 2004, pp. 111–124.

[2] Staats, B.R., Gino, F. and Pisano, G.P., "Varied Experience, Team Familiarity, and Learning: The Mediating Role of Psychological Safety," Working Paper 10-016, Harvard Business School, 2010.

[3] Myers, I.B. and Myers, P.B., *Gifts Differing: Understanding Personality Type*, 2nd edition, CPP, Palo Alto, Ca, 1995.

[4] Capretz, L., "Personality Types in Software Engineering," *International Journal of Human-Computer Studies*, 2003, Vol. 58, pp. 207–214.

[5] Bush, C. and Schkade, L., "In Search of the Perfect Programmer," *Datamation*, Vol. 31, No. 6, 1985, pp. 128–132.

[6] DeMarco, T. and Lister, T., *Peopleware*, Dorset House, New York, NY, 1999.

[7] Capretz, L., Varona, D. and Raza, A., "Influence of Personality Types in Software Tasks Choices," *Computers in Human Behavior*, Vol. 52, 2015, pp. 373–378.

[8] Schaubhut, N. and Thompson, R., *MBTI Type Tables for Occupations*, CPP, Mountain View, California, 2008.

Chapter 6

Motivating

"The best, most effective motivator is a simple 'Thank you'."

–Francesca Gino, Harvard University

6.1 Chapter Overview

You have laid out a project plan, put together a team you believe can do the job and now begin to ponder the question, "How do I get the team committed and motivated to this work?" Part of the answer lies in the interview process where you explained the work you are hiring them for so that they should have known what they were going to be doing and what would be expected of them. Why should we care if they are motivated? We should care because an unmotivated team will take longer and produce lower quality than a motivated one. As you will see in this chapter, we need to understand what work appeals to each software engineer and what are the many options at your disposal for getting them engaged in the project. This chapter explores the dimensions of this issue(s), providing some options for addressing it together with further resources for exploring available research further.

6.2 The Problem

For many years, managers in various industries and sports teams have grappled with the problem of motivating their teams to perform to the best of their ability. Several factors are involved in making that happen. Without training and science-based information, many software project managers have concluded that in order to get the team members motivated, offer money as an incentive since they see money as the primary motivator but it isn't. Money has been shown to be the primary motivator for repetitive work like factory work [1] and developing software is anything but repetitive. The software project managers' incorrect assumption about money as a motivator stems from their value system which places money as number one in importance [2] as shown in Table 6.1. In order to better understand what motivates people to work, we need to understand the nature of work and how people relate to it. What motivates people can vary greatly from person to person

DOI: 10.1201/9781003484288-6

Table 6.1 Value System Differences between Software Engineers and Their Managers [2]

Factor	Manager's Importance Rank	Nonmanager's Importance Rank
Salary	1	5
Job Security	2	4
Promotion/Growth Opportunities	3	7
Working Conditions	4	9
Interesting/Challenging Work	5	6
Personal Loyalty to Workers	6	8
Tactful Discipline	7	10
Appreciation for Work Done	8	1
Help with Personal Problems	9	3
Being in on Things	10	2

and profession to profession. It all depends on their value system. We will examine some of the most common factors mentioned earlier. A study of the psychological profiles of 60 professions [3] found that software engineers are unique in that they have:

1. High Growth Needs Strength – This is a need to solve challenging problems.
2. Low Social Needs Strength – This is the desire to solve these problems independently.

There are other studies which characterize software engineers which found less profound results. One particularly observant one showed that working on projects which are on the leading edge of the technology is a big motivator as well as working on projects that would impress their colleagues [4]. It should be noted that these and other studies do not mention money as a motivator and yet, software project managers still believe that money is a motivator. It turns out that money has been shown to be a motivator only in repetitive work like factory work but not in challenging, creative and innovative technical work like software engineering [2]. Granted, not all of us are managing projects which are state of the art or breaking new ground in the profession, but we can vary the work so that people will look forward to coming to work and doing a great job. For example, I was in charge of a team whose job was to debug codes written by others which was of poor quality. Of all the assignments software engineers probably dislike the most, it is cleaning up somebody else's poor-quality code. Also, at this time, there was an advanced research effort to develop three-dimensional viewing which was going unstaffed due to low priority and limited funding. Even though our group was tasked with code cleanup duties, literally everybody wanted to work on the experimental three-dimensional viewing glasses. What I did to remedy the situation was to rotate people from code cleanup to the three-dimensional effort for fixed periods of time negotiated with the team. That way, each team member knew they would only be doing the distasteful work for a known limited time before they would be doing something really interesting, then back again and so forth. This worked. The code cleanup effort improved, and morale improved measurably. While not every project management situation may have such a readily available solution, it is important to recognize that the morale of the team and each individual is vital to the success of your effort. You might try creating a technically challenging project to help give team members an alternative or, better yet, have each member of the team propose something and have the team vote on which to pursue.

In his speech upon being inducted into the Automotive Hall of Fame in 2006, Alan Mulally, former CEO of Ford Motor Company pointed out that in the United States at that time only 40% of workers were happy about their jobs and only 25% were engaged in their work. These are important productivity issues directly related to the role/behavior of management. Some senior managers believe "I am paying them to do a job. I am not paying them to be happy!" Hopefully, this group is in the minority since studies have shown that workers who are happy are up to 20% more productive and engaged in their work [5].

6.3 What Motivates Software Engineers

In general, software project managers see themselves as problem solvers. Motivating the software engineering team to perform at their best is often challenging and a significant problem whose solution is part of the key to a successful project. It is among the "soft skills" successful software project managers utilize [6]. This is where the differences between the manager's value system and that of the software engineer come into play with (potentially) negative outcomes [2]. Software project managers value money more highly than software engineers [2]. This creates a communication barrier between the software project manager and the software engineer (Table 6.2). Succumbing to a form of affinity bias, without questioning it, the software project manager assumes the software engineer highly prizes money as well and proceeds to employ it as a means of motivating team members. Unfortunately, this is not what actually works. What does work is a simple "Thank you" [7]. This doesn't need to be some sort of award ceremony but just a private meeting with an individual or even the whole team and thanking them for their efforts. This situation is something of a paradox, wherein the most expensive motivator is the least effective while the least expensive is the most effective. Let's just call this Peters' Paradox. The assumption that money is a motivator is true only in a limited arena which involves repetitive [1] work (e.g. factory work) but software engineering is creative, challenging and anything but repetitive.

Table 6.2 Known Demotivators of Software Engineers [8]

During the Development Phase	Comments
Technically High-Risk Requirements	Not anchored in what is possible
High-Risk Schedule	Market generated and not realistic
Inadequate Staffing	Not just head count but skill set, proficiency level and experience
Inadequate Resources	Hardware, software and communications
Software Quality	Just getting it done is not enough
During the Distribution Phase	
Poor Software Quality	Reflects badly on the development team
Feature Reduction	Reduces the importance of individual efforts

6.4 What Demotivates Software Engineers

It is important for us to recognize what actions demotivate the software engineering team. The problem often is that circumstances beyond our control may put us into a situation where there is nothing we can do but try to get through as best we can because the factors like those shown in Table 6.2 are thrust upon us. By looking at the table, we can see several of the usual complaints that software engineers have about the management of their projects. The content of the table should be considered the short list. If you review your own experiences, you will probably remember others.

The thing to remember about Table 6.2 is that it is only a representative list of actions which inhibit productivity. As a reminder [3], shipping poor quality just to meet a deadline is a productivity inhibitor of the first order. According to reviewers on the internet, Microsoft's Surface Duo was not really ready for release due to the large number of programming errors present in that product. Given that, it is unlikely that developers of that product would highlight producing it as a high point in their career. Also, reducing features is a demotivator because people who were working on those features have a lot of time and effort investing in them. Postponing them for a later release or canceling them altogether may be well intended (i.e. to shorten the schedule) but can have a significant impact on the motivation and productivity of those assigned to their creation.

6.5 Motivating Test and Maintenance Teams – Their Jobs Are (Almost) Thankless

Cleaning up someone else's poor-quality code is bad enough but testing it and having to notify the developer that the code was faulty and failed some test(s) in the mind of some worse. Remember that code is psychologically an extension of the developer's self [9] so there is a natural reluctance for the software engineer to simply accept the tester's verdict. In some firms, the people who test software are viewed unfavorably. In fact, they may be shunned socially. The challenge for the software project manager is to educate the software engineering team as to the value that finding (and removing) coding errors before the product ships saves the developing firm a considerable amount of money over emergency rework and even saves the product from receiving poor reviews which may ultimately cause the product to be abandoned.

6.6 The Role of Antipatterns

The software project manager is the ultimate problem solver. No matter what is going wrong in the project, the software project manager is expected to have some solution for it. The problem is, as we have discussed earlier, the software project manager is not likely to be trained for each and every eventuality that can occur. But since the problem feels something must be done about the problem, they make up something that may seem like a solution. Not all of these solutions fail to solve the problem but enough have that books have been written about them [10]. These ineffective solutions are referred to as "antipatterns" and, as their name implies, they not only do not work but generally make things worse. The best way to avoid falling into the "antipattern trap" is education. That means learning what constitutes an antipattern and refraining from engaging one when it seems like the action to take. One of the earliest published works in identifying an antipattern was Brooks' work titled "The Mythical Man-Month" [11]. In it, Brooks pointed out that adding people to a late project actually makes it later. It is fair for us to ask, why did we think it would help in the first place? This is where our humanity works against us. Our everyday experience tells us that if we have a task to do, the more people we have working on it, the less time it will take. The problem is these everyday tasks are simple and deterministic. For example, if we have to stack a load of firewood, two people working on it will get it done quicker than one and so forth. The important difference is that developing software is neither simple nor deterministic. That is, it does always have a definable end. Why? Because as the development process goes on, we begin to discover nuances in the requirements, the environment the system will run in changes, users' needs change and more. All of these factors and more make software engineering challenging for both the engineers and the project manager. It is a process constantly subject to change.

6.7 Peters' Paradox

As stated earlier, the most effective means of motivating software engineers is a simple "Thank you." This free but the most common means of motivating software engineers is money. But money has been shown to be ineffective at motivating software engineers over the longer term. So, we have a paradox of sorts in that the most expensive motivator is the least expensive while the least expensive motivator is the most effective.

6.8 The Nature of Work

For several decades, psychologists have been studying people's motivation to work. The obvious answer is that people work for money but that is only partially true. If you disagree, think of the worst, most disgusting job you can imagine. Now if someone offered you double the salary you are currently being paid to do that job for the rest of your career, would you accept the offer? I have posed that same question to, literally, hundreds of software engineers over the years and have not had a single taker. It turns out work is a deeply personal activity involving our image of ourselves, our goals in life, how we relate to colleagues and more. A good example of this money issue took place on the big screen in a 1954 movie titled "On the Waterfront." In it, Marlon Brando plays the part of Terry, a prizefighter who works on the docks in New York unloading ships. His brother Charlie is a lawyer for the crime syndicate that controls the docks and shipping. Terry and his brother are having an argument over why Brando was forced to throw (intentionally lose) a fight. Terry says, "You're my brother Charlie, you should look out for me" to which Charlie responds, "We had some bets down for you, you saw some money." To which Terry responds, "It's not about money Charlie, I could have had a shot at the title, I could have been somebody." All of this and more demonstrate that self-esteem and other needs are fulfilled by work. The three leading models of why people work are:

1. Herzberg [12] proposed a "Two Factor Theory" to explain why people work. These were *hygiene* defined as being survival related to having to do with pay, working conditions, respect and job stability. The other factor, *relationship to the job*, involves advancement, promotion, fair treatment and the potential for higher rewards.
2. Maslow [13] proposed that people have a hierarchy of needs and working satisfies the hierarchy. Starting at the top, these are psychological needs, safety and security, social needs, esteem needs and self-actualizations.
3. McClelland's [14] theory proposes that people work to satisfy three needs – achievement (to do something important), power (to have control over others and/or their own actions) and affiliation (friendly relationships).

While all three models involve some issue(s) related to self-esteem in one way or another, Herzberg's model may be the most widely accepted model of the three. Software project managers who rely on these factors (i.e. pay rate, working conditions and so forth) to control and motivate software engineers have high turnover rates [3]. It should be noted that turnover (i.e. leaving the project or company) increases development costs by as much as 60% [15]. Since no one wants to be associated with a failed project or poor quality, taking what amounts to shortcuts reduces productivity. In addition, more recent work [4] has shown that technology workers have a common value system which places a high priority on producing work that they can be proud of, that their colleagues will be impressed by and is at or near the state of the art. Producing work that incurs technical debt violates these goals and value systems. These factors can be extremely strong in some software engineers. For example, a software engineer whom I managed was part of a team on a very aggressive schedule. Some of the work involved fixing bugs in what might be most kindly described as "spaghetti code." He informed me that since his name was going to be associated with this code, he would go beyond just fixing the latest bug and restructure and retest the software assigned to him. Even though he voluntarily worked quite late some nights, he still met the schedule and, due to some requirements changes, actually saved himself and his successors a great deal of time to respond to these changes. The successors of his colleagues who just did the minimum bug fixes were not so fortunate. An environment in which doing the work less than the "correct" way reduces productivity and incurs "hidden" expenses in several ways:

- Loss of Productivity – When a person knows that what they are being asked to do is in conflict with what they know they should be doing, they are working at their lowest productivity level [9]. The phenomenon is called cognitive dissonance. Cognitive dissonance reduces productivity. In the case of software development, productivity is often equated to the production of source code. But source code production has only increased by less than one line of source code per programmer per month per year in the period from 1960 to 2000 [16]. This increase has been linear even though dozens of programming, analysis, design, testing and other methods and development tools were developed and engaged in over that period. Cognitive dissonance means that even though the coding practices being used are seen as justified because they will foreshorten development flow time, they may, in fact, increase it making this practice something of a self-fulfilling prophecy. Management may be inclined to speculate that even though shortcuts were taken, we still had trouble meeting the schedule. When people are able to fulfill their perception of being productive with work that reflects positively on them, they become highly motivated and are more productive. Therefore, technical debt may actually increase, not decrease, development time.
- Reduced commitment to quality practices – Cutting corners and/or abandoning our standard development process simply sends the wrong messages to the software engineering team. These negative messages all reduce productivity and motivation while undermining the self-confidence of the development team. They include:
  - The development process you so diligently spent time developing and refining is OK when things are going smoothly but must be abandoned when we get behind schedule and/or over budget.
  - We are committed to quality only when it is convenient.
  - Management does not believe we can do it right and finish on time, within budget.
- Reduced use of collective team experience – Most project managers try to compose development teams in such a way that each member possesses skills and experience that complement the skills and experience of the other team members. In this way, the team as a whole possesses the skills and experience needed to be successful. Schedule pressure may be the key

driver behind engaging in technical debt [17]. This practice amounts to telling the development team we have not got enough to do the job well, just less than well. This is a credibility problem because the software engineers know that the likelihood that they will ever be directed to go back to the source code and upgrade is low due to the (potentially) horrendous cost involved. But to overcome possible resistance to engaging in technical debt, a lot of pressure will have to be brought to bear on the team. We now know that if enough pressure is put on a team, they cease to work together as a team and revert back to working as a group of disconnected individuals [17]. Meaning that the collective knowledge and experience within the team is mostly lost.

■ Increased cost – We know that in most job markets, software engineers can experience a high degree of mobility. If they do not like working at one firm, there is often another one seeking to hire them or, in the case of larger firms, they can transfer to another organization. Experiencing cognitive dissonance, pressure to cut corners and so forth can increase turnover. As stated earlier, we now know that turnover can account for as much as 60% of the cost of a software project. So, we have a paradox, the very practice engaged in to reduce flow time and costs (technical debt) may actually increase both due to lower productivity via reduced motivation and increased turnover.

■ Putting off correcting/paying technical debt can be really expensive. We have known for decades that the later in a software system's life cycle we correct a problem or make a needed improvement, the more it costs and these costs increase exponentially [18]. Taking shortcuts now with the intent of correcting the problems they cause until later practically guarantees increased total system life costs. Besides, software engineers prefer to be creating new code, not cleaning up somebody else's mess. Also, the business case usually cannot be made to go back and change code that is, presumably, working in order to "pay off" the existing technical debt [19].

■ Undermining a culture of professionalism by setting a tone of just getting the code out when, in fact, people want to be associated with a culture in which getting quality results is the norm. We know the long-term benefits of generating quality code in terms of maintenance but the short-term benefits in terms of improved productivity have only more recently been identified [4]. Five factors were identified that affected the motivation of high-technology professionals [2] and are listed in Table 6.3.

Looking at Table 6.3, we can see that engaging in technical debt is the antithesis of several of the factors that enhance motivation thereby reducing productivity. Most tasks are going to be some combination (pro and con) of these motivating factors. It will be rare that all factors will be met but if enough are, the software engineer will likely be motivated.

Table 6.3 Motivating Factors in Software Tasks [2]

Factor	Description
Skill Variety	The task requires the use of multiple skills
Task Identity	The task is something the software engineer would like doing
Task Significance	The task is seen as important
Autonomy	The software engineer can accomplish the task as they see fit
Feedback	Management provides feedback on how well the task has been done

6.9 Keeping Successful Teams Together for Higher Productivity

More recent work with software organizations found that teams that worked well together should be kept together [20, 21]. While this may not always be possible due to organizational changes, product line evolution and other factors, the point is that effective, productive teams do not just happen. Such teams are the result of hard work on the part of the software project manager and the senior management team and sometimes just a matter of luck. The point is, once you have identified a high-performing team, do not just break it up at the end of a project and reassign the individuals to other projects. Instead, find a way to keep the team intact and assign them to another project. Keep in mind that sometimes, team members, particularly those who are in the early years of their careers, develop and mature in ways which may cause them to no longer be compatible with the other team members. I had this happen when one team member decided he no longer wanted to develop software. He decided to go back to school and obtained a Master's degree in Business Administration specializing in his first love, accounting. Another member decided they no longer wanted to develop the type of software we were working on at that time. They decided to go to work for Microsoft instead. All of this occurred after successfully completing a project that was deemed "impossible." But the remaining members of this five-person team pushed on, two new members were acquired and their successes continued.

6.10 Generational Differences

For a broad range of reasons, today software project managers are managing multiple generations. This can not only impact your project planning but may provide several unexpected challenges. The challenges are a result of different perceptions of work and the relationship of the employee to the employer as well as how to perform one's work assignment. The demographics worldwide are unique in history.

In the United States, several different categories of workers have been identified and studied (Table 6.4) based on the period in which they were born. The United States is used here because it is the easiest to obtain data for at this time.

In the United States, only one new worker will enter the workforce for every two that leave it via retirement, one in six workers turned 55 in 2008 and 7,916 Boomers turned 60 in 2006.

Table 6.4 Age Classifications in the United States [22]

Classification	Birthdate	% of the United States Population
Matures	Before 1945	10%
Boomers	Between 1946 and 1964	43%
Generation Xers	Between 1965 and 1977	33%
Millennials (Generation Y)	Between 1977 and 2000+	14%
Generation Z	Between 1995 and 2010	20%
Generation Alpha	2010–present	13%

Given that the nominal retirement age in the United States is 65, the workforce is shrinking, further intensifying the mixing of various age groups in the workforce. Similar figures apply to the countries comprising the European Union.

Each of these six groups displays common tendencies with respect to the values they bring to the job, their work ethic and company loyalty. These are described below but keep in mind that these are common tendencies, not absolute behavioral traits for any specific individual and the degree to which these tendencies manifest themselves will vary from one person to the next:

- Matures
  - Values – Respect for authority, doing a job well is important, usually patient.
  - Work Ethic – Efficiency is the standard and believe in *quid quo pro*. That is, receiving rewards from the company for working on its behalf. Sees job tenure as playing a role in receiving raises.
  - In the Workplace (pluses/minuses) – Stable, thorough, detailed, works hard, loyal, change and ambiguity are challenging, tends to not buck the system.
  - Motivating Matures – Feedback phrases like "What you have to say is valuable regarding what has or has not worked in the past;" "Your perseverance is valued and will be rewarded" and "We respect your experience(s)."
- Boomers
  - Values – Competitive, workaholic, optimistic and tries to balance work and family.
  - Work Ethic – To them, the hours worked represent a measure of value to the company, evaluate work ethic with respect to themselves and highly value teamwork, relationships and loyalty.
  - In the Workplace (pluses/minuses) – Service oriented, driven team players, avoid conflict, not budget oriented, process may supersede results and sensitive to feedback.
  - Motivating Boomers – Feedback phrases like "We need you;" "You are valued" and "Your contribution is unique/important."
- Gen Xers
  - Values – Work/life balance, independent, cynical, pessimistic, technically literate, global thinking and informal.
  - Work Ethic – Favor productivity, not tenure, communication, avoids the Boomer work ethic and is loyal to a person, not necessarily the company.
  - In the Workplace (pluses/minuses) – Creative, independent, not intimidated by authority, technically savvy, very adaptable, cynical, lack people skills, impatient and inexperienced.
  - Motivating GenXers – Feedback phrases like "We have a very open company culture;" "You will be provided the latest technology" and "We tend not to have a lot of red tape."
- Millennials (Gen Y)
  - Values – Need stimulating work, rely on authorities, optimistic, confident and ambitious.
  - Work Ethic – Need open, high-bandwidth communication with others, want a job that is personally fulfilling, need almost constant reinforcement from manager and works well with matures.
  - In the Workplace (pluses/minuses) – Multitask, technically literate, heroic style, optimistic and need rules, structure and discipline in the workplace.
  - Motivating Gen Y – Feedback phrases like "You (and/or your team) can play a major role here;" "You will be working with the best and brightest people in this field" and "Your manager is quite a bit older than you, in their 60s."

- Generation Z
  - What partly defines this group is its relationship to technology. They have not experienced a time when most of what we take as commonplace technically did not exist.
  - They expect technology to be able to do just about everything.
  - They don't see the need for an office they go to each day because they can do work from anywhere, even in an aircraft.
  - They prefer and, in some cases, will require remote work or at least partly remote (e.g. hybrid).
  - The pandemic highlighted the possibilities of this style of work.
- Generation Alpha
  - The research on this group is relatively new but what we do know is that they value collaboration and teamwork.
  - Managing them should emphasize group projects rather than single-person efforts.
  - Encourage communication among all team members.

6.11 Generational Issues – Summary

Opinions vary among researchers regarding the tendencies or characteristics of each of these groups and the research is ongoing. What has been presented above is, essentially, an amalgam of the various views. Similarly, most people are an amalgam of various characteristics and, depending on their background and experiences, may sometimes be mislabeled.

6.12 Cultural and Language Differences

Culture may be defined as "The beliefs, customs, arts, etc. of a particular society, group, place, or time" [23]. Believe it or not, a person's background, current behaviors and attitudes on the job are greatly determined by the culture they grew up in. Hence, without even thinking about it, if one comes out of a culture of discrimination or bigotry, behaviors occur which are not thought out but some form of nearly automatic response. Apart from psychological profiles and personality, it is likely that you, the software project manager, will be managing a software development team composed of software engineers from different cultures. This is true even if they all come from the same country. Add to this the fact that some members of the team do not speak, as their first language a language other than your own and you are in for some challenging communications and project control issues. Why the language problem? Because worldwide, countries have recognized the value of software technology and supported their students who wish to earn a degree in this subject even if it means they have to study overseas. Often, some then immigrate to a country with greater opportunities for employment in software engineering. This results in software development teams more frequently being composed of people from different countries and different cultures with different language skills.

If your first language is English, you might incorrectly assume that if people from other countries just worked at it, they could speak English much more understandably. You may be surprised to learn that some people whose first language was not English literally, do not have the muscular ability in their facial muscles to pronounce English words as well as those for whom English is a first language. Similar comments apply to other languages. It is true that no matter how hard they try or how much they practice, in most cases they will not speak as clearly as first-language speakers. It turns out the converse is true as well. That is, those whose first language is English (or some other national language) may not have the facial muscle control to be able to speak some other language(s) like a native, regardless of how much they practice. Over many generations, members of each culture have physiologically adapted to speaking their native language, often to the detriment of being able to speak some other language like a native. This fact alone can lead to communication problems, some so serious that on some projects they had to resort to communicating only by email. Both parties were able to understand written English and express themselves in written English, but the spoken word was not as easily comprehended. Other factors can come into play including attitudes regarding deadlines and costs that were an embedded part of each team member's culture that can put their value system into conflict with what was agreed to by the team regarding cost and deadlines.

6.13 Managing Teams Composed of Different Cultures

As we already know, software engineering training as well as self-taught software developers have resulted in software engineers from just about every country in the world. This means you are likely to be managing people from a broad range of cultures no matter what country you are working in. Data similar to what is presented below is likely available in your country. Let's look at two situations for which we have ample data to which we can extrapolate elsewhere [24]:

■ Nearly 40% of software engineers working in Seattle, Washington in the United States were born outside of the United States. A similar situation exists for other technology centers in the United States as shown in Table 6.5. The details of where Seattle's foreign-born workers come from highlight the diversity in cultures and backgrounds as shown in Table 6.6.

Table 6.5 Percentage of Technology Workers Born Elsewhere by Software Center in the United States [24]

Rank	City/Locale	State	Percentage
1	San Jose, Sunnyvale, Santa Clara	California	71%
2	San Francisco, Oakland–Hayward	California	50.3%
3	Seattle–Tacoma–Bellevue	Washington	39.8%
4	Washington–Arlington–Alexandria	Washington D.C.	33.6%
5	Dallas–Fort Worth–Arlington	Texas	31.4%
6	Boston–Cambridge–Newton	Massachusetts	30.8%
7	San Diego–Carlsbad	California	30.5%
8	Raleigh	North Carolina	27.2%
9	Minneapolis–St. Paul–Bloomington	Minnesota	24.9%
10	Austin–Round Rock	Texas	22%
11	Portland–Vancouver–Hillsboro	Oregon	20.9%
12	Denver–Aurora–Lakewood	Colorado	15.8%

Table 6.6   The Country of Origin of Software Engineers in the United States [24]

Rank	Country of Origin	Percentage
1	India	40.8%
2	China	13.5%
3	Canada	6.0%
4	Russia	5.9%
5	South Korea	3.5%
6	Vietnam	3.0%
7	Philippines	2.1%
8	Mexico	1.9%
9	England	1.7%
10	Germany	1.5%

As you can see from the table, both the location and the percentage of foreign-born software workers in the United States vary widely. Given that a similar situation exists in your country, it almost guarantees that the software engineering team you manage will be composed of people from various cultures each with their own value systems.

Although the development team may be viewed as working toward the same goal(s), each individual on the team comes at this task with a unique combination of skills, values and priorities. The skills issue is one which is relatively straightforward given the member's education, training, work experience and, in some cases, the reputation they have established at the firm or previous firms. But a team member's values and priorities are a direct result of the culture they come from. Some extreme examples I have worked with include:

- On Time – No Matter What – This individual's work was always on time but we quickly learned that the issue of quality was of a lesser value than being on time. The code that was turned in was frequently less than stable and not properly tested and debugged, often requiring rework by others before the build could proceed.
- Deliver Only the Best – This individual did not want his name associated with code he considered to be of poor quality. When assigned to correct a bug in a module which was of poor quality, he not only fixed the bug but rewrote, restructured and tested the module resulting in a much more stable and maintainable piece of software. The interesting thing about this was that his resulting code was delivered on time, bug free (as far as we could tell) and of remarkably high quality. Again, what drove him to do this was that he did not want his name associated with what he considered poor-quality code. In the interest of full disclosure, he often worked late into the night to meet deadlines due to the poor quality of some of the modules he worked on.

As you can see from the preceding as well as many others in my experience and yours, engineering software engages many aspects of the human psyche that are not often written about in software project management texts. The reasons why it should be studied and written about is the internationalization of software engineering. It is a fact that more than half the sales of software companies in the United States occur in other countries [25]. Although that data may seem outdated, the numbers are probably similar to today's data. The demand for information systems professionals continues to grow making it likely that multiple cultures will be increasingly involved in software engineering for the foreseeable future. This makes the ability to manage multiple cultures ever more valuable. As stated in [23], "Culture is characterized by a set of unique values that guides the behavior of people belonging to that culture." One model of cultural differences [26] posits that cultures can be categorized into four dimensions:

■ Individualism–Collectivism – Individualism refers to a preference for loosely knit societies in which people are expected to take care of themselves and their families. Collectivism refers to the converse – a society in which people can expect others to care for them in exchange for their loyalty.
■ Masculinity–Femininity – This dimension is an indication of the degree to which a culture emphasizes achievement over nurturing. Masculinity indicates the degree to which a society emphasizes distinct gender-based roles. In many countries, the trend has been toward equalizing or overlapping the "traditional" roles of male and female.
■ Power Distance – This refers to how people belonging to a certain culture view power relationships. That is, superior–subordinate and the degree to which people of that culture who are not in power accept the unequal distribution of power. So, if you are managing someone from a culture of low power distance, they will question authority (e.g. your authority) whereas those from high power distance cultures accept authority.
■ Uncertainty avoidance – This refers to situations (e.g. a software project) where the outcome of a process is either unknown or not reliably predictable. Hofstede developed an index of uncertainty avoidance and applied it to the cultures of several countries. Low uncertainty avoidance indicates a greater propensity for taking risks. Countries with low uncertainty avoidance scores include the United States, England, India, China and Singapore. Countries with high uncertainty avoidance (indicating an aversion to risk taking) scores include Italy, Korea, Mexico, Belgium and Russia.

As you can see from the previous discussion, the elements of all four dimensions are present in all cultures. The difference for us in managing software projects lies in the degree to which any specific individual presents these characteristics.

6.14 Effects of the Work Environment on Productivity

If you have ever wondered whether or not the office environment you and your team work in has an impact on how you and your team perform on the job, look no further. Although it has been updated since it was first published, companies continue to ignore some or all of these results. What the researchers set out to do was answer that question. After surveying many companies, their results are summarized in Table 6.7. What they sought to find out was how environmental factors helped or hurt people do their jobs. Some of what they measured was obvious. For example, people doing work like software development would be negatively impacted by a noisy environment, many interruptions and so forth. Here is what they found.

Table 6.7 The Impact of Environmental Factors on Productivity [27]

Environmental Factor	Highest Performers [% Yes]	Lowest Performers [% Yes]
Amount of dedicated workspace	78 square feet (7.2 square meters)	46 square feet (4.3 square meters)
Work area is acceptably quiet	57%	29%
Work area is acceptably private	62%	19%
Phone can be silenced	52%	10%
Phone can be diverted	76%	19%
People interrupt you needlessly	38%	76%

6.15 Outsourcing

For more than a decade, major corporations in the United States and elsewhere have tried to reduce the cost of software development. One popular approach has been to outsource development to firms in countries which have lower labor and operating costs. For example, the wages for IT professionals in India were approximately 50% less than a US-based subcontractor [28]. There are risks (some are also potentially beneficial). One team [29] identified and categorized these into several categories:

1. Geopolitical – How stable is the country in which the outsourcing is taking place?
2. Temporal Difference – Depending on where you choose to outsource to, there may be some serious coordination and communication problems due to time differences. Your firm may make an important request via email which may not get read by the outsource firm until your firm has quit for the day or worse, the issue is discussed via a telephone call where it is in the middle of the night for one of you. This leads to miscommunication and poorly coordinated responses to requests from both parties.
3. Human Capital – Do they have the people to do the job as well as a few who can fill in for those who may leave the firm, become ill or otherwise become unavailable?
4. IT Competency – Do they have the skills, knowledge, training, infrastructure and experience needed to be successful on your project? Do they have a reference client(s) for whom they have done similar work successfully? Can you contact the references?
5. Economical – How is the pricing and payment(s) to be implemented? What is the cost to be firm, fixed price, cost plus fixed fee with a not-to-exceed clause? Is there an escrow agreement in place? The way that works is the fee you plan to pay the outsource firm for the work is held by a bank which does business in both countries or at least has a presence in one and a correspondent bank in the other country. They hold the funds until you notify them to release the funds to the outsourced contractor, indicating the work was completed to your satisfaction. What happens if you do not believe the work was completed satisfactorily but the outsourced firm disagrees? What organization or mechanism resolves the dispute? In what country will depositions be taken? Who pays for the expenses associated with all of this? If there is a trial, in what country, state and city will it take place?
6. Legal – Who owns the results of this work? Does "work for hire" (or its equivalent) mean the same thing in the outsourced country as it does in your country? How and where will disputes be settled if the parties have to go to court? What are the criteria for acceptance/rejection of the work?

7. IT Infrastructure – How is the contractor organized internally? What precautions and safeguards are in place that will prevent a hacker or an employee from gaining access to your software and selling it to a competitor?
8. Cultural Risks – Does the term "deadline" mean the same thing in that country as it does in your country? Additionally, are delivery dates that appear in the contract legally binding in both countries?

I think you get the idea. There is a lot more to the act of outsourcing software development to another country than may appear at first glance.

6.16 Picking a Team Just Like You

You may have gotten into management because of your exemplary technical skills. That fact and the desire by most of us to work with people we are comfortable with and agree with (on most topics) can often cause software project managers to select team members who strongly resemble the software project manager in technical and procedural matters. There is a significant danger in this. It is that the manager's "blind spots" (e.g. errors in judgment) will be reflected in the team rather than having differing backgrounds and experiences which, taken together, form a more complete and effective set of policies and technical skills. This follows from Ashby's Law of Requisite Variety [30]. Although it was originally developed as a means of evaluating systems, its ramifications are applicable to the task of creating an effective technical team.

Chapter 6 Review Questions

1. What is the least effective form of motivation for software engineers?
2. What is the most effective form of motivation for software engineers?
3. What do software engineers really want to work on?
4. Why do software project managers continue to rely on money as a motivator?
5. What are three practices that demotivate software engineers?
6. Why do test teams need special attention to be motivated?
7. What is the motivation paradox?
8. Why do people work?
9. Why should we keep software engineering teams together?
10. Do all generations work the same way and have the same value systems?
11. How likely is it that you will be managing software engineers from different generations?
12. How does the physical environment the software engineers are working in impact productivity?
13. Name some aspects of outsourcing often overlooked.
14. How can you prevent creating a team just like yourself?

References

[1] Ryan, R.M. and Deci, E.L., "Intrinsic and Extrinsic Motivations: Classic Definitions and New Directions," *Contemporary Educational Psychology*, Vol. 25, 2000, pp. 54–67.
[2] Thamhain, H., "Team Leadership Effectiveness in Technology-Based Project Environments," *IEEE Engineering Management Review*, Vol. 36, No. 1, 2008, pp. 165–180. College, Cambridge, UK.

[3] Couger, D.J. and Zawacki, R.A., *Motivating and Managing Computer Personnel*, Wiley-Interscience, New York, NY, 1980.

[4] Katz, R., "Motivating Technical Professionals Today," *IEEE Engineering Management Review*, Vol. 41, No. 1, March, 2013, pp. 28–38.

[5] Forbes Magazine, 17 February, 2023.

[6] Capretz, L.F. and Ahmed, F., "A Call to Promote Soft Skills in Software Engineering," *Psychology and Cognitive Sciences*, Vol. 4, No. 1, pp. 207–214, 2018.

[7] Grant, A.M. and Gino, F., "A Little Thanks Goes a Long Way: Explaining Why Gratitude Expressions Motivate Prosocial Behavior," *Journal of Personality and Social Psychology*, Vol. 98, No. 6, June 2010, pp. 946–955.

[8] Thanhaim, H.J., "Changing Dynamics of Team Leadership in Global Project Environments," *American Journal of Industrial and Business Management*, Vol. 3, 2023, pp. 146–156.

[9] Weinberg, G. M., *The Psychology of Computer Programming*, Van Nostrand Reinhold, New York, NY, 1971.

[10] LaPlante, P., *Antipatterns: Identification, Refactoring and Management*, Auerbach Publications, New York, NY, 2005.

[11] Brooks, F.P. Jr., *The Mythical Man Month: Essays on Software Engineering*, Addison – Wesley, Reading, MA, 1995.

[12] Herzberg, F., *Work and the Nature of Man*, The World Publishing Company, Cleveland, OH, 1966.

[13] Maslow, A.H., *The Farther Reaches of Human Nature*, Viking Press, New York, NY, 1971.

[14] McClelland, D.C., *The Achieving Society*, Van Nostrand – Reinhold, Princeton, NJ, 1961.

[15] Cone, E., "Managing That Churning Sensation," *Information Week*, May 1998, No. 680, pp. 50–67.

[16] Jensen, R., "Don't Forget about Good Management," *CrossTalk Magazine*, August 2000, p. 30.

[17] Gardner, H.K., "Performance Pressure as a Double Edged Sword: Enhancing Team Motivation while Undermining the Use of Team Knowledge" Working Paper, 09-126, Harvard Business School, January, 2012.

[18] Boehm, B., *Software Engineering Economics*, Prentice-Hall, Englewood Cliffs, NJ, 1981.

[19] Peters, L.J., "Technical Debt: The Ultimate Antipattern," *6th Annual Conference on Managing Technical Debt*, Victoria, BC, Canada, 30 September, 2014.

[20] Huckman, R. and Staats, B., "The Hidden Benefits of Keeping Teams Intact," *Harvard Business Review*, December, 2013.

[21] Gardner, H., Gino, F. and Staats, B.R., "Dynamically Integrating Knowledge in Teams: Transforming Resources into Performance," Working Paper 11-009, Harvard Business School, September 7, 2011.

[22] Knight, R., "Managing People from 5 Generations," *Harvard Business Review*, September 25, 2014.

[23] Merriam-Webster Online Dictionary, March, 2015.

[24] Balk, E., "More Than Half of Seattle's Software Developers Were Born Outside U.S.," *Seattle Times*, January 19, 2018 based on latest census data.

[25] Software and Information Industry Association, *Building the Net: Trends Report*, 2001.

[26] Hofstede, G., *Cultures Consequences: Comparing Values, Behaviors, Institutions and Organizations across Nations*, Sage Publishing, 2nd edition, 2003.

[27] DeMarco, T. and Lister, T., *Peopleware*, Dorset House, New York, NY, 1999.

[28] Igbaria, M. and Shayo, C., *Strategies for Managing IS/IT Personnel*, Idea Group Publishing, Hershey, PA, 2004.

[29] Minevich, M. and Richter, F., "The Global Outsourcing Report – Opportunities, Costs and Risks," The CIO Insight Whiteboard, 2005.

[30] Ashby, W. R., *Introduction to Cybernetics*, Chapman and Hall, London, England, January, 2015.

Chapter 7

Project Closeout

"When a project ends, there is a plethora of valuable information that should be preserved."

–L. Peters

7.1 Chapter Overview

When a project ends, much of the team proceeds to other assignments, subcontractors seek other projects to work on and assuming the project resulted in a working system, the project moves into maintenance and enhancement mode. This chapter describes the actions that should be taken in order to prevent the project experience from being lost as a learning experience which may help to avoid some mistakes in the future. One of the key learning mechanisms is a review of the pre-project checklist created at the start of the project. Having each member review their initial evaluation of the items listed and then contrasting them with what actually occurred can provide valuable insights into one's ability to assess the various factors. This chapter also provides guidance on what project-specific variables are to be collected and conveyed to future projects.

7.2 Project Closeout Review and Learning

If we look at a software project as an opportunity for learning as well as a commercial venture, then it is incumbent upon us to record what occurs during the project as part of a continuous process improvement effort. As we saw earlier, the Reference Class Forecasting method has many benefits but they can only be had if we have recorded our estimates and how they were done on previous projects constituting a class. Without this referential data, we are left to the typical estimating methods which have not been proven to be accurate. Looking at this aspect of the project, it is important for us to document how we arrived at the estimate, what changes to the requirements or at least our interpretation of them occurred over the course of the project, when they occurred and what adjustments, if any, we made to the project estimate. But there is much more to be recorded such as how much turnover in personnel occurred (note: as much as 60% of software project costs can be attributed to personnel turnover [1]). We need to record who the members of the software engineering

DOI: 10.1201/9781003484288-7

team were and who the members of the client team were, what role each played, what were their skill levels, education and so forth. On and on it goes. What we are recording is the history of the project from start to finish including how it was viewed upon by the client as a success or failure or something in between. What we are trying to do is identify what worked and what didn't to improve the chances of success or at least better results on the next project. In order to ensure that key elements are recorded, a list of items to record is provided which could act as a starting point to create one unique to your company for future use. It is given that over time the closeout information that is collected will evolve as items are added or deleted based on experience and their perceived value. A review of the results of the pre-project checklist (Appendix 20) results should also be reported in this project closeout document as part of a learning experience for all members of the team.

7.3 The Advantage of Keeping Extemporaneous Notes

Think of a software project as a journey, a trip of sorts. Creating a journal and maintaining it throughout the journey will help document what happened and when. In this case, its purpose is to identify what went well and what didn't as well as enough information to better ensure that in future projects, we can avoid some of the problems we encountered. Even failed projects have valuable information and "lessons learned" that can be beneficial in the future. Many new management practices may seem to make sense in theory but may not work out when actually applied. What we are trying to achieve in generating extemporaneous notes is to capture useful practices which worked and may be transferable to other projects in the future as well as identify those which did not so we can avoid making the same mistake(s) in future software projects.

7.4 Identifying/Archiving Lessons Learned

When the software project ends, the most common question asked may be "Was it a success?" That is certainly a fair question to ask but what exactly is success? The most common interpretation of that question is whether or not it finished on time, within schedule and meeting the requirements set forth at the outset. Back at the start of the project, one of the tasks was to set forth in writing what the success criteria were. The three just mentioned are considered by some to be the minimal success criteria. Others that may have been included include whether or not the delivered software system is easy to use, an improvement over previous systems and maintainable by software engineers other than its developers. Granted, we are generally struggling to meet the minimum success criteria (i.e. on time, on budget and meeting requirements) but delivering a technically superior system that users dislike and won't use can't really be considered a success. This is partly why the Agile method has been so widely accepted. Right from the start, the users are involved in the system's development – its look and feel. Psychologically, during its development, it becomes their system. Throughout the development, user preferences have been incorporated into the system. Some people would say "Careful what you wish for" but acceptance of the deliverable depends largely on how well the user community recognizes its features as what they requested. So, success or failure needs to be documented in advance but may fall victim to political infighting within the contracting organization. In addition to success or failure evaluation, an extemporaneous log of what the contracting firm was directed to be done, what was done and what the software engineering team advised may be invaluable if a lawsuit ensues.

7.5 Sample List of Variables to Record for a Project Closeout Document

The items discussed here constitute what some might refer to as "boilerplate" in that much of this information could have been derived from the legal, contractual documents associated with the project. While this is useful, what might be more useful are observations from the manager of this previous project regarding the client's propensity for pushing the scope of the effort to include work not part of the original requirements. Doing this extra work can drive project costs over the estimated amount no matter what estimating method we used. Why do project managers agree to such requests? They agree to the extra work because they want to maintain a good relationship with the client. Also, some project managers see these "extras" as no-cost items but remember, anything that requires labor costs the project money. This means that "free" extra work isn't free at all.

7.6 Reviewing the Pre-Project Checklist

Early in the project, the team reviewed the pre-project checklist arriving at a consensus value for each item. Now that the project has ended, it is time for the team to review that checklist but this time comparing what they see as having actually occurred versus what they expected to occur. In this way, each member of the team learns more about their predictive and evaluative skills, their biases and so forth. Over time, this can result in more accurate assessments of projects in their early stages through the use of the pre-project checklist.

References

[1] Cone, E., "Managing that Churning Sensation," *Information Week*, Vol. 2, May 1998, No. 680, pp. 50–67.

ADDITIONAL SOFTWARE PROJECT MANAGEMENT RESOURCES

Managing software projects differs in significant ways from managing other types of engineering projects. One important aspect of this is that software project management has not received the kind of attention from university research and the industry at large to have matured and grown into a stable, well-defined professional practice. It is this aspect that results in just about any model of software project management being only temporarily accurate but incomplete. This section addresses the "incompleteness" issue by providing several narrow-focus discussions on topics that may be useful to the software project manager at various points in a project. These should best be viewed as tools which are available for use as the situation calls for their use. Some topics have been adapted from other fields worldwide but still have applicability to software projects. Many represent principles and techniques developed outside of software project management, but which are applicable just the same. The topics are presented as appendices. As a group, they represent the tools and techniques likely to come into play during the actual conduct of the software project. Since all software projects are unique in some ways, it is not realistic for me to prescribe which narrow focus topics will be needed by your project. This is for you to decide. References are provided throughout to support further research.

Appendix 1

A Word from Our Sponsor – The Brain

This is a book about managing software projects. Why are we discussing a topic from neuroscience? Successfully managing a team of software engineers is first and foremost about relationships. Our relationships, our motivation to work, our self-esteem, our pride in our work, how strongly we engage with our work and more are established and maintained by our brains. So, understanding how our brains do this and why it can help us successfully manage software projects is at the foundation of nearly everything related to management. In order to achieve great things or even engage our team members, we need to understand just what it is that works to engage them and why. Our brains control just about everything about us. They are extremely complex. So much so, that there is less information on how they work than on the geology of the moon, and there are more connections in our brains than there are stars in our galaxy [1]. The brain controls everything including our motivation to work. It generates an important hormone – oxytocin – which affects many things. If you want your team to become engaged and achieve quality results in spite of obstacles, then we need to take actions which foster the production of oxytocin.

A.1.1 Actions Which Can Help Our Cause

As a software project manager, we have a certain amount of control over what the team does but not over what they think. What we are looking to do is take actions which have been shown to induce a higher production of oxytocin which, in turn, will produce positive results within the team. This will result in a higher level of oxytocin which in turn will result in greater engagement of team members to the project which will result in higher productivity – not just in the volume of source code but its quality as well. So, what are these actions? As we discussed earlier, increasing a team member's pay does not result in the intended increase in loyalty, retention and productivity that many companies expect [2]. We now know that the number one thing we want to improve is trust. Although a few software engineers may be dishonest [3], we should be concerned about establishing trust between ourselves and the team members. From the work in this regard [2], compared with people at low-trust companies, people at high-trust companies exhibit several desirable characteristics including:

- 74% less stress
- 106% more energy at work
- 50% higher productivity
- 13% fewer sick days
- 76% more engagement
- 29% more satisfaction with their lives and 40% less burnout

Those statistics may be impressive, but they do not happen by accident. They require the creation and maintenance of an environment of trust. Actions we can take to improve trust include:

- Recognizing Excellence – This goes beyond what was mentioned earlier in this text. It can be private recognition but rather public recognition within the development team. It is not only beneficial to the individual but to the team at large. It also gives the best performers an opportunity to share their approach(s) that resulted in their success.
- Inducing "Challenge Stress" – Challenging the team to attempt to meet a challenge they are unlikely to achieve is detrimental to productivity. Now we know why. What is suggested here is the imposition of makeable challenges. This results in team members being able to see progress toward these makeable goals. One study by Harvard professor Teresa Amabile [2] found that 76% of people reported that their best days involved making progress toward goals. Regardless of which type of life cycle your project is using, it will contain milestones (e.g. in the waterfall model), stories (e.g. in Agile) or some other indicator of the attainment of some predefined hopefully makeable goal. Along the way, there will be points in time at which certain achievements are planned for. These mark progress but, more importantly, they impart a sense of accomplishment to team members.
- Give Team Members the Freedom to Do Their Work the Way They Choose – This is one of the biggest challenges all project managers are faced with. It is the temptation to not only assign work but to tell the team members how that work should be done as well. This robs the software engineer of the autonomy needed to establish and maintain trust. As cited by Zak [4], in a study at Citigroup, almost half of employees would give up a 20% raise in exchange for greater control of how they work. That amount of salary is certainly significant but more importantly it indicates how important it is to employees to have autonomy over how they perform their job. This is not the result of being stubborn or uncooperative but rather another indication of how important our work is since it is an extension of ourselves. This is particularly true in the case of software engineers [5]. The onset of the COVID-19 pandemic introduced many software engineers to the pros and cons of working from home. Now that the pandemic has subsided somewhat, many software engineers do not want to go back to having to work in an office setting. This has setup a conflict of sorts between management and the software engineering team(s). Rather than demanding that software engineers return to the office setting or risk being fired, many companies have worked out a hybrid model. A negotiated number of days working at home and a number of days in the office each week. In this way, important large-scale coordination meetings can take place among the teams face to face while maintaining the personal preference for working from home.
- Enable Job Crafting – When allowed to pick what projects to work on or a role within a large project employees tend to pick tasks that interest them, ones they are passionate about and/or

believe they can learn from. In such situations, employee performance is measurably higher and so is retention.

■ Share Information Broadly – Only 40% of employees report that they are familiar with their company's goals [6, 7], strategies and tactics. Working in such an environment leads to chronic stress and other negative outcomes such as taking an action thought to be beneficial but which is contrary to corporate goals.

■ Intentionally Build Relationships – A Google study found that managers who show an interest in and concern for team members' success and personal well-being outperform others in terms of the quantity and quality of the team member's work. Different software project managers have found ways to achieve this. One of the most common is social interactions with the team members such as a group luncheon at company expense, taking in a movie as a group and other activities that are often away from the office that allow relaxed interactions among all members of the team.

■ Facilitate Whole-Person Growth – High-trust organizations favor their people growing both personally and professionally. For example, not standing in the way of a team member taking a college class in a subject unrelated to software engineering. This is the approach taken by Accenture, Adobe Systems and others with positive results. There, managers ask questions like "Am I helping you get your next job?" This can be a touchy subject in that the outside educational study may be oriented toward starting a different career but is often oriented toward getting a degree in another subject area or an advanced degree in software engineering. I once worked for a very effective software project manager who encouraged every member of his team to apply for other jobs within or outside of the company at least monthly. In two years, contrary to what you might think, very few people left his group.

■ Show Vulnerability – The technical aspects of software engineering as well as the complexity of the problems we are asked to solve are increasingly complex. Leaders in high-trust organizations ask for help from their team members as opposed to just telling them what to do. This stimulates oxytocin production in others. This, in turn, increases trust and cooperation. Although some managers believe that asking for help is a sign of weakness, the findings of researchers are that seeking help is a symptom of a secure leader – one who engages everyone to reach goals. Jim Whitehurst, the CEO of Red Hat said, "I found that being very open about the things I did not know actually had the opposite effect than I would have thought. It helped me build credibility." Again, trust is damaged if the software project manager tries to make everyone believe that they know all there is to know about the technology involved in the project when in reality they don't. The truth will eventually become known only to have trust suffer.

A.1.2 The Return on Investment in Trust

A survey of the United States as of 2017 showed that the U.S. average for organizational trust was 70%. 47% of respondents worked in organizations where trust was below the average with one firm scoring 15%. Overall, companies scored lowest on recognizing excellence and sharing information (67% and 68%, respectively). The bottom line here is that organizations with higher levels of trust have employees who enjoy their work, are more productive and stay with the firm longer. Perhaps, the best summary of this issue is a quote from the CEO of the Herman Miller Corporation, "The first responsibility of a leader is to define reality. The last is to say thank you. In between the two, the leader must become a servant."

References

[1] Smith, O. *Private Communications with Professor Emeritus Orville Smith in Neuro Biology*, University of Washington, Seattle, Washington, 2022 and 2023.

[2] Grant, A.M. and Gino, F., "A Little Thanks Goes a Long Way: Explaining Why Gratitude Expressions Motivate Prosocial Behavior," *Journal of Personality and Social Psychology*, Vol. 98, No. 6, June 2010, pp. 946–955.

[3] Gino, F and Ariely, D., "The Dark Side of Creativity: Original Thinkers Can Be More Dishonest," *Journal of Personality and Social Psychology*, Vol. 102, No. 3, 2012, pp. 445–459.

[4] Zak, P.J., "The Neuroscience of Trust," from "Management Behaviors That Foster Employee Engagement," *Harvard Business Review*, January-February, 2017.

[5] Weinberg, G.M. *The Psychology of Computer Programming*, Van Nostrand Rheinhold, New York, NY, 1971.

[6] Amabile, T. and Kramer, S., *The Progress Principle: Using Small Wins to Ignite Joy, Engagement, and Creativity at Work*, Harvard Business Review Press, Boston, MA, 2011.

[7] Kaplan, R.S. and Norton, D.P., "Linking the Balanced Scorecard to Strategy," *California Management Review*, Vol. 39, No. 1, pp. 242–253, Fall 1996.

Appendix 2

Basics of Negotiation

No matter how well or poorly your project is progressing there will be times when there is an important difference of opinion regarding some aspect of the project. These differences can occur between the client and you, between you and your team or a member of it or other combinations. Often, we don't see a way out of, essentially, trying to bully our way to get the other party to agree to what we are asking. Unfortunately, that sets us up for future hard feelings and increased difficulties in getting cooperation. A successful negotiation is one in which both sides come away feeling they won because they achieved what they wanted to or at least as much of it as they thought they could. Although it is rare, sometimes the negotiation ends with both sides happy. Over the years, various researchers have developed recommended actions and advisories for negotiating. A few are listed below but keep in mind that much like writing code different researchers have developed different lists – all of which are tacitly claimed to work:

1. **Research the issue** – Knowing what to expect (instead of guessing or "seeing what you can get") will give you more confidence when you open the conversation. For example, before you try to discuss the cost of rent with a current landlord, find out what it might cost to move into a comparable building.
2. **Build rapport** – The last thing we want to happen is the negotiation turns into an "us versus them" battle which likely results in hard feelings on both sides. Try to find some common interests like sports to talk about. The goal here is to learn more about the people we are negotiating with while sharing with them or while providing them with some insights into ourselves. Be sure to be an active listener in order to better understand what they are seeking to achieve in the negotiation. Be sure to respect the other person and avoid any form of disrespect such as treating their viewpoint as foolish or ill-informed.
3. **Listen carefully** – There is often a temptation to unwittingly take control of the conversation by talking too much. This means we are not getting the input we need because we can't talk and listen at the same time. Listen to the other party and ask relevant questions in order to identify and better understand the issues as the other party sees them. Again, we learn more from listening than speaking.
4. **Make sure you know your priorities** – If we are looking for highest quality or shortest delivery time or whatever, we need to keep this in mind right from the start.
5. **Be prepared to make a decision** – If you see what appears to be an acceptable deal, make it. Putting the decision off could result in that deal being "off the table" when you meet again.
6. **Seek to Arrive at a Win-Win** – Instead of seeing this as a battle with a winner and a loser seek to identify a deal that results in both parties being better off than before.

7. **Keep your emotions under control** – Some negotiators will attempt to get you to lose your temper or in other ways lose control. Keep your focus on the issue(s) at hand and don't fall into the emotional trap.
8. **Be mindful of your timeline and that of the other party** – Understand your timeline and the other party's timeline. Remember, the longer the negotiations go on, the higher the likelihood that new issues may be identified that could potentially cause the deal to fall through or progress that was previously made lost.
9. **Be prepared to walk** – If the other side has unrealistic demands or is unwilling to make any compromises, walk away from it as it is not going to result in a positive outcome.
10. **A Time For a Post Reflection** – Whether the negotiation works out or not, take some time to review how things went, what might have been done differently and so forth. This is an invaluable learning experience.

Whether the negotiation works out or not, take time at the end to reflect on how it went. We've all had successes and failures in our attempts to reach a deal, so try to learn from every negotiation, because there will always be a next time. There are many books and university courses available with which to acquire negotiation skills. In addition, the Harvard Business Review has a website from which you can obtain free resource materials on negotiating.

Appendix 3

Brainstorming

It is often the case that the software engineering team needs to generate some ideas quickly in order to solve a particularly serious and difficult-to-solve problem quickly. This can happen for many and varied reasons. The problem-solving power of the team can be greatly enhanced or reduced depending on how the team approaches the activity of "brainstorming" to arrive at a solution. Although the concept is decades old, it is still used effectively today and can be effective provided a few guidelines are employed. But first, let's take a look at what can hinder the effectiveness of brainstorming [1]. Factors that can hinder the effectiveness of brainstorming:

- Evaluation Apprehension – Working in a group makes each person's contribution visible to the rest of the group. Despite the admonition not to criticize, people can be reluctant to participate for fear of being criticized regarding the lack of quality of their ideas.
- Free Riding – Some members of your team may not participate because others are making good suggestions. They may not view their own ideas as being as good and don't want to embarrass themselves. Also, they may not see any value in the activity.
- Limited Air Time – Only one person speaks at a time so there is only a limited amount of time for each team member to speak. This may cause some to not contribute due to the need to be concise.
- Production Blocking – At any moment, only one line of ideas is being generated, since they are reported serially, groups will tend to pursue fewer different kinds of ideas.
- Cognitive Inertia – While waiting to speak, some people may forget what they were going to contribute.
- Time Constraints – Pressure to arrive at a solution quickly [2, 3]

Now that we have seen what to avoid, let's take a look at what to do.

Microsoft was studied regarding its use of brainstorming. Brainstorming teams were typically composed of a software project manager or program manager (PM), software development engineer(s) (SDEs) and software development test engineer(s) (SDET). The "life cycle" of their sessions was composed of four stages:

1. Planning
   - The PM and possibly others gather.
   - The entire team meets to achieve a general agreement on specifications.
   - The SDEs define an architecture plan.
   - SDETs describe the features in the test plan.
   - The team reaches an agreement on the specifications.

2. Implementation
   - SDEs start implementing features.
   - SDETs implement object models and begin writing test cases.
   - Test cases are run as features are developed.

3. Stabilization
   - SDEs fix bugs
   - SDETs analyze test failures and retest bug fixes.

4. Future Planning
   - The team meets to discuss customer(s) feedback, requirements changes, feature support and bugs.

One issue of interest is how does this approach relate to software development stages and related matters. Tables A3.1, A3.2 and A3.3 layout time flows as well.

It should be made clear to the team that a brainstorming meeting is not a sign that any individual or by inference, the team, is incompetent [2,3]. Rather the message should be that some of the programming problems that will be encountered are going to be just too complex for any single individual to solve and will require a team effort to solve them.

Table A3.1 Brainstorming versus Development Phase

Development Phase	Percent of Brainstorming Sessions Devoted To
1 – Planning	89.5%
2 – Implementation	42.1%
3 – Stabilization	36.8%
4 – Future Planning	23.7%

Table A3.2 Frequency of Brainstorming Meetings

Time Period	Percentage
Daily	21.1%
Weekly	34.2%
Monthly	21.1%
Yearly	10.5%
At Every Milestone	23.7
As Needed	13.2%

Table A3.3   Time Spent in Meetings [2]

Activity	Planning	Implementation	Stabilization
Identify Problem	1.8%	7.5%	14.8%
Gather Information	2.6%	4.4%	5.5%
Idea Generation	14.5%	19.4%	12.3%
Evaluation	39.3%	29.7%	44.8%
Logistics	21.5%	11.9%	12.2%
Recap & Scenario Development	17.6%	20.0%	2.7%
Miscellaneous	15.0%	7.1%	7.7%

References

[1] Diehl, M. and Stroebe, W., "Productivity Loss in Brainstorming Groups: Toward the Solution of a Riddle," *Journal of Personality and Social Psychology*, Vol. 53, No. 3, September 1987, pp. 497–509.

[2] Osborn, A.F., Venolia, G. and Olson, G., "Brainstorming under Constraints: Why Software Developers Brainstorm in Groups," *Proceedings of the 25th British Columbia Society on Human-Computer Interaction*, January, 2011, pp. 74–83.

[3] Osborn, A.F., *Applied Imagination*, Charles Scribner & Sons, New York, NY, 1953.

Appendix 4

Characteristics of Successful High-Technology Teams

One aspect of preparations to begin a software project is the composition of the software engineering team. Each software project manager has their own opinion on who makes a "good" team member and by extension, what makes a "good" team. It is fair to say that software project managers believe that a team composed of the best and brightest software engineers stands the highest chance of being successful. But a study of the characteristics of successful teams in high-technology projects produced, for some, surprising results [1]. What they found was that successful teams had three characteristics in common:

- **Knowledge of the technology involved** – Note that to be successful, team members only had to be "familiar" with the technology involved, not experts. This is consistent with the notion that team members will support each other. Since each team member will have some knowledge others may not have, together they have a comprehensive, more complete knowledge set.
- **Experience working as a member of a team** – Being part of a software engineering team means that at times there will be differences of opinion. In order for the differences to be resolved, some degree of compromise on the part of all team members will be necessary. Having experience with this process and recognizing its benefits is a necessary attribute. A member who only worked as an independent developer may have difficulty with the give and take involved in teamwork.
- **Compatible personalities** – If team members cannot get along due to personality differences, the project will be jeopardized. The Myers-Briggs Type Inventory [2] or some other personality profiling system can identify compatible and incompatible personality types. The point is that incompatible personalities on the team can create friction thereby reducing team effectiveness and jeopardizing success.

A.4.1 What the Data Indicate

A study of projects and multidisciplinary teams [3] described the fundamental properties a team needs to have in order for them to potentially be successful. These "winning" teams were composed of people who shared three characteristics:

1. They had knowledge of the technology involved – they did not have to be experts in their field but had some experience in it.
2. They had worked as part of a team before – not necessarily with these team members but had experienced the give and take of negotiating what happens when teams make decisions. More recent work [4–6] found that the ideal situation occurs when the team members have worked together as a team before.
3. The team members had psychological profiles which were compatible – Using Myers-Briggs or some other personality type/inventory system, the personalities of the team members were deemed to range from reasonably compatible to incompatible. We have all experienced instances in work situations where some people we worked with seemed easier to work with than others. It turns out that, at least part of the nature of this was the personality profile of the individuals involved.

A.4.2 Psychological Compatibility

No matter what line of work you are in or have been in, there are people you have worked with easily and others you simply had a difficult time working with but could not explain why in either case satisfactorily. One team studied thousands of successful and failed high-technology projects in an attempt to find what made teams work or not work [5]. They found, as stated above, that psychological compatibility was one of three primary factors present in successful high-technology projects. As a software project manager, you have probably figured out ways to establish whether or not a prospective team member possesses the training, technical knowledge and experience your team will need on a given project but what about compatibility with other team members? It turns out that for more than 2,000 years, various people have been trying to understand human personality well enough to do just that. One of the most widely used methods is the Myers-Briggs Type Indicator (MBTI). It views personality as having four dimensions with each dimension having two opposing factors. The dimensions and their opposing factors are:

- **Focus of Attention** – The two opposing forms this dimension takes are:
  - Extravert (E) – These are people who are at ease talking to and sharing with others. They gain energy from working with groups.
  - Introvert (I) – These people relate best to their inner self. Their energy is drained from working with groups.
- **Seeking Information** – The two opposing forms this dimension can take are:
  - Sensing (S) – These people rely on facts, reality and are no-nonsense individuals. When they review documents, they are most likely to find typographical errors and misspellings.
  - Intuitive (N) – These are people who use/rely on their intuition, speculation and imagination. When they review a document, they are most likely to find problems in how the document was developed.
- **Decision-Making** – The two opposing forms this dimension can take are:
  - Thinking (T) – These people make decisions based primarily on sound principles, laws and so forth. Thinkers are analytical, logical and objective.
  - Feeling (F) – These people make decisions based on values, devotion, sympathy and harmony. Feelers will take the emotions and opinions of others into consideration. They strive to maintain harmony in the group.

■ **Relationship with the World** – The two opposing forms this dimension can take are:
  - Judging (J) – These people are outcome-oriented, regulated and decisive. They make decisions quickly and drive toward getting closure of issues and settlement.
  - Perceiving (P) – Process-oriented, flexible, open-minded, make decisions slowly. They like to get new information or consider other possibilities.

Each person is a combination of one of the two possibilities in each of the four categories (e.g. INTJ), giving us 16 possibilities. Some possible types work better or are more compatible with others as shown in Table A4.1. To use the table, select a type on the vertical that corresponds to one person and then move to the right to the column representing a second person's type. The higher the compatibility index, the more compatible the type is with another type. For example, an INTJ type would be very compatible with an ESFJ type (0.83) but not very compatible with an ENTP (0.17).

Some advisories are in order here. Regardless of the model used (MBTI is only one of several available), personality type should not be the only factor used to select team members. Besides, work rules in some countries and organizations may preclude the administering of the Myers-Briggs Type Inventory or some other typing instrument, even if it is put forward as a condition of employment. Also, this information must be retained in the strictest confidence unless the team member explicitly gives permission to share it. There are other factors as well so it would be wise to check your local laws and organization's rules.

Interviewing prospective members of the development team should involve all current members – if they do not believe they can work with the interviewee, then find someone else who can.

For a variety of reasons, you may end up having to manage a team with members who are incompatible. There are several things you can do to mitigate the situation:

Try working with the individuals involved directly, privately and together. The key issue here is whether or not they are willing to set aside their differences for the good of the project.

Do not single anybody out as a troublemaker. The rest of the team probably already knows who this person(s) is.

Make sure everyone on the team puts the success of the project ahead of their personal agendas.

A gentle reminder on the merit or annual performance review may help in some circumstances.

If you have tried everything you can think of, enlist the help of a psychology professional who specializes in team development. I had this exact situation before, and the cost was money well spent.

The most common software types are ISTJ and INTJ. To use the table, go to the intersection of two types. For example, ESTP and INTJ have a compatibility index of 0.33. Recalling that the higher the compatibility index, the more compatible the personalities, 0.33 is not highly compatible.

A.4.3 Keep Successful Teams Together for Higher Productivity

More recent work with software organizations found that teams that worked well together should be kept together [6]. While this may not always be possible due to organizational changes, product line evolution and other factors, the point is that effective, productive teams do not just happen.

Table A4.1   Normalized Personality Compatibility

	ESTJ	ESTP	ESFJ	ESFP	ENTJ	ENTP	ENFJ	ENFP	ISTJ	ISTP	ISFJ	ISFP	INTJ	INTP	INFJ	INFP
ESTJ	0.67															
ESTP	0.33	0.67														
ESFJ	0.83	0.50	0.67													
ESFP	0.50	0.83	0.33	0.67												
ENTJ	0.83	0.50	1.00	0.67	0.67											
ENTP	0.50	0.83	0.67	1.00	0.33	0.67										
ENFJ	1.00	0.67	0.83	0.50	0.83	0.50	0.67									
ENFP	0.67	1.00	0.50	0.83	0.50	0.83	0.33	0.67								
ISTJ	0.50	0.17	0.67	0.33	0.67	0.33	0.50	0.50	0.33							
ISTP	0.17	0.50	0.33	0.67	0.33	0.67	0.67	0.83	0.00	0.33						
ISFJ	0.67	0.33	0.50	0.17	0.83	0.50	0.33	0.33	0.50	0.17	0.33					
ISFP	0.33	0.67	0.17	0.50	0.50	0.83	0.67	0.67	0.17	0.50	0.00	0.33				
INTJ	0.67	0.33	0.83	0.50	0.50	0.17	0.33	0.33	0.50	0.17	0.67	0.33	0.33			
INTP	0.33	0.67	0.50	0.83	0.17	0.50	0.67	0.67	0.17	0.50	0.33	0.67	0.00	0.33		
INFJ	0.83	0.50	0.67	0.33	0.67	0.33	0.50	0.17	0.67	0.33	0.50	0.17	0.50	0.17	0.33	
INFP	0.50	0.83	0.33	0.67	0.33	0.67	0.17	0.50	0.33	0.67	0.17	0.50	0.17	0.50	0.00	0.33

Such teams are the result of hard work on the part of the software project manager and the senior management team and sometimes just a matter of luck. The point is, once you have identified a high-performing team, do not just break it up at the end of a project and reassign the individuals to other projects. Instead, find a way to keep the team intact and assign them to another project. Keep in mind that sometimes, team members, particularly those who are in the early years of their careers, develop and mature in ways which may cause them to no longer be compatible with the other team members. I had this happen when one team member decided he no longer wanted to develop software. He decided to go back to school and obtained a Master's degree in Business Administration specializing in his first love, accounting. Another member decided they no longer wanted to develop the type of software we were working on at that time. They decided to go to work for Microsoft instead. All of this occurred after successfully completing a project that was deemed "impossible." But the remaining members of this five-person team pushed on, two new members were acquired and their successes continued.

References

[1] Chen, J. and Lin, L., "Modeling Team Member Characteristics for the Formation of a Multifunctional Team in Concurrent Engineering," *IEEE Transactions on Engineering Management*, Vol. 15, No. 2, 2004, pp. 111–124.

[2] Briggs-Myers, I., *Gifts Differing: Understanding Personality Type*, Nicholas Brealey, 2nd edition, Boston, MA, 2010.

[3] Gardner, H., Gino, F. and Staats, B.R., "Dynamically Integrating Knowledge in Teams: Transforming Resources into Performance," Working Paper 11-009, Harvard Business School, September 7, 2011.

[4] Bayne, R. "A New Direction for the Mers-Briggs Type Indicator," *Personnel Management*, volume 22, No. 3, pp. 48–51, 1990.

[5] Blackwell, G.W. et al, "Multidisciplinary Team Research," Interdisciplinary Analysis and Research, D.E. Chubin et al, Eds: Lomond, 1986, pp. 103–114.

[6] Campion, M.A., Medsker, G.J. and Higgs, A.C., "Relations Between Work Group Characteristics and Effectiveness: Implications for Designing Effective Work Groups," *Pers. Psychology*, Vol. 46, pp. 823–850, 1993.

Appendix 5

Computing the Cost of a Change

Well before the software profession "discovered" it, project managers in other professions had known since before the Roman Empire that changes made to a project increased cost and that the later in the project that they occurred, the greater the cost. The increase in cost with lateness in the project is due to the fact that some work will have to be undone in order to make the change. But changes throughout the course of software projects will have to be made. While some are inevitable (e.g. to correct programming errors – bugs, miscommunication regarding user interface preferences), others could be best described as changes. For example, modifications of the user interface requested by the customer, changes in how taxes or interest rates are computed due to changes in tax law, privacy and security changes and so on. These changes tend to increase development costs in real time and are often unforeseeable. A study of several thousand projects in the construction industry [1] provides some much-needed insights into what the total cost of a project will be when we include the cost(s) associated with making changes. This method requires that we keep records specific to each project as to the cost of a change on that project. The mathematical relationships developed in that study are not specific to the type of project and are applicable to software. A side effect of the formulation that the study developed is that it gives us the opportunity to provide ourselves and our customer with a realistic estimate of the cost of the change being proposed. This provides our customer with some semblance of control over the total cost of the project. This result is formulated along two lines. One is the average cost of a change. The other is the relative cost of a change with respect to the total cost of the project. For example, if the burdened cost (this includes all direct and indirect costs) of a software engineer is €50/hour based on a 2,000-hour work year, the cost for an average change which we estimate to be 8 hours (development, debugging, testing and so forth) gives us an average change cost of €400. The formula for estimating the impact of the changes that may occur over the life of a project [1] is:

$$CV = \left(n^2 \, f_c^{\,2} \, u_c^{\,2} \right) \big/ C^2$$

where

N = our estimate of the number of changes which will occur during the project.
f_c = coefficient of variation of cost change.

u_c = average cost of a change expressed as a decimal – it is the ratio of the cost of the change to the estimated total project cost.

C = original project cost estimate.

CV = the cost variance.

If we originally estimated the total project cost to be €100,000 and estimate there will be 100 changes, each costing €1,000 then,

$$C = 100,000, n = 1000, f_c = 1000, u_c = .01 \text{ substituting into our formula}$$

$$CV = \left[1.000^2 \; 2000^2 \; 0.01^2\right]/100.000^2 = 0.04$$

CV is .04 or 4% meaning that the projected project cost will be between €100,000 and € 104,000. Again, cost estimating is not an exact science. This method gives us a value or range of values that are within the realm of possibility. The obvious but incorrect answer would be to simply multiply the 100 changes by the cost per change and add it to our original estimate. But the research work showed that would be fallacious because changes occur while development is occurring so some economies can be wrought.

References

[1] Touran, A., "Calculation of Contingency in Construction Projects," *IEEE Transactions on Engineering Management*, Vol. 50, no. 2, May 2003, pp. 135–140.

Appendix 6

Developing a Business Case

A.6.1 The Basics

Whether we are refining an existing project plan or creating a new one, the elements of the engineering model of a project [1] will need to be satisfied. The format and content for project plans vary from one company and industry to another. For example, in the United States, HIPAA (The Health Insurance Portability and Accountability Act) requires that the privacy of patient health information not be distributed without the patient's permission. This requirement makes security, control and limited access to such information a prominent element of any software project plan in the health industry in the United States. Other industries (e.g. Financial Services) have their own unique requirements and these also vary from country to country. The most common elements of a project plan and its justification (the justification is often called a "business case"), regardless of the location (note that titles for these elements may vary internationally but the content remains the same), include:

■ The Business Case – This is the economic justification for doing the project. In general, if you cannot make a business case for an effort, it isn't going to go forward. In simple terms, the business case states the problem this project intends to solve, if the project is successful, what the savings will be, what the return on investment (ROI) will be (this describes how long it will take the firm or customer to recover the funds expended, the assumptions made in this analysis and so forth), an overall strategy that will be applied (frequently, this is one that has worked before), the staff to be used and equipment needed and so forth.

A.6.2 Business Case Defined

There are many different definitions of just what constitutes a business case. According to the United States General Accounting Office (May, 2000), a business case is:

> A structured method for organizing and presenting a business improvement proposal. Organizational decision makers typically compare business cases when deciding to expend resources. A business case typically includes an analysis of business process performance and associated needs or problems, proposed alternative solutions, assumptions, constraints and a risk adjusted cost/benefit analysis.

There is no fixed format for business cases so they vary from organization to organization. They are a vital part of go–no-go decisions on projects and assist greatly in helping to prevent the project from expanding into a different project than originally envisioned (e.g. scope creep). However, it can happen in spite of our best efforts.

Generally, there are five categories of issues that need to be considered:

- The problem to be solved or opportunity (e.g. to create a new product)
- Changes that must be made to an existing system or product
- Benefits of the changes
- Costs and risks associated with the changes
- Measure(s) of success

Although profitability is the most common criterion used in evaluating a business case, it is not the only one. Social responsibility, corporate image, community welfare and other criteria not related to profit may be employed. There are many other business case models presented in the literature but we have enough here to demonstrate the application of the concept from a project I actually consulted on.

A.6.3 Business Case Example

A few years ago, a kindergarten through high school educational facility was being built by a Native American tribe. Their goal was to provide their children and young adults with a state-of-the-art educational facility while at the same time demonstrating the tribe's commitment to core values that included respect for the environment. The school would be utilizing more than 400 personal computers. The era in which this development occurred was such that personal computers (PCs) consumed much more electricity than they do today generating heat which required the HVAC (Heating, Ventilation and Air Conditioning) systems to remove heat from the classroom(s) during warm weather. A second factor associated with the use of these PCs was the fact that electric rates from the company serving the area where the school was located were going up. The simple, obvious solution was to have teachers and students turn off their PCs before leaving for the day. This could not be guaranteed in all cases. Besides teachers and students complained about boot-up times since many of them were rushing to complete an assignment late. A vendor was identified that sold software that would put a PC central processor into a state which drew very little current from which it could be awakened quickly into an operational state. It could install itself via push technology and allowed each user to set a schedule for their PC to "go to sleep" or defer to the default. Without getting into all the cost and savings details, Table A6.1 shows the results of our analysis.

Some of the elements are listed below. Also, projects may not always be justified based on profit. Many projects are justified based on their benefit to society or the community in general or a segment of the population (e.g. those with disabilities, reducing our impact on the environment).

Explanation of Notation

- Amounts are in Euros.
- An amount surrounded by parentheses is a negative amount.
- A period is used instead of a comma consistent with European conventions.
- ROI represents Return On Investment if the original purchase price was invested at 5% or 10% compounded.

Table A6.1 Data Developed for Our Business Case

Item	Year 0	Year 1	Year 2	Year 3	Year 4	Total
Energy Savings	€3.968	€4.167	€4.375	€4.593	€4.823	€21.926
HVAC Savings	€595	€625	€656	€689	€726	€3.291
Product Cost	(€8.000)	€0	€0	€0	€0	(€8.000)
To Date Totals	(€3.437)	€1.355	€6.386	€11.668	€17.217	€17.217
ROI @ 5%	€8.000	€8.400	€8.820	€9.261	€9.724	€9.724
ROI @ 10%	€8.000	€8.800	€9.680	€10.648	€11.713	€11.713

In the preceding example, the total positive cash flow of €17,217 being greater than what would have been received via a simple investment at 5% or 10% means the business case is a viable one both from a financial and an environmental standpoint.

Project Charter – The Project Charter legitimizes the project in that it authorizes the expenditure of company funds to specific ends. It bounds the project and attempts to reduce "scope creep." It states what the project will and will not do. It is necessitated by the fact that software often touches so many other aspects of the enterprise. Not bounding the project in some way almost guarantees that the scope of the project will expand to include some of the systems it interfaces with perhaps resulting in the budget and/or schedule exceeding the plan. Most importantly, the project's charter gets everyone related to this effort to think about what will and will not be addressed by this project. There have been many formats published for project charters. Most software companies will have their own, possibly unique, format. Regardless, the project charter should contain at least the following elements:

Project Name – This is how this project will be referenced.

Owner(s) – Who, in the organization, is responsible for maintaining this document (it will be under change control)?

Executive Summary – This section lists the measurable objectives of this project, proposed start and end dates, estimated costs, assumptions, risks, project overview, scope and any other factors senior management may need to know in order to make an informed decision about approving this effort.

Approvals List – This is a list of the people, by job title, who are approving this effort as signified by their signature. Typically, this list would include the Project Manager (who usually prepares this document), Project Sponsor, Senior Manager (the Executive) who is sponsoring this effort, Client Representative.

Stated another way, the project charter is a high-level view of the proposed project – the project described without all the details

■ Measures of Success – This item is one of great importance and often overlooked. It states clearly and (hopefully) simply what the resulting system must do in order for the project to be deemed successful. These must be stated in a measurable way, including the current baseline from which we may be measuring improvement. For example, "With all hardware and operating system software in working order, the system shall prompt the user for a password within 60 seconds after a 'Power On' event has been detected." Certainly, there is a lot more to that one but the essence of this item is there. The conditions under which this acceptability requirement must be met are stated together with acceptable performance under those conditions.

■ Risk Analysis – What are the risks associated with developing this system, its use and so forth? How are or will these risks be mitigated? For example, if we are developing a system to automatically park an automobile, how will the driver regain control in the event of a failure of the software? How will the driver know the system has failed? How many different ways could the system fail and how can we prevent them from occurring?

■ A Multidimensional View – The best policy to have regarding business case development is to consider all the various dimensions a new or revised system can engage. The best system for this right now is "The Balanced Scorecard" [2]. It considers the entire spectrum of impacts organized into four dimensions or viewpoints:
  – Financial – What will this cost versus what will it save the company? What confidence level do we attribute to this estimate?
  – Customer – How will this impact the customer? Is it likely to be well received by our customers? What are the acceptance criteria?
  – Internal – Are we organized or structured in a way that will support this change? If not, what changes will we need to put in place?
  – Learning – Will we have to train some of our people in this new technique(s)? If so, who and what will this cost?

Anyone who has called a company's technical support team with a problem that needs some explanation only to encounter an automated answering system that requests you press a number for this type of problem or that then requests another selection and so forth none of which seem to match your issue has experienced what can happen when a company only considers profit and loss issues. These systems can be frustrating, particularly if they do not have the option of pressing zero in order to speak to a human being to explain the nature of the problem you are calling about.

The Balanced Scorecard [2] is discussed in more detail in Chapter 3.

References

[1] Peters, L., *Getting Results from Software Development Teams*, Microsoft Press Best Practices Series, Redmond, WA, 2008.
[2] Kaplan, R.S. and Norton, D.P., "Linking the Balanced Scorecard to Strategy," *California Management Review*, Vol. 39, No. 1, pp. 53–79, Fall 1996.

Appendix 7

Developing the Project Closeout Plan

Every software project, successful or not, represents an important learning opportunity. Not all software engineers and engineering organizations recognize this as such and, as a result, leave themselves vulnerable to committing the same mistakes and encountering the same difficulties on the next project while being ignorant of some practices that could have avoided problems. Documenting what worked and what didn't work may not eliminate the chance of the next project being unsuccessful but it at least provides an opportunity to avoid some of the difficulties we experienced on our current or previous project. There are many software project closeout templates published on the internet from which to choose. If your team or your company does not have a software project template that is in current use, it is suggested that you take a look at a few of the ones published on the internet and see which one(s) best suits your team and projects. Don't be reluctant to change the one(s) you select because none may be ideal for your situation.

A.7.1 What Do We Want to Capture at Project Closeout?

In a very real sense, every software project is a unique undertaking. It is not like building out a 100 home subdivision which has just five floor plans. In that case, there are usually better flow times and fewer errors with each successive building of the same floor plan including possible alterations of the plan to reduce waste, decrease construction time and so forth. Software projects tend to be considerably less repeatable and predictable. What we are trying to do with the closeout document is officially declare the software to be at a level of development to be released to operations, document events, practices and discoveries that could be useful to some other projects in the future and document lessons learned. For this final developmental phase of this project, we need to capture at least the following:

- How does the outcome of the project compare with the pre-project checklist developed prior to the start of the project? – Comparing what we initially perceived about the project before it started with what we now believe here, at the end of the project, will reveal our misconceptions as well as other influencers on our judgment such as overoptimism or pessimism. In this way, the pre-project checklist becomes part of a learning experience.

- What were the checklist items with the greatest differences in pre-project versus post-project? Try to explain the difference.

Whether the project was considered a success or not, each and every software project experience should result in the team and each member learning more about themselves and the process of software engineering.

Appendix 8

The Effect of Cultural Differences (on Software Development Teams)

Why is this important? Due to the worldwide demand for software engineers combined with ease of travel as the COVID pandemic and other factors subsided, today software engineers are finding it easier to move from one country to another. A contributing factor is the worldwide availability of training in software engineering in various forms from university curricula to private training organizations. This has resulted in software development teams being composed of software engineers from different countries, different backgrounds and different cultures. While such mixed groups offer the promise of unusually innovative solutions they bring with them, problems stem from cultural differences. First and foremost among these problems is communication. As has been noted elsewhere [outsourcing discussion], this has severely impacted offshore IT projects. An early negative result of this was that at least 40% of offshore projects failed to deliver results [1]. Studies of global teams in virtual settings show cultural differences affect at least these areas:

- Work ethic – The principle that hard work is a virtue and should be rewarded.
- Work hours – The number of hours per day that are required by the employer.
- Preferred method of communication and how administrative tasks are viewed, the role of the software project manager and authority are perceived.

More recently, both offshore firms and domestic ones have matured – they have made significant changes to improve results, lower costs and become more reliable. Studies have shown that pre-pandemic outsourcing has been increasing at an exponential rate. Companies that are outsourcing expected productivity in terms of source lines in delivered product, but it actually went down. The United States approaches software development differently as compared to the Middle East [1] – United States teams will get to work quickly while Middle East teams will spend time getting to know each other before beginning work. This discussion applies to co-located teams composed of people from different cultures, virtual teams that may have never been together in one place as well as a mixture of these circumstances.

A.8.1 Culture

Researchers have been studying the effects of cultural backgrounds in the workplace possibly before software engineering was born. This is a delicate topic to discuss because it is closely related to various kinds of discrimination and racism. As much as I can, this discussion will be based on "facts and data." A challenge for most software project managers is to avoid viewing all members of a particular culture as being the same. The studies cited make the point that each person is an individual, and cultural characteristics represent "tendencies" [2]. An analysis of eight different research studies found a common core among their definitions of culture:

> *Culture is learned, culture is associated with values, beliefs and behaviors that are shared by a group and these values are passed along from generation to generation.*

In order to better understand what is meant by culture, a study [3] was conducted of cultures from the perspective of value systems resulting in five areas or dimensions into which all cultural groups have in common though they differ in their beliefs. The beliefs and their relative positions are:

1. Human Nature – People are born good, evil or a mixture of both.
2. Person versus Nature – People value their subjugation to nature, mastery over nature or harmony with nature.
3. Time Sense – Priority is given to traditional customs, future plans or present events.
4. Social Relations – Society is organized around a linear hierarchy of authority, collateral interests or individual goals.
5. Space – Business and life are conducted publicly, privately or a combination of both.

In the field of high-technology workers, Hofstede [4] might be the most widely quoted. He conducted a large-scale study (approximately 70,000 people) of IBM employees located in more than 40 countries and developed the following cultural dimensions based on these employees:

1. Individualism/collectivism – This dimension describes how an individual is perceived in a culture – according to individual characteristics or by the characteristics of the group to which he or she belongs. An individualistic culture is one where individual interests take precedence over collective ones and everyone is expected to look after themselves.
2. Power Distance (PD) – Measures the extent to which a culture embraces social inequality. High-PD cultures embrace a strong sense of hierarchy whereas low-PD cultures consider every individual as an equal.
3. Uncertainty Avoidance – It is the level of risk accepted by a culture.
4. Masculinity/Femininity – Reflects that either masculine norms such as success and material orientation or feminine norms like relationships, people orientation and quality of life are important in a culture.
5. Long-Term/Short-Term Orientation – This is the level to which a society takes a long-term versus a short-term orientation in life. A long-term culture prescribes long-term commitments and perseverance towards slow producing results.

A summary of Hofstede's National Culture Dimensions is presented in Table A8.1.

The European Software Institute (ESI) surveyed best practices adoption throughout Europe, Asia and the United States. What they found reflects the composition and behavioral tendencies of the countries listed in Table A8.2.

Table A8.1 Hofstede's National Culture Dimensions [4]

Dimension	Low Score Value	High Score Value
Power Distance	Society deemphasizes differences between citizens' power and wealth	Inequalities of power and wealth within society
Individualism versus Collectivism	Collectivist nature with close ties between individuals	Individualism and individual rights are paramount
Uncertainty Avoidance	Tolerance for a variety of opinions and less concern about ambiguity and uncertainty	Low tolerance for uncertainty and ambiguity
Masculinity versus Femininity	Value social relevance, quality of life and welfare of others	Aggressive goal behavior, high gender differentiation and males dominate
Long-Term vs Short-Term Orientation	Place less emphasis on hard work and perseverance	Embraces long-term devotion to traditional, forward-thinking values

Table A8.2 Adoption Rates by European Countries with More than Four Responses [5]

Country	N	Organization Issues	Standards & Processes	Metrics	Control	Tools	Overall Average Adoption %
France	18	72	62	61	76	58	65%
United Kingdom	52	66	63	52	67	50	60%
Greece	18	63	57	49	65	50	57%
Denmark	17	64	53	46	63	53	55%
Finland	4	63	56	50	54	50	55%
Austria	16	66	50	42	60	46	53%
Norway	6	60	53	44	61	48	53%
Italy	77	57	52	50	61	40	52%
Germany	62	55	48	43	52	47	49%
Netherlands	30	57	49	41	51	48	49%
Australia	205	48	54	35	49	47	48%
Israel	11	57	47	38	55	34	46%

(*Continued*)

Table A8.2 (Continued) Adoption Rates by European Countries with More than Four Responses [5]

Country	N	Organization Issues	Standards & Processes	Metrics	Control	Tools	Overall Average Adoption %
Ireland	12	51	43	36	51	45	45%
Spain	34	53	44	36	57	35	44%
Belgium	15	52	41	40	46	40	43%
Sweden	13	38	36	25	33	26	32%

As you can see from Table A8.2, many countries residing in climatically different parts of the world are adopting software engineering tools and techniques. While software engineers from these countries represent an asset to your project, they can constitute a challenge which, if met effectively, will enhance the effectiveness of the software engineering team and increase the software project's chances of success.

References

[1] Olson, J. and Olson, G., "Culture Surprises in Remote Software Development Teams," *Queue*, December 2003, Vol. 1, pp. 52–59.
[2] Rebello, K., "The Impact of Culture in the Workplace," *Forbes*, December, 1, 2021.
[3] Aberle, D., *Culture and Behavior: Collected Essays of Clyde Kluckhohn*, Wiley Publishing, Hoboken, New Jersey, August 1963.
[4] Hofstede, G., *Cultures Consequences: Comparing Values, Behaviors, Institutions and Organizations across Nations*, 2nd edition, Sage Publishing, Thousand Oaks, California, 2003.
[5] European Software Institute, *Software Best Practice Questionnaire*, Bilboa, Spain, 1997.

Appendix 9

Emotional Intelligence

Emotional intelligence is most often defined as the ability to perceive, use, understand, manage and handle emotions. It may sound like an oxymoron because most of us have witnessed bursts of emotion that were anything but intelligent. But understanding and controlling your emotions are an important part of being an effective leader and definitely required to be an effective software project manager. In fact, emotional intelligence is seen by many researchers as a key competence for all project managers [1]. This is particularly true in organizations with several generations [2] working together. Emotional intelligence is especially important in team collaboration, trust and satisfaction, conflict management, project manager leadership style and project results/success [1]. It is considered a necessary skill for all project managers to possess. Part of the reason for this "importance" is that project managers spend a significant portion (60–80%) of their time communicating but emotional intelligence abilities are not something we are born with but skills that must be learned and improved through use [3]. In general, the professional success of the project manager is related to their knowledge, communication skills and thinking ability. Emotional intelligence may be broadly understood as a person's ability to understand people's emotions and the ability to react to their emotional condition [4]. Research has shown that a high level of emotional intelligence enables professional development and success overall [5].

A.9.1 Models of Emotional Intelligence

Different researchers have developed their own models of emotional intelligence in order to help understand the phenomenon and convey why it is important for project managers to understand it and to develop their emotional intelligence. While each model is unique, they do have some commonalities. The five elements of the emotional intelligence model developed by Daniel Goleman, who helped to popularize the concept of emotional intelligence, are:

1. Self-awareness
2. Self-regulation
3. Motivation
4. Empathy
5. Social skills

Note that none of these elements involves technology but deals with interpersonal actions [6]. Consider two incidents I observed watching NFL football one afternoon. Late in the game, one

123

team had an opportunity to win the game by kicking a field goal with very little time left in the game. If the kick was good, there was so little time left in the game they would probably win by a point but the kicker missed. When he returned to the sideline, the coach told him, "OK, you'll make the next one." Then the unlikely happened, the team recovered a fumble and had another chance to kick a field goal and win the game. Sure enough, the kicker made it and they won. I watched another game the previous week with a similar situation. After the miss, the coach was livid. He was screaming and yelling at the kicker and obviously angry at what happened. So the question is, which coach displayed more refined emotional intelligence? Obviously, the first one but more importantly consider the effect his behavior had on the self-confidence of the placekicker. The message being conveyed was "I have confidence in you" while the message being conveyed by the second coach was just the opposite. In managing a software team, there will be many situations which could cause the software project manager to be angry but not giving in to the temptation to scream and yell but instead calmly convey confidence in the individual and the team can work wonders for the performance of your team.

References

[1] Ciutiene, R., Meilene, E., Daunoriene, A. and Surgelyte, I., "Project Managers of Different Generations: How to Deal with Emotional Intelligence Issues," *Project Management Development – Practice and Perspectives, 8th International Scientific Conference on Project Management in the Baltic Countries*, April 25–26, 2019, Riga, University of Latvia.

[2] Moss, D., "5 Generations + 7 Values = Endless Opportunities," *Society for Human Resource Management Newsletters*, June 20, 2017.

[3] Goleman, D., *The Brain and Emotional Intelligence*, More Than Sound Publishing, Florence, MA, 2011.

[4] Derevyanko, S.P., "The Role of Emotional Intelligence in the Process of Social-Psyhclogical Adaptation of Students," *Innovative Education Technologies*, Vol. 1, 2007, pp. 92–95.

[5] Meshcheryakova, I.N., "Formation of Emotional Intelligence of Psuchology Students during Their University Study," *Tambo University Bulletin*, Humanities Series, Vol. I, No. 81, 2010, pp. 157–161.

[6] Thamhain, H. "Critical Success Factors for Managing Technology-Intensive Teams in the Global Enterprise," *Engineering Management Journal*, Vol. 23, No. 3, April 2015, pp. 30–36.

Appendix 10

Environmental Factors Affecting Productivity

Most managers underestimate the power of familiarity. Use it to drive performance.

[1]

Productivity is a topic that has been a consistent topic of discussion in software engineering literature for many decades. It seems every few years another "new" method or software tool is introduced with the promise of increasing software engineering productivity equated to code production. The problem with that type of equivalence is that it is not how many lines of code one produces but whether or not it meets requirements, is stable, is maintainable, makes it through to the source code for the released product and so forth. The mental state of the people producing that code is increasingly being seen as an important factor in the search for productivity. There are some senior software project managers who believe that software engineers' happiness isn't important. The attitude of some I have worked with is, "Who cares if they are happy – they are being paid to do a job, they are not being paid to be happy!" This attitude has manifested itself in software engineers rating their career happiness at 3.2 out of 5.0 which puts them at the bottom 46% of careers [2]. Hopefully, these senior managers may be a distinct minority but the attitude expressed is more widespread than you might think. It is present in subtle ways. For example, resistance to improving working conditions, increasing pay rate, not being included in scheduling decisions and commitments and more are all areas that software engineers have found to be frustrating. Those frustrations equate to unhappiness which equates to lower productivity [3] and lower product quality. It may also equate to higher turnover which can increase development costs by as much as 60% or more [4]. For more than a century, academics have studied how working conditions and related factors affect worker productivity. But much of that work is related to factory work – repetitive work often requiring very little in the way of mentally challenging problem-solving. The relatively recent introduction of software engineering into the workplace has become a new domain of research since this profession involves mentally challenging work involving creativity and technical proficiency in the context of often frequently changing requirements. Software project managers are focused on making their project effort successful with the people resources they have. New programming languages, analysis and design methods and other aids all held out the promise of solving "the software engineering problem" but it remains unsolved with the productivity improvements being disappointingly modest – one source line per programmer per month per year [5]. One reason is that this is not the same problem from project to project but the issue that remains the same from project to project is that software engineers are doing the work. As stated many times in this book, they may be the most important and least addressed factor in this endeavor. If your software engineers are not working together as a collaborative team, your project is likely doomed to failure. Worse, many senior managers believe that successful software engineering teams could benefit the company better if they were broken up and spread throughout the organization so that what was successful can be learned by other teams. Once again, nothing could be further from the truth as data refute this belief [6]. Experience shows that keeping teams together improves performance and increases their chances of success. Why? For one thing, over time team members learn which members possess certain kinds of knowledge so that when they have a particularly challenging problem they know who best to get help from. This works both ways so what is happening is that a team composed of *n* members becomes analogous to a single software engineer with the skills and experience of all *n* software engineers on that team. What would be far more effective than breaking up a team would be to have other software project managers emulate what the software project manager of that successful team did [6]. Besides keeping teams together, the physical environment the team is working in can and does impact productivity where productivity is not just the number of lines of code produced but the quality of the code, responsiveness of the team to requested changes and so forth. Table A10.1 lists the results from a study by DeMarco and Lister [7] on the impact of the physical environment on software engineering team performance. What they did was to compare the two extremes of performance – highest and lowest with their physical environments. The COVID pandemic also highlighted this issue as many workers now prefer to work from home rather than in an office. What appears to be evolving from this experience is a hybrid work environment wherein workers work from their home so many days a week and go into the office to link up with other team members on specific days of the week. It remains to be seen how well this works out but for now in 2024, some firms are adopting the hybrid model and adjusting the finer details as problems occur.

Table A10.1   Impact of Environmental Factors on Productivity [7]

Environmental Factor	Highest Performers [% Yes]	Lowest Performers [% Yes]
Amount of dedicated workspace	78 square feet (7.2 square meters)	46 square feet (4.3 square meters)
Work area is acceptably quiet	57%	29%
Work area is acceptably private	62%	19%
Phone can be silenced	52%	10%
Phone can be diverted	76%	19%
People interrupt you needlessly	38%	76%

References

[1] Huckman, R. and Staats, B., "The Hidden Benefits of Keeping Teams Intact," *Harvard Business Review*, December, 2013.

[2] Business Insider, October 2021.

[3] Lester, P.B., Diener, E. and Seligman, M., "Happiness Drives Performance," *MIT Sloan Management Review*, February 16, 2022.

[4] Cone, E., "Managing that Churning Sensation," *Information Week*, May 1998, No. 680, pp. 50–67.

[5] Jensen, R., "Don't Forget about Good Management," *CrossTalk Magazine*, August, 2000, p. 30.

[6] Staats, B., "Unpacking Team Familiarity: The Effects of Geographic Location and Hierarchical Role," *Production and Operations Management*, Vol. 21, No. 3, 2022, pp. 619–635. doi:10.1111/j.1937-5956.2011.01254

[7] DeMarco, T. and Lister, T., *Peopleware*, Dorset House, New York, NY, 1999.

Appendix 11

How Software Project Managers Are Evaluated

Skilled software project managers trained in project management are a key element in a successful software project. As discussed elsewhere in this text, success involves much more than bringing a software project in on time and within budget but even so, it is important for the software project manager to understand how he or she will be evaluated in order to avoid the shock of a significantly poor evaluation which may lead to a demotion or worse. Several groups that the software project manager interacts with may be involved in evaluating the manager's performance [1]. Each of these groups has their own value systems, preferences and images of what a "good" software project manager is like. Since there are no absolute rights or wrongs with regard to evaluating software project managers, the use of Likert scale evaluation criteria is probably the best mechanism to use. The Likert scale in this case could range from 1 (Strongly Disagree) to 5 (Strongly Agree) and increase monotonically. A series of statements would be contributed by each of the following groups and evaluated by them [1]:

- Senior Managers – These are the people who made the decision to put this person into a management position. Their evaluation of software project managers may be defined by company policy but their own evaluation often takes the large view regarding the software project manager's value to the company.
- The Client (or customer) – This is the person or group that is paying for the software to be developed. They are the ones who are specifying what the software should do (define requirements) and interface with the software engineering team during development. The client may be internal to the company and not an outside entity.
- Software Engineers – As the Google organization found out [2], it is essential that the software engineers on the team be able to honestly evaluate their manager which is one of the techniques used by the Google organization to sell their engineers on the value and role of managers [2].

A.11.1 Evaluation Perspectives

Each of the groups that are interacting with the software project manager has their own set of criteria by which they judge the manager to be capable and to what degree. An overview of these relationships is presented in the subparagraphs which follow.

A.11.2 The Senior Manager Perspective

Table A11.1 lists the main criteria suggested for the assessment of software project managers from the senior management perspective. Possibly more than anyone, the senior managers' perspective is clearly focused on what is best for the company and in simple terms, the priorities are clear – complete the project satisfying the client while ensuring a profit on the contract. This is even true when the work is being done "in house."

For that reason, an adequate planning and risk management strategy are crucial. These two issues are also discussed by Thomas [3] as being among the most relevant causes of software project failures according to senior managers. Therefore, such issues must be assessed. Note that adequate planning does not mean detailed planning, but a plan with the level of detail needed at the time.

Team management is another critical task of software project managers, reflected by several criteria in Table A11.1. For some time, personnel turnover has been identified among the main causes of software project failures, while the software project manager has been identified as the primary reason for personal turnover [4]. Therefore, adequate team management and motivation skills are crucial qualities for software project managers. In our experience, some software project managers tend to be too proud to ask for help when needed. Recognizing our own limitations is an acquired skill.

Table A11.1   Senior Manager Evaluation

Senior Manager Evaluation Criteria	Likert Evaluation (1 = Poor, 5 = Excellent)				
The software project manager controlled costs acceptably	1	2	3	4	5
Maintained "good" relations with client	1	2	3	4	5
The plan was sufficiently detailed	1	2	3	4	5
Mitigated risk in advance of it happening	1	2	3	4	5
Requested help when needed	1	2	3	4	5
Was able to get support from the development team	1	2	3	4	5
Had relatively low personnel turnover	1	2	3	4	5
Motivated the development team	1	2	3	4	5
Maintained/improved team performance	1	2	3	4	5
Complied with company policy	1	2	3	4	5

Finally, company policy exists for a reason (e.g. legal, financial), diverging from it would need to be justified – conversely, if company policy is contributing to failures, it needs to be modified. So feedback about this issue is also beneficial.

The people who would be filling out this evaluation are the senior managers who might have sponsored the software project manager to become a project manager. Their perspective may be biased toward the positive because they do not want to be seen as having put someone into management who was not really qualified. It is expected that over time, senior managers will come to recognize areas that specific software project managers need to improve upon which will be reflected in their regularly scheduled evaluation.

A.11.3 The Client Perspective

Whether part of a larger organization which includes the software development team or a separate entity, the client or customer is the one who is paying for the work being done, and therefore their satisfaction is directly related to the adequacy of the final product. Additionally, according to our experience, the attitude and relationship with the software project manager during the development process are also a very relevant factor. Therefore, as shown in Table A11.2, the client evaluator is in an excellent position to assess the quality and effectiveness of communication between the organization and the software project manager. These evaluation criteria are consistent with findings elsewhere, particularly with [5]. Even when the project is experiencing difficulties, maintaining open and honest communications with the client organization can lead to mutual understanding with few unpleasant "surprises."

Table A11.2   Client Perspective Evaluation

Client Evaluation Criteria	Likert Evaluation (1 = Poor, 5 = Excellent)				
The delivered system met/exceeded expectations	1	2	3	4	5
The project delivered value for the cost	1	2	3	4	5
The software project manager kept us informed regarding progress	1	2	3	4	5
Kept us appraised of difficulties and possible solutions	1	2	3	4	5
Informed us of scheduling issues	1	2	3	4	5
Explained technical issues understandably	1	2	3	4	5
There were a few surprises during the project	1	2	3	4	5
We will be able to manage the maintainability of the system	1	2	3	4	5
We want to work with this manager again	1	2	3	4	5
Overall, the project was a positive experience	1	2	3	4	5

This communication is not usually easy as there exists a natural communication gap requiring the project manager to speak in the client's language to explain complex technical issues in terms the customer can understand.

Table A11.2 also deals with maintainability; not ensuring the maintainability of the system by those other than its originators will not contribute to client satisfaction. Finally, Table A11.2 includes a couple of items related to the general impression of the clients with the software project manager and the project. They don't have to coincide and, in our experience, represent quite well the overall satisfaction of the client, and can provide very useful information in the subsequent analysis.

A.11.4 The Software Engineer Perspective

Table A11.3 lists the evaluation criteria of software project managers by software engineers. Like other high technology and knowledge workers, software engineers seek to work on projects which are at or advancing the state of the art [6]. Recognizing this need lets practitioners develop their own technical and professional careers in a supportive working environment. In this context, team management aspects are also valuable from the software engineering perspective, as shown in Table A11.3.

Notice that this concern for technical superiority is frequently in direct opposition to the client view. To a large extent, what they most often want is a system that provides the functionality, reliability, maintainability, security and ease of use they need. This difference between the goals of the software engineer and those of the client, and sometimes of the software project manager,

Table A11.3   Software Engineer Evaluation

Software Engineer Evaluator Criteria	Likert Evaluation (1 = Poor, 5 = Excellent)				
The software project manager empowered the team and did not micromanage	1	2	3	4	5
Expressed interest in and concern for team members' success and personal well-being	1	2	3	4	5
Encouraged quality results and practices	1	2	3	4	5
Was productive and results oriented	1	2	3	4	5
Was a good communicator – listened and shared information	1	2	3	4	5
Was a good coach	1	2	3	4	5
Had a clear vision and strategy for the team	1	2	3	4	5
Had key technical skills that help him/her to advise the team	1	2	3	4	5
The project was a positive learning experience	1	2	3	4	5
I want to work with this software project manager again	1	2	3	4	5

who finally wants the system to work, can make the software project manager's intentions and even their qualifications suspicious in the eyes of the software engineer.

A.11.5 Evaluation as a Learning Mechanism

While some software project managers may fear or resent being evaluated by others, that evaluation offers an opportunity to learn just what is or is not working with respect to how the manager interacts with others.

A.11.6 Software Project Manager's Perspective

The other three perspectives all involve assessing how others view the software project manager. However, how the software project manager "sees" himself/herself with respect to the other evaluators may be just as important to reveal discrepancies between the manager and the other groups.

So software project managers should assess from their own perspective equivalent criteria to the ones assessed by the other agents involved in the process. Table A11.4 partially shows the equivalent criteria to be assessed according to the three previous perspectives; in practice, all equivalent criteria in Tables A11.1, A11.2 and A11.3 should be considered. Reflecting upon and analyzing this information will provide useful data for the evaluation.

Table A11.4 Software Project Manager Self-Evaluation

Senior Manager Equivalent Evaluation	Likert Evaluation (1 = Poor, 5 = Excellent)				
I controlled costs acceptably	1	2	3	4	5
I maintained "good" relations with the client	1	2	3	4	5
The plan was sufficiently detailed	1	2	3	4	5
…….	1	2	3	4	5
Client Equivalent Evaluation	Likert Evaluation (1 = Poor, 5 = Excellent)				
The delivered system met/exceeded the client's expectations	1	2	3	4	5
The project delivered value for the cost	1	2	3	4	5
I kept the client informed regarding progress and issues	1	2	3	4	5
Software Engineer Equivalent Evaluation	Likert Evaluation (1 = Poor, 5 = Excellent)				
I empowered the team and did not micromanage	1	2	3	4	5
I expressed interest in and concern for team members' success and personal well-being	1	2	3	4	5
I encouraged quality software practices and discouraged shortcuts……	1	2	3	4	5

A key element in the evolution of a software project manager is the narrowing of any gaps between how the software project manager sees themselves versus how others view them. The larger the gap, the greater the communication and effectiveness.

A.11.7 Proficiency Levels in Software Project Management

Acquiring knowledge about managing software projects is less than half the challenge but is necessary to become proficient. Knowledge includes the facts and data needed but the competency needed to adequately apply that knowledge is another matter altogether. It often requires a "leap of faith" meaning that you lead your team using some method or system you have not used before which you believe will be effective.

One model of software project manager proficiency [3] is summarized in Table A11.5. Eight characteristics are listed vertically with levels of proficiency characterized from Novice to Master horizontally. A few of the terms that appear in the table need some explanation:

- Cognitive Intelligence – This is what most of us would agree is what "intelligence" is. It involves our ability to plan, solve problems including complex problems and so forth. Just about all software engineers have to have at least a reasonable level of this type of intelligence.
- Emotional Intelligence – As described by [4] it is, "the ability to monitor one's own and others' feelings and emotions to discriminate among them and to use this information to guide one's thinking and actions." In other words, it involves having empathy with your team and each individual member to the extent that you know when to inquire as to whether or not there is a problem, push for better performance and so forth. This level of understanding of your team and each of its members does not come about easily for most but is necessary for all software project managers.
- Spiritual Intelligence – The ability to behave with wisdom and compassion while maintaining inner and outer peace regardless of the situation [5]. In practical terms, this means that even when things are going badly, you as the software project manager do not throw a temper tantrum. Looking at it another way, watch the coach of a successful sports team. The most successful tend to rarely scream and yell at the officials even when things are not going well. In fact, they refrain from yelling at their players when they fail to execute as planned. After all, the player does not need to be yelled at. They know they made a mistake or failed to perform at the level required. A good example is the management style of Pete Carroll, coach of the Seattle Seahawks professional (American style) football team. A few years ago, in a game crucial to the team getting into the championship playoffs, late in the game, the placekicker missed a field goal that was well within his range. It was unlikely the team would get possession again so the game might be lost at that point. What did the coach say to the placekicker? He said, "That's OK – you'll make the next one." Luckily, the team got the ball back on a turnover and in the final play of the game, the placekicker made the kick to win it for the team. Self-confidence is very fragile. Berating a team member for failure not only impacts their self-esteem but sends a message to the rest of the team that negatively impacts their productivity.

Notice how the progression from Novice to Master tends to move away from what might be considered technical expertise and toward a more intuitive functionality while becoming effective in more complex projects.

Table A11.5 Proficiency Levels in Managing Projects

Characteristic	Novice	Journeyman	Master
Knowledge Level	Novice and Advanced Beginners	Competent and Proficient Performer	Emotionally and& Spiritually intelligent expert
Nature of knowledge	Context-independent rules and situational elements	Categorizations of context-dependent and independent rules based on experience & education	Intuitive, holistic, synchronic and synthetic
Nature of intelligence employed	Cognitive Intelligence	Emotional intelligence	Spiritual intelligence
Development of	Know What	Know How, Know Where, when and who	Know why
Relation to the external environment	Reactive to context environment	Relational and responsive to context environment	Orientational, interpreting and transforming context
Role and Types of projects	Team leader	Manager of systems type projects	Leaders of complex adaptive projects in uncertain environments
Method of application	Analytical deliberation	Analytical interpretation	Intuitive leaps
Method of movement from one level to another	Significant levels of project experience under an experienced practitioner; formal education in Project Management fundamentals	Significant levels of project management experience; additional formal training in advanced topics of project management	Maintaining a position at this level requires "giving back" to the occupation through mentoring, training and researching practice

Source: Adapted from [1].

References

[1] Peters, L. and Moreno, A.M., "Evaluating Software Project Managers: A Multi-Dimensional Perspective," *IEEE Software*, Vol. 34, No. 6, November 2017, pp. 104–108.

[2] Garvin, D.A., "How Google Sold Its Engineers on Management," *Harvard Business Review*, December, 2013.

[3] Thomas, J. and Mengel, T., "Preparing Project Managers to Deal with Complexity – Advanced Project Management Education," *International Journal of Project Management*, Vol. 26, 2008, pp. 304–315.

[4] Salovey, P. and Mayer, J.D., *Emotional Intelligence*, Baywood Publishing Company, Amityville, New York, 1990.

[5] Wigglesworth, C., "Spiritual Intelligence: Living as Your Higher Self," *Huffpost blog*, April 03, 2015.

[6] Katz, R., "Motivating Technical Professionals Today," *IEEE Engineering Management Review*, Vol. 41, No. 1, March 2013, pp. 28–38.

Appendix 12

How to Run Effective Meetings

We've all been there. The department head or team manager has called a meeting to discuss some important issue or problem in order to identify possible solutions or at least make the audience aware of the seriousness of some issue(s). As you look around the room, some attendees are staring into space, barely able to stay awake, while others are frantically sending emails or text messages and others are actually trying to contribute to this event. When you compute the cost of such meetings based on the true hourly cost of the attendees, you have to ask yourself was it worth to the project, the company and/or the client? Obviously, there must be a better way and there is. Here is a list of guidelines for ensuring that your meetings are effective and not a waste of time [1]:

1. Why are we having this meeting? What do you hope to accomplish by calling the attendees together? If you don't know why your team is meeting other than the fact that you have a meeting every Monday, maybe you should rethink why this meeting is being called. Conversely, if you do know why this meeting is necessary, say so in the meeting's announcement. This is the purpose of the meeting, its reason for happening and the people being invited need to know that.

2. Consider who should attend – Inviting everyone in the group might seem like a good idea but if the meeting is an announcement for all employees but not such a good idea if the meeting has a specific, narrow focus such as a reported serious software bug or response timing issue or other technical problem. In the case of technical issue discussions, only the people who could contribute to a solution should be in attendance; otherwise, some people will literally be wasting their time.

3. Stick to the Schedule – Create an agenda and stick to it. It frequently happens that some attendees will take this as an opportunity to introduce off-agenda items that are important to them but not relevant to the problem at hand. Put the agenda up on a screen and follow it. Extraneous items could be addressed once everything else has been discussed. This keeps the focus on the topics at hand. The extraneous issues raised may provide agenda items for a future meeting.

4. Be ruthless when it comes to the amount of time someone takes to go on and on – If this happens, you might suggest that this topic is important but we need to hear from everyone within the time allocated for this event. I once worked with a manager who made it clear each person had a maximum of 10 minutes to make their point. He would signal when

you were at 8 minutes and at 10 minutes cut you off with, "Thank you for your insightful contribution but we need to hear from others regarding this issue." It didn't take long before everyone in the group began to revise their comments to just the essential points.

5. Be punctual – Start and end your meetings on time. A maximum of 60 minutes is recommended. If topics come up during the meeting that will require the meeting to be extended beyond that, have those interested in the topic take their discussion offline (after the meeting).

6. Ban the use of mobile phones and other technology – Nothing can sabotage a meeting more effectively than having phones going off during the meeting and or people texting during it. Make it clear that phones are to be turned off, texting is not to be done and so forth. One exception I recall was a fellow who asked to keep his phone on because his wife was about to have a baby any day now. Sure enough, his phone went off during the meeting telling him his wife was taken to the hospital by a neighbor and he left the meeting announcing he was the father of a baby boy.

7. Follow up on the outcome of the meeting – Often, there will be action items or tasks assigned, decisions made and so forth. Put these into an email to the group in order to reduce misunderstandings as to who was supposed to do what and by what date. This statement of outcomes should be distributed within 24 hours of the meeting.

Finally, meeting just to update status may be a poor use of people's time but this is a judgment call on your part. The question you should ask yourself is "Is this a necessary expenditure of project funds?" A second question is, "Who absolutely needs to attend."

References

[1] Hartman, N., "Seven Steps to Running the Most Effective Meeting Possible," *Forbes Leadership Forum, Forbes Magazine*, February 5, 2014.

Appendix 13

Ishikawa (Fishbone) Diagrams

So-called "Fishbone diagrams" were developed by Kaoru Ishikawa in 1969. They are also often referred to as "Cause and Effect" diagrams. They have been used effectively to identify the source(s) of problems in a broad range of processes from office paperwork to the manufacturing of automobiles and other products. To create a Fishbone diagram:

1. Put the main problem in a box on the right.
2. Identify potential sources of the problem.
3. Sort out the process variables.
4. Place them on the Ishikawa diagram.
5. Ensure that each "bone" is measurable, controllable and specific.

As an example, consider a software project that has fallen behind schedule. Using the preceding five steps, a simple Fishbone diagram might look like this.

Although Ishikawa diagrams [1] can get much more complex than the one shown in Figure A13.1, even simpler ones can provide much-needed insights into our project. We generated the figure because

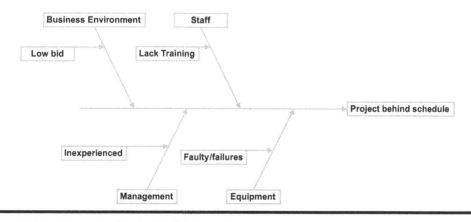

Figure A13.1   Example of a simple fishbone diagram.

we are trying to get to the root cause(s) of the project being behind schedule. The major ones we have identified as:

- Equipment
- Management
- Staff
- Business Environment

Then, we take each of these and document what it is about that item that could be a contributing factor to the problem. For example, in the figure Lack of Training is conjectured as being a contributing factor. Regardless of how extensive or detailed these diagrams become, the most important thing to note is that they get us to focus on solving the stated problem by identifying what is causing it. This is something the software engineering team members can all participate in and contribute to.

References

[1] Reqillard, M., *How to Create an Ishikawa Diagram*, Maine et Loire, France, 2020.

Appendix 14

Knowing When It Is Time to Cancel a Project

Putting a software engineering team together and developing the project plan and other documents and deliverables involve a commitment to the project on the part of all parties. In so doing, the project becomes more than a work product but becomes a part of the team. In many cases, it is affectionately viewed upon by the team members. Remember, even the partial results achieved are seen psychologically by the team members as extensions of themselves [1]. That is partly why it is so difficult for the software project manager to face reality and come to the realization that the project must be cancelled. Fortunately, some guidelines have been published which provide us with advice on how to reach the cancellation decision if it is an appropriate one [2]. Here are some reasons from that paper for not cancelling a project:

- The manager does not pay attention.
- The manager cannot decide.
- The manager is in denial.
- The manager does not know how to communicate with the project team.
- The manager thinks that if the project is canceled, her/his resources will be taken away.
- The manager thinks canceling would look bad to senior management.
- The manager lacks the courage to make difficult decisions.

Conversely, Tarim [2] lists some reasons for canceling a project:

- Cancellation by the customer.
- The project is no longer on the priority list.
- Customers are moving *en masse* to a new product concept or technology.
- Strategic changes have occurred in the marketplace.
- Competitors have produced a better product.
- The original Return on Investment (ROI) which originally justified the project no longer exists.

Either way, continuing or canceling a project involves risk at least in part because the decision will be reviewed by others, sometimes to slant facts in order to further their own agenda.

References

[1] Weinberg, G.M. *The Psychology of Computer Programming*, Van Nostrand Rheinhold, New York, NY, 1971.

[2] Tarim, T.B., "Managing Technical Professionals: Knowing When It Is Time to Cancel a Project," *IEEE Engineering Management Review*, Vol. 41, No. 3, Third Quarter, September 2013, pp. 3–4.

Appendix 15

Lying and Software Projects

Software engineers have been described by some as being the most optimistic people on the planet. A symptom of this optimism often occurs in the project status review. When asked the status of their portion of the system under development, the team lead will often state that there are just a few bugs to clear but they should be done on time. In fact, no one really knows how long it will take to clear any given bug. I have seen one which had no reliable reproducible scenario. It caused a "blue screen of death" (rolling hexadecimal output across a blue background screen) and took several months to find and clear. At least the optimistic approach is honest. That is, to the best of the team lead's knowledge and belief, this is the situation. What is much more problematic is a situation in which the software engineer lies about the status, usually to claim the situation is better than it really is. This may be due to a desire to avoid the wrath of senior management or some other reason but it is hardly justified. The goal of a review at any level is to establish the state of health of the project or some portion of it. Lying about it is a lot like going to your doctor and lying about some symptoms you are experiencing; it is not going to help your condition. To understand this phenomenon better, we first need a reasonable definition of lying. The one we will use is "To knowingly misrepresent what we know to be true." The problem of course is that we often believe that we can clear those few remaining bugs but the fact remains that the code is not functional at the time of the review and should be characterized as such.

A15.1 The Study

A study published in IEEE Software in 2008 [1] showed the prevalence of lying in software projects as well as the motivation for lying. It also described several of the circumstances in which lying occurred. The problem with lying is that the truth will eventually come out which damages your creditability. One project I learned about was done for the United States Department of Defense. It was a two-year effort and required a monthly status report. Each month's report showed that milestones were being met, costs were exactly as planned and the project was proceeding according to plan with respect to completion of tasks and expenditures. Six weeks before final delivery, the contracting firm notified their client that it would be another six to 12 months before the software would be delivered. Obviously, that project had not proceeded as smoothly as represented by the contracting firm. The difficulty with determining the status of a software project as compared to a construction project is there is little in the way of tangible evidence as to what progress has been made. In construction, the client can visit the site and see what is being done but in the case of software, that is difficult to determine. Agile has helped to keep vendors honest partly because the client can use some very early version of the software right from the start of the project and with each milestone or update experience the progress that is being made. The study referred to above [1] involved responses from Europe, the United States and Australia. What they found reveals the extent to which software engineers may lie but also how the software project manager may inadvertently cause software engineers to see lying as the best way to keep from being admonished due to unexpectedly slow progress. Let's take a look at their findings.

Some of the motivations for lying:

■ Increasing sales in order to obtain larger market share.
■ Lying being more advantageous than telling the truth to maintain optimism.
■ Appearing competent in the eyes of colleagues, senior management and/or customer.
■ Overconfidence that obstacles can be overcome.
■ Hiding mistakes.
■ Trying to get the workload decreased.

In examining the preceding list, note how the issue of management's perception comes into the picture. If you want to reduce lying, demonstrate the emotional intelligence needed to ensure that if things are not going according to plan, you, as the project manager, focus on fixing the problem, not fixing the blame. My standing rule with the teams I managed was that I wanted to be the first, not the last, to know if there is a problem and there will be no repercussions to the messenger (i.e. I will not "shoot the messenger"). Another part of the study addressed what areas of software engineering accounted for most of the lying (Table A15.1).

The importance of establishing an environment which encourages honesty and does not penalize software engineers for being honest supports self-esteem and self-worth and promotes a rewarding work environment. All of these benefits and more improve productivity, code quality and cost reduction (Table A15.2).

The research being cited here also asked respondents to describe how lying could be reduced or eliminated in software engineering efforts. The responses were telling with respect to the practice of managing software engineers and software projects. 22% of the responses were about management. They noted that managers should focus on solving the problems that were causing the difficulties rather than placing blame. In other words, "fix the problem, not the blame." Also, making reporting verifiable would help. About 10% were pessimistic because we are dealing with human nature and nobody wants to be the bearer of bad news even if there are no consequences personally.

Table A15.1 Lying Frequency [1]

Category	Respondents Who Experienced Lying (%)	Number of Projects on Which Lying Occurred (%)
Cost or schedule estimation	66	50
Status reporting	65	50
Political maneuvering	58	10
Hyperbole	32	30

Table A15.2   Who Lied and Who Knew [1]

Category	Management	Project Lead	Developer	Marketing	Customer
Cost/Schedule Estimate					
Who lied	53%	48%	45%	40%	11%
Who knew	47%	60%	66%	36%	13%
Status Reporting					
Who lied	49%	54%	30%	20%	12%
Who knew	43%	59%	59%	23%	16%
Political Maneuvering					
Who lied	44%	34%	19%	26%	13%
Who knew	42%	45%	48%	29%	16%
Hypeperbole					
Who lied	31%	32%	29%	36%	16%
Who knew	31%	36%	44%	34%	19%

References

[1] Glass, R.L. Rost, J. and Matook, M.S., "Lying on Software Projects," *IEEE Software*, Vol. 25, No. 6, Nov.–Dec. 2008, pp. 90–95. doi: 10.1109/MS.2008.150

Appendix 16

Managing Multiple Generations

Starting in the late twentieth century, possibly for the first time in history, multiple generations of software professionals began working side by side. The reasons for this cultural and employment shift include the fact that people are living longer (prior to the pandemic), are staying active longer and engineering software does not take an obvious physical toll on our bodies. This presents software project managers with both challenges and opportunities [1]. Challenges because different generations view technology and its use in different ways, the value systems differ between/among generations and technical skills vary from one generation to the next. This means that nearly every decision made by the software project manager will be challenged by members of one or more generational groups. It needs to be kept in mind that while all members may have similar value systems, these values are present to varying degrees further complicating this issue. Managing multiple generations presents us with opportunities in that the multiple experiences and viewpoints represent a tremendous problem-solving capability. In order to meet the challenge of managing different generations working together:

- Be cognizant of the different value systems held by each group.
- Observe your various team members to determine what their values are.
- Be aware of the degree of collaboration each member may commit to.
- Work to keep the team unified.

A.16.1 How Many Generational Groups Are There?

Different authors have broken today's workforce down into four, five or even six generations. We will focus our attention on the groups in the United States since this is the country for which we have the best data. Furthermore, we will break the generational groups down into four groups which have been studied (Table A16.1) [1]:

Table A16.1 Generation Birthdate Ranges and Approximate Percent Occurrence

Generational Classification	Birthdate Range	% of the United States Population
Matures	Born before 1945	10%
Boomers	Born Between 1946 and 1964	43%
Generation X	Born Between 1965 and 1977	33%
Millennials (Generation Y)	Born Between 1978 and 2000+	14%

A16.2 Generational Characteristics

It should be noted that not everyone in a given generation exhibits the same set of characteristics strongly. What is presented here is a set of generalizations that hold true for each generational group:

Characteristics of Matures
- Values
  - Respects authority, usually patient.
  - Doing a job well is important.
- Work ethic
  - Efficient, believes in *quid quo pro*.
- In the Workplace
  - Stable, detailed, works hard, loyal and ambiguity is challenging.
- Motivating Matures
  - Generally, feedback is important.
  - Phrases like "What you have to say regarding what has or has not worked in the past is valuable to our project?"

Characteristics of Boomers
- Values
  - Competitive and workaholic.
  - Optimistic and tries to balance work and family.
- Work Ethic
  - The hours worked represent value to the company.
  - Highly values teamwork, relationships and loyalty.
- In the Workplace
  - Service oriented and driven team player.
  - Avoids conflict and not budget oriented.
  - Process supersedes results.
  - Sensitive to feedback.
- Motivating Boomers
  - Positive feedback like "We need you" are effective motivating actions.

Characteristics of Generation Xers
- Values
  - Work–life balance is important.
  - Technically literate.

- Thinks globally.
- Is informal.
■ Work Ethic
- Favors productivity over tenure.
- Communicates well.
- Avoids Boomer work ethic.
■ In the Workplace
- Creative and independent.
- Not intimidated by authority.
- Technically savvy and very adaptable.
- Lack people skills, impatient and inexperienced.
■ Motivating Generation Xers
- Provide the latest technology.
- "We don't have a lot of red tape."

Characteristics of Millennials (Generation Y)
■ Values
- Must have stimulating work.
- Optimistic, confident and ambitious.
■ Work Ethic
- Wants a job that is personally fulfilling.
- Needs high-bandwidth communication with others.
- Needs almost constant reinforcement from manager.
- Works well with matures.
■ In the Workplace
- Multitasking heroic style.
- Needs rules, structures and discipline in the workplace.
■ Motivating Generation Y
- Phrases like "You and your team can play a major role here."
- "You will be working with some of the best and brightest people in this field."

A complicating factor to managing multiple generations in a single team is that you may also have multiple cultures represented in your team. These cultural differences and their implications are discussed elsewhere in this text. In other words, it is not prudent to consider just one factor apart from others because they all impact each other.

Reference

[1] Knight, R., "Managing People from 5 Generations," *Harvard Business Review*, September, 25, 2014.

Appendix 17

Outsourcing (Offshoring)

With the advent of software engineering education worldwide and the availability of lower-cost personal computers and various programming languages, many companies have sought to reduce their software development costs by having some software development done in another country that has lower labor costs. Anecdotal results more than two decades ago indicated that the results were good as the responsiveness to changes and fixes for bugs were better than expected. But as time went on, code quality, responsiveness to change requests and other factors began to make outsourcing less and less attractive [1, 2]. Some of the factors that have led to the reduction in the use of outsourcing include:

- Cultural
  Differences in value systems between people from different countries are a fact of life. While you may see delivering the contracted elements of the system on time, not everyone from every culture you may outsource to will see it that way [3]. In some cultures, delivering, even if late, is the goal. In other cultures, it doesn't get delivered until it has been established that the quality is high. In others, the cost is paramount. And on and on it goes in various combinations of the preceding. Also, in some cultures, the aggressive, hard driving style of some software project managers is seen as insulting. Remember, when one becomes a software engineer, they bring their culture with them – there is no way to escape it. So keep this in mind if/when you seek to offshore some part of your project.
- Legal
  Depending on the country the outsourcing is being done in, the most common protections under copyright law in the home country may be missing, poorly enforced or otherwise put your intellectual property at risk. When code development is outsourced, that constitutes "work for hire." This means that the company that lets the contract owns the rights to the developed code. Intellectual property rights attorneys have indicated that some countries have impressive laws covering this topic but they are poorly enforced and/or the judges charged with enforcing them are eminently bribable. The other extreme also exists wherein the laws do not appear very stringent but enforcement is stellar. The best strategy here is to engage the services of a law firm with offices in both the home country and the outsourced country which deals with intellectual property rights such as software.
- Risk(s)
  The outsourced software not only represents an investment but also may contain some company proprietary information. This information may constitute a competitive edge. Placing it in the hands of another firm whose security and reliability may be unknown represents a

Table A17.1 Outsource Motivations

Determining Factor/Motivation to Outsource	Percentage Due to This Factor
Upgrading current service levels	14%
Inability to staff appropriately	12%
Focusing on core business	27%
Avoiding needed investments	15%
Reducing operating costs	28%

real risk to the contracting firm. However, there are firms that are trustworthy and capable. An experienced law firm may have some recommendations.

Summaries of the motivation to outsource have been developed. The results from one of these studies [4] are presented in Table A17.1.

Over the last two decades, major corporations have chosen to contract with firms in parts of the world which have software engineering talent and lower wages than where the corporation is located. Many of these arrangements appear to be quite beneficial for both parties. They are frequently fixed-price contracts meaning that the work will be done for a certain, unchanging price. Many of the early offshore software development efforts turned out quite well. The quality was high, changes due to errors or alteration of requirements were made in a timely manner and customers pleased with the results. But in more recent years, clients have told me that delivery dates were missed, response to requested changes (even when accompanied by bonus payments) was slow and sometimes nonexistent and the quality of the deliverables is not what it used to be. Upon further investigation, it was determined that in some cases key people in the contractor organization had left it to form their own company and lacked the business knowledge, managerial skills, experience and organizational skills to deliver on commitments. These factors plus cultural differences between organizations have greatly reduced the advantages of outsourcing that were experienced in its early years.

References

[1] Laplante, P.A., Costello, T., Singh, P., Bindiganavile, S. and Landon, M., "The Who, What, Why, Where, and When of IT Outsourcing," *IT Pro*, Published by the IEEE, January|February 2004, pp. 19–23.

[2] Casey, V., "Developing Trust in Virtual Software Development Teams," *Journal of Theoretical and Applied Electronic Commerce Research*, Vol. 5, No. 2, August 2010, pp. 41–58.

[3] Kankanhalli, A., Tan, B.C.Y., Wei, K and Holmes, M.C., "Cross-Cultural Difference and Information Systems Developer Values," *Decision Support Systems*, Vol. 38, 2004, pp. 183–195.

[4] Pai, A.K. and Basu, S., "Offshore Technology Outsourcing: Overview of Management and Legal Issues," *Business Process Management Journal*, Vol. 13, No. 1, 2007, pp. 21–46.

Appendix 18

PERT [Program Evaluation Review Technique]

The Program Evaluation Review Technique [PERT] is a tool for project planning developed in the 1950s. It was originally developed by the United States Navy as part of the effort to develop the first nuclear-powered submarine – Nautilus. Contrary to the experience with many first-time technical projects, it finished on time and within budget. At that point, many management organizations began to believe that the problems associated with managing projects would be solved if PERT was used. As history has shown, the rejoicing was premature. However, some new ideas were the result of this project [1]. One was an estimating approach. In it, three estimated values were considered and blended into one. The three values associated with the cost or flow time were:

- O = the optimistic estimated value.
- M = the most likely estimated value.
- P = the most pessimistic estimated value.
- E = the estimate was computed as $E = (O + 4M + P)/6$.

As you can see from the formula, it is weighted toward the most likely value (M). Most software project management software systems support PERT represented as a network as well as Gantt chart depictions of a project plan.

References

1 Evdokimov, I.V., et al., "Using PERT and Gantt Charts for Planning Software Projects on the Basis of Distributed Digital Ecosystems," *Journal of Physics: Conference Series*, Vol. 1074, 2018, 012127.

Appendix 19

Planning using Integrated Cost and Schedule Work Packages

We all use some means of breaking a project down into smaller tasks so that we can "see" what needs to be done, what should be done first and so forth. One issue we all face is the larger the number of tasks we have to deal with, the greater the chances are that we will leave out some tasks, get the order of task initiation/completion wrong or otherwise make some mistakes due to the sheer volume of tasks we identify. One effective way to reduce the volume of tasks and to increase our chances of success is to consolidate tasks into groups by breaking the project into work packages. To do this, we try to break the project down into the largest tasks we can, layout the order in which they should occur, estimate their duration and their interdependencies. Some tasks must be completed sequentially, while others can be performed in parallel. That may sound like a lot but, as we shall see, it isn't. These tasks constitute the project. They can be viewed from a high level or macro level down to something approaching a micro view as long as we do not go beyond the recommended eight-hour (or whatever constitutes a full working day in your locale) limit as recommended by the Project Management Institute [1]. Many of these steps constitute mini projects consuming flow time, labor and other resources. One serious difficulty that all planning efforts experience is linking cost and schedule. That is, we think we know how long a task will take and when it should take place but its relationship to the other tasks in our plan and overall costs are often seen as separate issues. Also, the Gantt chart may show us that a task is late but it is not obvious how other tasks and those on the critical path may be impacted. Fortunately, there is a method complete with notation that aids both our planning and our management of the project. It involves the utilization of the concept of a "work package." A work package may be defined in different ways but for our purposes, a work package will be defined as "A cohesive set of subtasks defining a step in the process of completing the project." Regardless of the definition you may choose to use, a unique notation and some valuable insights demonstrate how to document the relationship among work packages as part of actively managing a software project [2]. The reference cited integrates cost and schedule into a project planning and management notation. It offers us a new and different perspective of our project dwelling heavily on the relationships between work packages and emphasizing ranges of time spans to complete a work package. Before we get into the details of using this notation, it is important to set forth some definitions which we can use regardless of the planning method we utilize. These are more precise than those we commonly read about or may currently believe:

■ Float – This is frequently also referred to as total float, slack or total slack. It is calculated for each work package individually. It is incorrect to state how much float a project has. It is calculated using either of the following equations and adopting whichever value is less:

$$\text{Total Float} = \text{Late Start} - \text{Early Start}$$

or

$$\text{Total Float} = \text{Late Finish} - \text{Early Finish}$$

From a management standpoint, doing this for each work package can help us identify which packages could be assigned to less-skilled members of the team, which packages are the most critical in terms of on time delivery and so forth.

■ The Critical Path – This is an important piece of information every successful software project manager tracks continuously. The work packages that are on the critical path are vital to the success of a project. This method views a software project as a network of work packages. Some of these packages are in such a location within the network that if they are delayed, the final project deliverable(s) will be delivered late. Knowing the packages that lie on the critical path also provides us with added insight as to which packages should be assigned to our best software engineers and/or team. The critical path consists of all of the following [2]:
  - The longest path through our network schedule
  - The shortest time to complete the project as planned
  - The path(s) with tasks that have zero float
  - Not the only path of work requiring management control

■ Calculating Free Float – Free float is also known as free slack. It is the amount of time a work package can be delayed before that delay impacts any other work package in the network. The notation and an example of its use are presented in Figure A19.1.

■ The Notation – The Integrated Cost and Schedule Control method utilizes a network of rectangles representing work packages each of which is annotated as shown below. Each represents a work package and is composed of six parts:
  - Work package title
  - Work package scheduled time to complete, usually in days
  - Early start in days since project start
  - Early finish in days since project start
  - Late start in days since project start
  - Late finish in days since project start

It should be noted that in creating a network of these work packages, the focus is not on simply relying on everything happening on time but allowing for not just early finishes but late starts and so forth. Here is an example of a single work package using a generic label:

One aspect of this method that should not be overlooked is the fact that it only requires us to estimate the most optimistic and the most pessimistic flow times to complete a task. Also, you should be sure to establish whether or not you are specifying work days and not including weekends or other days on which work will not be performed.

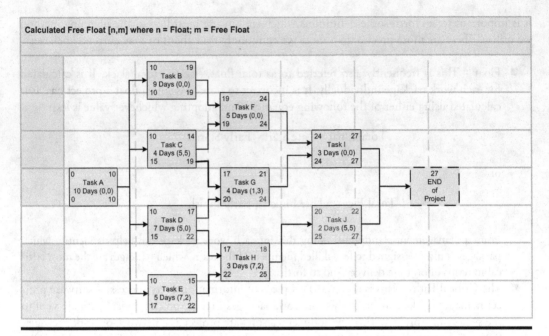

Figure A19.1   Example of free float.

A19.1 Applying the Forward Pass Method

The Forward Pass Method gets its name from the fact that the network of work packages is organized starting at the beginning of the project and working toward the end of the project (i.e. working "Forward"). It consists of executing four steps:

1. Start with t = 0 as the "Early Start" at the beginning of the project.
2. Add the task's duration to get the early finish of the task.
3. Recognize that the early start of each successor task will be the latest early finish of each of its predecessor's tasks.
4. Repeat steps 2 and 3 until you find the early finish of the last work package or the end milestone of the project.

A generic example of applying this method is shown in Figure A19.2.
  Let's look at how Figure A19.2 was developed:

- We have determined that this work package is composed of 10 tasks (Task A through Task J) plus the END of the Project task to which we have not assigned.
- Using the Forward Pass Process, we start with Task A which starts at zero and completes in 10 days.
- Tasks B, C, D and E can all be done in parallel but cannot start until Task A is completed on day 10.
- Recalling that a subsequent task cannot start until the latest finish for its predecessor(s) n identifier means Task F must have an early start of 19 days.
- In a similar manner, Task G must have an early start of 17 days.

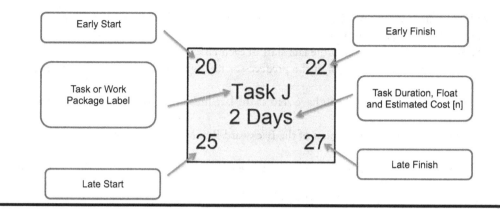

Figure A19.2   Single work package notation.

- Also, Task H will have an early start of 17 days.
- Task I will have an early start of 24 days and Task J will have an early start of 20 days.

Upon examining Figure A19.3, if we wanted to shorten the total flow time for this effort, we will have to focus on tasks much earlier than tasks I and J. This is one advantage of developing the network view of the overall effort.

The Backward Pass Method works in the opposite direction from the Forward Pass Method. It identifies the latest a work package can start and finish. It also uses a four-step process:

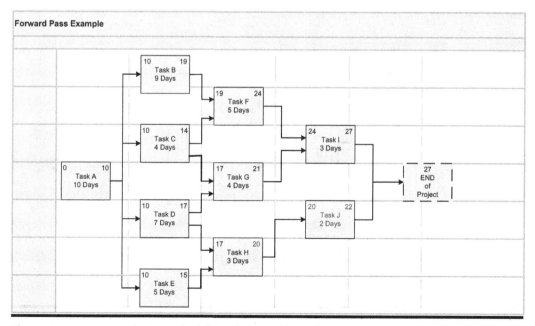

Figure A19.3   A generic example using the forward pass method.

1. Identify the latest early finish found during the forward pass of the end of the network (i.e. reverse forward pass approach).
2. Subtract the duration to find the late start of each task.
3. Recognize that the late finish of the predecessor task will be the earliest of the late starts of each of the successor tasks.
4. Repeat steps 2 and 3 until you have zero as the late finish of the start milestone or the late.

Some rules regarding the development of the Backward Pass Method (Figure A19.4):

1. Start with the end date and set that as the late finish of each task that has the "End" task as its successor.
2. Subtract the task duration from the late finish to determine when the task "must" start.
3. When a task is a predecessor to more than one successor, it must be finished in time for the earliest late start of all its successors.

Note that both the Forward and Backward Pass Methods may bear some bad news regarding the project. Specifically, it cannot be completed in the timeframe originally envisioned or we should have started on this effort way before the planned start. But the news is not always bad.

This method gives us the choice of modeling the project from start to finish (the "Forward Pass Model" or from the end of the project back toward the start (the "Backward Pass Model"). In some cases, the Forward Pass network may result in a project end date beyond what we had planned. In that case, adjustments need to be made to our plan such as deferring some features. Similar comments apply to the Backward Pass network if it ends up showing that the project needed to be started prior to the originally planned start date.

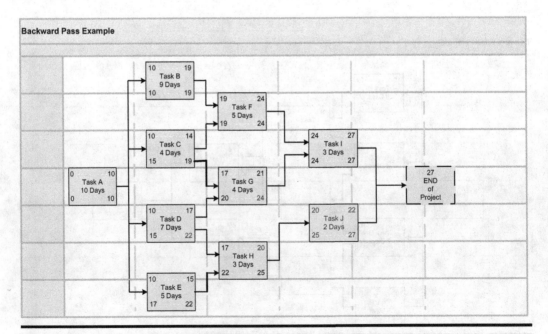

Figure A19.4 Generic example of applying the backward pass process.

A19.2 Some Definitions and Observations

The work packages that comprise the network(s) of our project can be detailed at another level down. In other words, decomposed and represented by another network of work packages detailing what is going on in the upper level or parent work package.

A19.3 Definitions with Examples

Float – This is also referred to as Slack. It is the amount of time that a task can be delayed without causing a delay to subsequent tasks. Building some Float into our network enables us to build in some flow time in our project plan to accommodate the unforeseen such as delay(s) in completing a work package due to a particularly difficult software error which could take additional time to correct. Total Float is calculated as follows:

$$\text{Total Float} = \text{Late Start} - \text{Early Start}$$

Or alternately,

$$\text{Total Float} = \text{Late Finish} - \text{Early Finish}$$

A generic example of Total Float computation is presented in Figure A19.5.

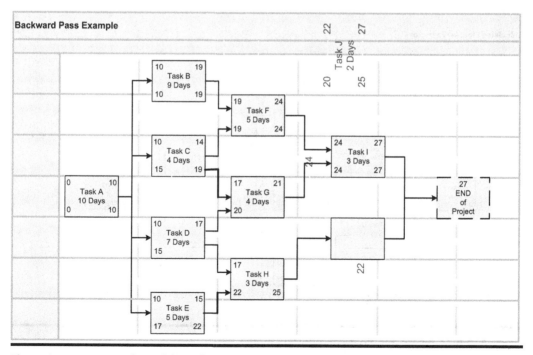

Figure A19.5 Network used for calculating total float.

A19.4 Calculating Free Float

Free Float is more useful than "Float" because it is the amount of time a work package can be delayed before it impacts any other work package in the schedule. It is computed as follows:

$$Free\ Float = Early\ Start_j - Early\ Finish_i$$

where

$$Early\ Start_j = the\ successor\ task/work\ package$$

$$Early\ Finish_i = the\ task\ being\ analyzed$$

If there is more than one successor, the minimum difference will equal the Free Float for the task.

A19.5 Calculating Free Float

- If there is more than one successor, the minimum difference will equal the Free Float for the task.
- A generic model of Free Float Computation is presented in Figure A19.6.

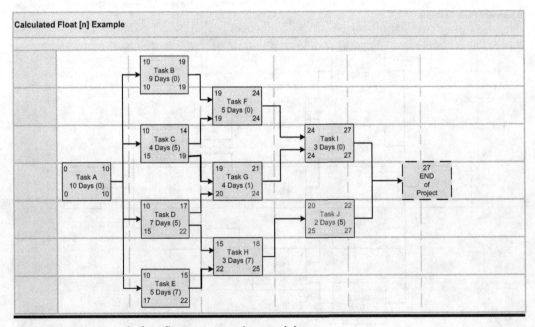

Figure A19.6 Generic free float computation model.

Critical Path – This is the path of work packages such that any delay could cause the project to miss its completion date. An example of how to detect work packages that lie on the critical path from Figure A19.7 involves the use of Table A19.1. In reviewing the table, note the amount of Total Float. Work packages with zero Total Float are the obvious candidates for lying on the Critical Path because they have to execute exactly as planned.

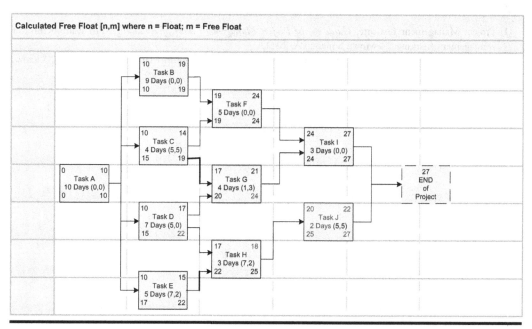

Figure A19.7   Generic example of a network used to compute free float.

Table A19.1   Identifying the Critical Path

Task	Total Float	On the Critical Path?
A	0	Yes
B	0	Yes
C	5	No
D	3	No
E	7	No
F	0	Yes
G	1	No
H	7	No
I	0	Yes
J	5	No

Summary

Planning using the integrated cost and schedule notation and underlying conceptual basis represents an efficient, disciplined and information-rich scheme for planning software projects.

References

[1] Project Management Institute, *Guide to the Project Management Body of Knowledge*, 7th Edition, Project Management Institute, Newtown Square, PA, 2021.

[2] Kuehn, U., *Integrated Cost and Schedule Control in Project Management*, Management Concepts, Vienna, VA, 2006.

Appendix 20

A Pre-Project Launch Checklist

"Nearly every aspect of software project management involves some form of risk."

–Michael Deutsch

Running a software project can be as complex and demanding as flying an aircraft. In a very real sense, complexity equates to risk. The basic definition of complexity we will use here is:

"Complexity is a subjective notion, reflecting the lived experience of the people involved."

[1]

Unlike the pilots' checklist, software project managers do not have a comprehensive list of the factors that could affect the success of their project to review before the project starts. Just like the aircraft analogy, the purpose of a checklist of factors is to ensure that success is at least possible and known issues are noted and corrected, a workaround is planned for or a decision is made to delay or even cancel the project. A significant difference between the aircraft analogy and the use of a checklist before a software project launches is that many of the software project-related items involve judgment and opinions whereas the aircraft inspection is generally binary. For example, if a pilot spots a hydraulic fluid leak, they usually can't ignore it by forming an opinion that it won't endanger the aircraft's flight. As in the case of the aircraft, such a list does not guarantee a successful software project but it at least enables the software project manager and the development team to conscientiously decide to go forward in spite of the potential risks or to decide the risks are too great to overcome and resign from the project or seek relief from the most serious risks. This appendix presents a checklist based upon many of the published risk factors software project managers have cited as potentially jeopardizing their projects. The checklist is intended to be evaluated by both the software project manager and each member of the software development team. Just as in the case of the aircraft checklist, wide discrepancies between team members' evaluation(s) and the software project manager's evaluations highlight issues that represent significant potential risks, requiring special attention, discussion and resolution. The value of this list lies in the fact that it may cause team members (especially the software project manager) and senior management to raise questions regarding the status of one or more of the listed items and its impact on the project under consideration.

A.20.1 The Concept

When a project is first considered, the software project manager and the development team all have their own perceptions of the challenges that lie ahead. For example, the software engineers concern themselves with the technical issues that will have to be resolved while the software project manager is focused on whether or not the funding, flow time and skilled personnel are sufficient to complete the project successfully. These differences in perceptions, individual priorities and value systems can lead to friction among the team members with each trying to convince others that their own concept(s) and most important issue (in their opinion) is the most important. This leads to team members becoming somewhat alienated from each other resulting in not working together as a team and not taking advantage of their complementary skills. While changing the value systems of team members is unlikely, previewing where problems may occur is well within the realm of possibility. For example, a simple statement "this project is extremely complex" may produce differing responses from team members depending on their training, experience and to what extent they want to be seen as having a superior intellect as compared to their colleagues. Probing why some see the project's complexity very differently from others is vitally important with respect to creating and maintaining an effective team. Stated another way, the project manager should seek to determine what one software engineer sees or misses that shapes their conclusion regarding complexity. A goal of a pre-project checklist is to engage the software project manager and software engineers in evaluating a list of common project variables and risks to discuss the ones with wide differences of opinion among the team members. This exercise would help to unify the team regarding how to address the pending issues. Another goal of this exercise is to adhere to the adage "Forewarned is forearmed." This enables the software project manager to prepare for events which could endanger the project's successful completion and be sensitive to issues on which there is a wide difference of opinion as to their importance.

"Perhaps the biggest challenge facing executives today is how to define success (or failure) on projects." – Harold Kerzner, author of "Project Management: A Systems Approach to Planning, Scheduling, and Controlling [2]."

The issue of success in software project management is like any other project management endeavor: it is ethereal. That is, it is subject to change without advanced notice and it is what we and/or others say it is at a specific point in time. During my consulting engagements, I have seen projects that the teams thought were successful be deemed disasters and conversely. So what happened? In general, the political winds of fortune shifted. In one particularly memorable project, a high-level executive was briefed on a significant change in how software was to be developed in a forthcoming project. The software engineering group had a particularly poor record of delivering on time, let alone on budget. After the briefing, this executive went on record as stating that there was no way the software group could successfully complete this project (i.e. on time and on budget). When they actually pulled off this seemingly impossible feat, the embarrassed executive was so angry that he saw to it that the head of software engineering was fired together with the project manager in charge of the project. Success really can be dangerous!

When you ask software project managers what the most difficult part of their job is, right after saying "personnel issues," they usually say "complexity." We will refine this further but for now, what complexity is varies from one software project manager to the next. These viewpoints revolve around the number of activities taking place all at once, the various changes occurring in the requirements without warning, the shifting political situation both within their own organization and the customer's organization (even when they both work for the same company), and many others. What disturbs most software project managers is the unexpected level of (apparent) chaos embodied in their projects. In a real way, they did not know what they were getting into when they agreed to manage this effort. Fortunately, several researchers [1] have refined what complexity is all about and developed a questionnaire that will help you, the prospective software project manager, to assess the level of complexity you will be expected to deal with effectively. It is called, the Complexity Assessment Tool (CAT). But before we describe its contents and how to use it, we need to understand how it helps us to manage complexity by organizing various complexity factors into three categories. Each category is described briefly below [1]:

A.20.2 Structural Complexity

This type of complexity involves dealing with the sheer volume of tasks, processes, events, milestones, interactions and coordination comprising the project. Planning tools like Gantt charts are especially effective at helping to cope with this type of complexity. It may be the most written about and most discussed type of complexity in textbooks and management training.

A.20.3 Sociopolitical Complexity

This is the area most project managers find to be the most difficult to deal with 68% of respondents [1]. This type of complexity is most apparent in projects of significant importance to the client in involving people, power and company politics both within the project team and the client's team. Each of these groups and even individuals may have their own agendas. Unfortunately, 86% of project manager training and available resources (e.g. textbooks) are focused on structural complexity [1].

A.20.4 Emergent Complexity

As the name of this type of complexity implies, it occurs without predictability during the project. A very common source of this type of complexity in software projects is the fact that the requirements will change either due to an actual change order or clarification of what was contained in the original requirements statement. This makes requirements definition and comprehension a discovery process.

A.20.5 Complexity Assessment Tool (CAT)

Maylor et al. [1] developed a questionnaire which they referred to as the Complexity Assessment Tool to help us focus attention on project factors which can make a project complex. As one might guess, there is no single formulation which could work for all projects. However, this questionnaire will help us to focus on those elements which we may be able to deal with right from the start or at least be prepared for them as we begin the project or proceed with it. This questionnaire should be reviewed on a regular basis during the course of the project. One item which software project managers often cite as the reason for project problems is that requirements changed after the project began. However, this is practically given in any project of any significance whether it be construction, road building or software. In effect requirements change partly because our understanding of them changes during the project, the client did not understand the ramifications of some of the statements, what was being built met the requirements but not the intent or goal of the new feature(s) or system under development.

The goal of the CAT is not to make complexity disappear but to identify factors which may lend themselves to some form of preemptive action thereby reducing complexity. Here is how:

1. Before project start, have each team member complete the survey. This includes the project manager.
2. Get the team together and develop a master or consensus version of the CAT.
3. Identify the most common items on the CAT that seem particularly worrisome. In general, these will be items to which one or more team members answered "No" to. For example, item 14 regarding key personnel. If key personnel will be splitting their time between projects, this represents a serious risk to the project increasing the complexity the team has to deal with.
4. Discuss with the team how to deal with, eliminate or reduce the impact of the "No" items and implement the plan. A key strategy here is to keep the number of items to be addressed to a minimum. Keep in mind that there will be some factors that are beyond our control.
5. Repeat items 1 through 4 at regularly scheduled points in the project and include a review of how well the complexity mitigation strategy(s) worked, revising them as necessary.

A.20.6 Discussion

Some of the statements in Table A20.1 may need some explanation while others should be obvious. To make sure, let's take a brief look at some of these statements and the issues they raise. Each statement number precedes the brief discussion:

3-If the development team is not familiar with the technology that will be employed, a learning curve must be overcome. In addition, once the team has become familiar with the technology, errors are more likely during its application than would occur if they were experts in it right from the start. This issue becomes even more serious if the technology is likely to undergo change during the course of the project.

5-One of the more popular excuses for software project failure is often referred to as, "scope creep." This usually refers to the project expanding beyond what was originally planned and scheduled for causing budget and schedule overruns. If we do not know the scope from the start and/or it is likely to change, complexity will definitely increase.

13-If the software project manager cannot prevent people from being reassigned or shared with other projects, complexity increases but so do the chances that the project will fail.

14-Key personnel really should not be shared with one or more other projects. Why? Because sharing a human resource in knowledge work results in lower productivity. This goes against our experience with machines but people are not machines. The studies vary in their estimation, but sharing someone among three projects really results in their total output being reduced by 40% of what would occur if they were dedicated to a single project [3]. The reason lies in the effect of context switching. Estimates vary for three projects and two projects but the effects of splitting time may be even worse than these estimates. For example, the software engineer involved may be needed in a meeting to make some important architectural or procedural decision. If they are splitting their time between just two projects, the chances are 50–50 that they will not be available to participate. When they return to the

Table A20.1   Pre-Project Assessment Checklist

Category/Statement	Agree with This Statement? (Y/N)	Is This Expected to Not Change? (Y/N)
Structural Complexity Assessment		
1-The vision and benefits of the project have been clearly stated		
2-Success criteria have been agreed upon with the client		
3-The development team is familiar with the technology		
4-The commercial arrangements are familiar to us		
5-The scope of the project is well defined		
6-Acceptance criteria for quality and regulatory requirements can be well defined		
7-A schedule and resource plan can be well defined		
8-The supply chain is in place		
9-Lines of responsibility for tasks and deliverables can be defined		
10-Accurate, timely and comprehensive data reporting is possible		
11-Existing management tools can support the project		
12-Sufficient people with appropriate skills are available		
13-The project manager has direct control of the needed human resources (i.e. they report directly to her/him)		
14-Key personnel are assigned 100% to the project		
15-Integration across multiple technical disciplines is not required		
16-The project budget is sufficient		
17-The budget can be used flexibly (i.e. reallocated among cost categories, as necessary)		

(Continued)

Table A20.1 (Continued)   Pre-Project Assessment Checklist

Category/Statement	Agree with This Statement? (Y/N)	Is This Expected to Not Change? (Y/N)
18-The project will be carried out in a single country/time zone		
19-The project is independent of other projects and established business operations		
20-The schedule is makeable		
21-Resources (e.g. test facilities, equipment, high-speed network access) will be available		
Sociopolitical Complexity		
Sociopolitical Complexity Assessment		
22-The project has sponsorship consistent with its importance		
23-The project has a clearly stated business case		
24-The project's goals align with the organization's strategic vision		
25-Senior management supports the project		
26-The project team is motivated and works well together		
27-The project manager(s) have experience with this type of project		
28-The project does not involve significant organizational and/or cultural change		
29-The project will be unaffected by significant organizational and/or cultural change		
30-The project's external stakeholders (i.e. those who are not members of the project team) are aligned, supportive and committed to the project and have sufficient time for the work		
31-External stakeholders have a realistic, shared understanding of the implications of the project		
32-The project team has the authority to make decisions		

Source: Adapted from [1] with the permission of its authors.

project, the decision made by the rest of the team may have to be reversed or revised due to some issue it creates. In addition, the efforts of this software engineer on all projects that share their attention will display a lack of cohesiveness. Sharing people between projects seriously impacts flow time estimates for all projects involved. Once you adjust estimates for this loss of productivity, you may reconsider whether or not this was a good idea.

18-Conducting a project over multiple time zones can vary from minor inconvenience to a major issue. For example, in the United States, as many as three time zones could be involved but conducting a project over nine time zones can raise serious coordination and performance issues. Conducting a project with teams on the West Coast of the United States and teams in Western Europe means coordination calls made in the morning on the West Coast occur in the late afternoon in Europe. So we have one team just starting their day, presumably fresh and ready to go, while their counterparts are nearing the end of their day and are likely tired and ready to go home. Conducting a project over multiple countries is compounded by cultural differences as well. For example, in Spain, it is the custom to take Monday as a "Puente (bridge)" day if a holiday falls on a Tuesday. Simply looking up the national or local holidays for various countries would not reveal such practices.

Some may look at the list of structural or sociopolitical complexity statements and conclude that a "Yes" to all items in the left-hand column and a "No" to all the items in the right-hand column practically guarantees success. But it doesn't. That is the point isn't it? The resolution of those issues reduces complexity leaving this simpler, more easily managed project to be successfully executed. Also, in reviewing this list, note how dependent the possible "Yes" answer is on the actions of the software project manager.

The key benefit of the pre-project checklist is the fact that it presents a list of issues which can raise or lower the chances of success of a project due to its inherent complexity. As most experienced software project managers will attest, there is no magic formula or method which will transform a complex project with a low probability of success into a simple project with a high probability of success. The complexity assessment tool helps in identifying the issues which are likely to increase complexity and implying what needs to be done to make them less difficult to deal with. It is like an early warning system which encourages strategic initiatives focused on what matters most.

A.20.7 Building Your Own Checklist

The checklist presented earlier is intended as a generic example. Your project situation may differ significantly from the generic example and so you are encouraged to create your own checklist, tailored to the specifics of your situation. Remember, what we are attempting to do with such a list is to create a form of an early warning system to help us preemptively address factors which could jeopardize the project.

References

[1] Maylor, H.R., Turner, N.W. and Murray-Webster, R., "How Hard Can It Be? – Actively Managing Complexity in Technology Projects," Research-Technology Management, July-August, 2013, pp. 45–50. [Used here with the permission of the authors]

[2] Kerzner, H., *Project Planning, Scheduling and Controlling*, Wiley, Hoboken, New Jersey, 12th edition, 2017.

[3] Weinberg, G.M., *Quality Software Management, Volume 1: Systems Thinking*, Dorset House Publishing, New York, NY, 1992.

Appendix 21

Putting Pressure on the Team Can Reduce Productivity

There exists an almost unquestioned belief among software project managers that if a team is not performing up to expectations or previously demonstrated ability, bringing this to their attention in an unpleasant way (e.g. a show of anger or disappointment by the manager, threats of firing, cutting hours and so forth) will act as a "wake up call" resulting in better performance. In fact, the opposite effect has been documented and is more likely [1]. What happens is the team members who may have been working together as a complementary team amounting to a "super software engineer" alter their behavior. Prior to pressure being applied by the manager, team members sought and got help from other team members when needed but when pressure has been applied, they begin to rely on their own knowledge and experience ignoring the knowledge and experience available from other team members. What this means is that instead of the team working together in a collegial manner to form a "super" performing group, each person does their own thing resulting in the team just being a group of people each working independently. So how much pressure is the right amount? Making sure that everyone is aware of the importance of the project to the company and encouraging all team members to seek and accept the assistance of their colleagues is an excellent start. Tracking how the team is progressing will document whether the team is responding positively or falling further behind. Remember, when using Earned Value Management to track progress, if the project is 15% complete and over budget and/or behind schedule, your chances of getting back on schedule or budget without changing requirements, schedule or budget are nil [2]. While we do not know the exact reason for this, we might speculate that the 700 projects studied were so poorly planned and estimated that they were, in a sense, doomed from the start. Regardless of the cause, the fact remains that knowing this outcome makes keeping your project on track right from the start is even more important. In most cases, if you have maintained open communications with your team, they already know that the effort is falling behind schedule and/or over budget and are applying their own pressure on themselves to improve the situation. Negotiating with the team and seeking to identify and resolve factors which may be impeding performance is preferred to any form of threats or other pressure.

References

[1] Gardner, H.K., "Performance Pressure as a Double Edged Sword: Enhancing Team Motivation while Undermining the Use of Team Knowledge" Working Paper, 09-126, Harvard Business School, January, 2012.

[2] Fleming, Q.W. and Koppelman, J.M., *Earned Value Project Management*, Project Management Institute, Newtown Square, PA, 2010.

Appendix 22

Reducing Affinity Bias

Whether you are hiring, making job assignments, making friends or ordering food at a restaurant, our personal preferences come into play. For example, when hiring, we consciously tell ourselves to focus on the skills and achievements of the job candidate and how they could contribute to our project but often we select people who are very similar to ourselves. In rare cases, this may be a good match for achieving the work at hand, but as noted by some [1], it more often results in our discarding qualified candidates in favor of those less qualified due to our often subconscious biases. This "affinity bias" (favoring that which is similar to us) is quite natural but as noted it may result in not hiring the most qualified candidates. Fortunately, there are some steps we can take that can mitigate this tendency [2]:

- Seek to Understand – Standardizing the process and (possibly) getting training is a way to achieve an organizational-level awareness of the need to reduce affinity bias as well as how reducing it benefits the organization.
- Revise job descriptions – Review the wording of job descriptions to make them as "neutral" as possible by reducing the use of pronouns like "he" and "she" and incorporating terms like "cooperative" and "collaborative" while reducing terms like "determined" and "competitive" which attract more men.
- Do Blind Resume Reviews – There are software programs available which will "sanitize" a resume to remove or revise names and terms with cultural significance. The process for this must be set into motion a priori.
- Use a Work Sample Test – This provides a consistent evaluation criterion by which to rank candidates.
- Standardize Interviews – Using a standard set of questions and scoring helps to create what amounts to a third party in the interviewing process.
- Consider Likability Issues – All most interviewees want is a fair chance of landing the job they are applying for. They all expect and deserve equal treatment. One issue that often comes up is the fact that some applicants seem to establish an instant rapport with the interview team – they have that kind of personality. This can lead to hiring someone who is less qualified than other applicants which could lead to a lawsuit. This is why it is so important to focus on skills, suitability for the work and so forth in writing during the interview.
- Set Diversity Goals – Many successful software companies started out as a bunch of people who are all very similar culturally and so forth forming a company. Without taking the time

to consider the value that diversity brings to companies in creative, innovative solutions they grow using members of traditionally advantaged groups. This ignores the fact that research shows that diversity in the workforce results in "significant business advantages" [2].

An approach I used that resulted in a very effective software engineering team involved a four-step process:

1. Candidates whose resumes looked promising were given a proficiency test to determine their ability to solve programming problems in the C language. They were given a set of 10 code snippets. Each showed the source code together with a statement as to what the code was supposed to do as well as what that piece of code did do. The candidate was instructed to verbally state what they observed and what they were thinking about what went wrong. Our senior software engineer and I watched. What we were interested in most was how they went about solving problems.
2. They were interviewed individually by each member of the team for 20 minutes.
3. We all went out to lunch together.
4. We got together as a team after the candidate left to discuss each person's impressions. The goals of the meeting were to determine if they could do the work, and more importantly, if each member felt they could work with this person.

Variations of the above process are certainly possible but the key point is that I, the software project manager, was not the only person making this decision. In fact, I did that once and it was an unmitigated disaster – lesson learned!

References

[1] Tulshyan, R., "How to Reduce Personal Bias When Hiring," *Harvard Business Review*, June 28, 2019.
[2] Knight, R., "7 Practical Ways to Reduce Bias in Your Hiring Process," *Harvard Business Review*, June 2017.

Appendix 23

Risk Management Methods

"Nearly every aspect of software project management involves some form of risk."

–**Michael Deutch**

The risks that must be overcome or avoided altogether in order for a project to be successful constitute a topic many software project managers and software engineers would rather avoid. The process is described generically in Figure A23.1. It is an uncomfortable topic involving how our project could be negatively impacted or even fail due to some event or condition which we usually have no control over. Thus, risk management suffers from at least one fundamental problem: The desire to be successful. In many arenas, it is socially unacceptable to focus on or even mention how things could go wrong resulting in project failure. Curiously enough, this attitude actually increases our vulnerability to failure if a risk "fires" (i.e. it actually occurs) since we might not have planned for it and how to mitigate its effects. The home construction industry has adopted a standard way of dealing with the risk of a project overrunning its budget. They set aside a fixed percentage (most often 10%) of the project budget to cope with unforeseen expenses or cost increases. Various companies have developed variations of this approach and have their own percentage formulations. Generally, risk management as a process looks something like Figure A23.2.

Keep in mind that most risk management approaches have been developed in response to an unanticipated situation that occurred during a project. Some of them may not be applicable to any other project. However, a few can be applied beyond their original context. The methods presented here fall into this second category. In some cases, they can be used exactly as presented here. In others, it might be necessary to alter them to accommodate your special circumstances. Regardless, it is advisable to utilize more than one risk management method, if you can. This will give you alternative results from which to make decisions. Note that the most common form of risk involves cost overrun(s). So, most risk management methods focus on determining how much money should be set aside right from the start to accommodate a possible overrun.

The five approaches presented here are all based on experience and have been published. References are provided should you need more detail.

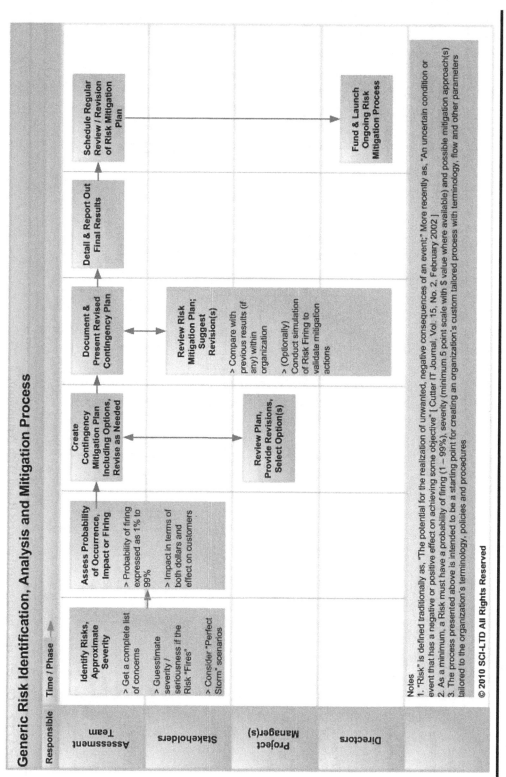

Figure A23.1 Generic risk management phases (Used With Permission).

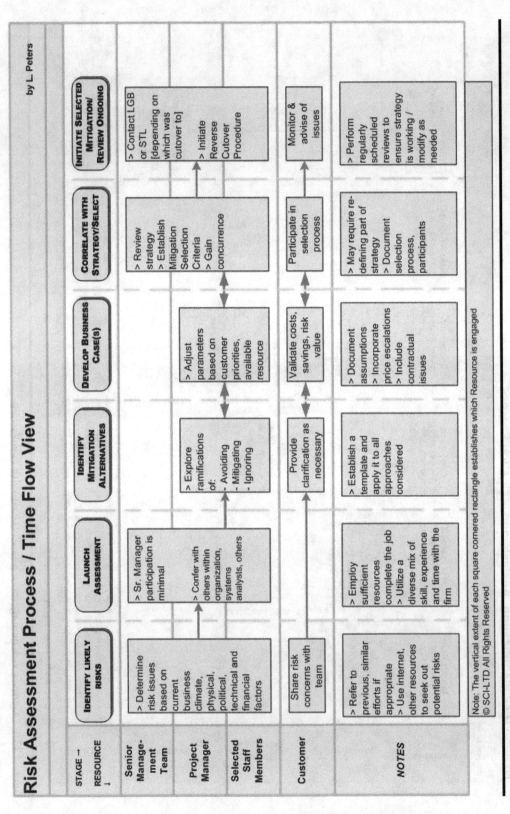

Figure A23.2   Generic risk management process (Used With Permission).

A.23.1 Identify, Rank, Evaluate (IRE) Method

Action/Goal:

Deploy resources to reduce Risk [1].

The Development Scenario: A product is to be developed, based on a significant extension of an existing simulation technology. The new product will support a derived proprietary methodology. The new methodology is still evolving. A Classic Waterfall model was used and the risk was evaluated on a phase-by-phase basis. A scoring range was set at 1–7 to correspond to the seven life cycle phases. The risk and the probability of occurrence were considered separately. At various points during development, risk was evaluated and discussed with the project sponsor as part of the regularly scheduled project status review series. The findings of the development team regarding risk are presented later in Table A23.2. The project sponsor concurred and was receptive to the fact that we had considered events that could have jeopardized their investment and had ways to cope with or prevent them.

Table A23.1 documents the relative probability of each risk firing as well as a judgment call as to its relative negative impact on the effect – its severity. Since these two factors should not be considered separately, they were multiplied to get a composite score and ranked as shown in Table A23.2. Note that the higher the composite score, the less impactful that risk is if it fires.

From the table, we can see that testing constitutes the highest risk level. This was deemed the most complex part of the effort due to the nature of the system being tested.

Table A23.1   Raw Data for IRE Estimate

Relative Severity	Relative Probability	Project Phase	Description	Mitigation
5	7	Requirements	Well-defined and stable	Monitor
3	6	Design	Proof of concept done	Ensure design and as-built are synchronized
2	2	Coding	Not done before	Acquire advanced skills
1	1	Testing	Stochastic system	Use analytic and *brute force* methods
6	3	Installation	Damage during shipment is possible	Take hard drive as carry on
4	4	Training	User knowledge level unknown	Survey users and create a relevant course
7	5	Support	Cost not known	Minimize error content

Table A23.2 Computation of Relative Ranking of Risk using IRE

Relative Severity (R)	Relative Probability (p)	Project Phase	Relative Severity X Probability [R*p]	Relative Ranking Based on Computation
5	7	Requirements	35	5
3	6	Design	18	4
2	2	Coding	4	2
1	1	Testing	1	1
6	3	Installation	18	4
4	4	Training	16	3
7	5	Support	35	5

A.23.2 Simple Risk/Breakeven Estimate of Risk Mitigation

This approach [2] is based on answering the following questions: "How much risk mitigation is too much?" and "How much mitigation is enough?" In other words, at what point are we spending more money to avoid a risk than we would spend if that risk fired (it actually happened)? The basis for this method lies partly in the Standish Group Chaos Report from 2004 [3] but is still applicable today. That report classified software projects as belonging to one of three categories:

- Type 1 – Completely Successful – 29% of projects reported on fell into this category.
- Type 2 – Experienced Significant Delays or Overruns – 53% of projects reported fell into this category.
- Type 3 – Cancelled – 18% of projects fell into this category.

Utilizing the statistics developed in the Standish Report, a formulation was developed to help us determine what the budget of our project should be if we were to account for risk. The variables are:

- P_f = Probability that our project turns out to be a Type 2 or Type 3 = 71% (this is the sum of 18% and 53%).
- R_0 = The ratio of the projects overrun to the original budget (approximately 56%).
- R_f = The ratio of the cost of the projects to their original budget (approximately 156%).

To demonstrate, the application of this published approach, let's compute the breakeven effectiveness, E_e, for a €10 million software project,

$$E_e = P_f B R_f + (1 - P_f) B \text{ solving for B,}$$

$$B = E_e / (P_f R_0 + 1) \text{ or approximately, €17 million}$$

where
  E_e is the breakeven point.
  B is the set-aside amount plus the estimated project cost.

Some issues this "set aside" of €7 million raises include whether or not we can afford this large set-aside budget to cover potential cost overruns. According to Section A23.3, if a risk mitigation action costs 5% of the total project cost, it only needs to have an 8.9% positive effect to be justified. What if we or our client cannot afford the previous amount or the 5%? In that case, we have a couple of options. One is to set aside what we can, begin the project and hope for the best. Another is to just start work and again, hope for the best. In any case, this method has done its job. It has demonstrated to us the size of the (potential) risk leaving the go-ahead decision to us and our client.

A.23.3 Risk-Based Contingency Budgeting

This approach is based on the assumption that the greater the number of risk contingencies we can identify, the larger the amount of set aside needed to overcome risk firings. Of course, there are some projects that even an enormous amount of money could not save but we will put that issue aside. As mentioned earlier, some project managers set aside a fixed percentage of the total budget. Where this percentage comes from in some firms is a closely guarded secret. But we might assume that experience on previous projects has something to do with it. In this case [4], several thousand projects were studied and a mathematical model was developed, validated and revised based on real-world data.

A simplified overview of the process:

1. Identify potential risks.
2. Estimate the probability of each firing.
3. Associate a cost with each risk firing.
4. Identify how many of the most expensive risks must be accounted for based on project confidence level.
5. Set a contingency budget based on the population of selected risks.

Some of the key features of this method include:

- It encourages finding as many of the risks to project success as we can think of simultaneously raising the question of how it can be prevented or overcome if it occurs.
- The research that produced this method showed that even if the number of identified risks is low, the results are still valid.
- It enables us to effectively budget for a subset of risks as it is unlikely that all the identified risks will fire.
- It works on single projects or programs composed of many projects.

The formula used by this method is:

$$a = 1.2 \times n \times p + 3.5$$

where
a = the number of risks (in order of descending cost) to provide for.
n = the total number of risks considered.
p = the average of the firing probabilities.

To demonstrate the use of this method, let's look at a hypothetical example as shown in Table A23.3 (the values are for demonstration purposes only):

Granted, some of these probabilities and even some of the costs are based on our best information or "guesstimates" at the time but the accuracy is less important than the fact that we identified each of the risks, ranked them and estimated their relative impact. That awareness could prove invaluable.

Following the steps outlined above, we have

The average probability is approximately 0.00235.

Computing item "a" from the equation above, we get a value of 3.6, rounding to the nearest whole number, we get 4. So, it appears we need to fund the top four most expensive risks. This gives us a set aside amount of €380,000. Note that this set aside is just that. It may never be used.

How do we apply this method to a program composed of several projects? We find the average probability for all of the identified risks. Then compute "a" as though this set of projects was actually a single project as shown above.

Although this method is beneficial even with a small number of identified risks, the confidence level increases as we increase the number of risks as shown in Table A23.4.

If we cannot afford to set aside the amount indicated by this method, we at least can see what our exposure will be by only financing what we can afford. Also, these probabilities and costs do not remain static, changing over time as equipment ages, policies change and liability laws and court decisions alter our liabilities in the event of a firing. Where it has been used, this method has been reported to have had a high success rate [4].

Table A23.3   Example of Data Needed

Firing Event	Probability	Cost (in thousands)
Server Failure	0.0010	10
Power Loss > 2 hours	0.0020	20
Weather prevents shift change	0.0100	5
Hacker/Malware intrusion	0.0010	250
Law changes without notice	0.0001	100

Table A23.4   Effect on Confidence Level as Identified Risk Count Increases

	Confidence Level ->		
Risk Count	90%	95%	99%
5	–	–	–
10	2	3	3
20	4	4	5

(Continued)

Table A23.4 (Continued)   Effect on Confidence Level as Identified Risk Count Increases

Risk Count	Confidence Level ->		
	90%	*95%*	*99%*
30	5	6	7
40	6	7	9
50	8	9	10
100	14	15	17
200	25	27	30
500	58	61	65

A.23.4 Risk Reduction via Bias Removal

Civilization has been building roads, tunnels and bridges for thousands of years but getting costs right still eludes us as shown in Table A23.5. The reason why we can't seem to accurately estimate such projects and, in fact, all projects was researched over a 20-year period resulting in a Nobel prize in Economics. Those findings resulted in a method that has worked so well, that the American Planning Association has recommended that its members use it and not use traditional planning methods alone (Table A23.5). What the prize-winning work showed was that "Human judgment is generally optimistic due to overconfidence and insufficient regard to distributional information. Thus, people will underestimate cost, completion times and risks of planned actions, whereas they will overestimate the benefits of the same actions" [6]. As evidence of this inability to accurately estimate, consider this. Even though hundreds of roads, bridges and tunnels have been developed over the centuries, we still have trouble accurately estimating their costs (Table A23.5).

The method which adjusts estimates to account for our human biases is called Reference Class Forecasting. In simplified terms, it amounts to basing our estimates of the new project on how we estimated previous, similar projects constituting our Reference Class. The more projects we have recorded information on, the more statically significant and accurate our results. Note that this approach does not result in a single cost number but rather, a cost estimate and a contingency amount based on the degree of confidence we desire for finishing within that combined cost (i.e. cost estimate + contingency). To use this method, for previous, similar software projects, we need:

- The original cost estimate for each project
- The actual final cost of each project

Table A23.5   Overrun Data from Industries Other than Software

Type of Project World Wide	Average % Overrun	Overrun % Range
Railways	45	7 to 83
Bridges and Tunnels	34	−28 to 96
Roads	20	−10 to 50

Source: Adapted from [6].

Be careful to avoid mixing different types of projects together. Reduce the data to percentiles and form a plot (in this example, a least squares fit) of the Acceptable Chance of Cost Overrun (x-axis) versus the Required Increase in Estimate/Contingency (y-axis). For this example, I was only able to locate a company with 18 similar projects that had collected the required data. The percentile range and aggregate percentages are shown in Table A23.6.

Reducing this data to a plot results in Figure A23.3. What the plot tells us is, if we want approximately a 70% confidence level, we need to increase our estimate by approximately 50%. Note

Table A23.6 Collected Data Reduced to Percentiles

Percentile Range	Aggregate Percentage
–30% to –20%	06%
–20% to –10%	17%
0% to 10%	33%
10% to 20%	44%
20% to 30%	72%
30% to 40%	89%
90% to 100%	94%
100% to 170%	100%

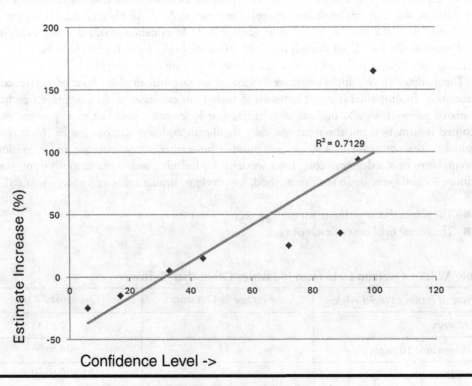

Figure A23.3 Example of Project Estimate versus Confidence Level.

that since this plot is in terms of percentages, it is not dependent on the actual amount of the initial estimate we arrived at by whatever other means we may have used. Furthermore, this inherent bias is in all humans and hence affects any method we use (e.g. Function Points, COCOMO II). So, if we were to estimate our project at €100,000 and want to have a 70% confidence that it will finish at or below that amount, using this chart as our experience guide, we would have to increase our estimate by €50,000 or simply hope for the best. The problem for most software companies is that competitive bids tend to cause firms to keep bids low in hopes of winning the contract by engaging in the overly optimistic pursuit of new business to the extent that the risks are ignored or significantly downplayed.

A.23.5 Northrup Grumman Risk Management System

I decided to refer to this approach [7] as a system because it goes far beyond the other approaches in the risk management category. This more comprehensive view includes definitions of risk, definitions of levels or severity of risk(s), and a categorization scheme involving more than a simple "winner takes all" voting scheme [8].

A23.5.1 Definition of Risk Levels in the Northrup-Grumman Scheme

This method separates risks into five categories (Table A23.7). Note how each category has a ranking level from 5 to 1. The fact that not all team members may agree on the level to be associated with a given event or firing is addressed via the Borda voting scheme which we will explain subsequently.

A23.5.2 Probability of Occurrence

As mentioned earlier, the severity of the firing of a risk is only part of the issue of risk. Another is its likelihood or probability of occurrence. This method also categorizes risks by their probability (Table A23.8).

A23.5.4 The Borda Voting System

All members of the team, the project sponsors and others are likely to disagree about just about every aspect of risk evaluation. This method does not subscribe to "the tyranny of the majority."

Table A23.7   Risk Levels in the Northrup Grumman System

Impact Category (Level)	Description
Critical (5)	System or program failure – may not meet primary requirements
Serious (4)	Significant cost and/or schedule overrun(s) – may not meet secondary requirements
Moderate (3)	Minor cost and/or schedule overrun(s) – requirements still met
Minor (2)	Small cost and/or schedule overrun(s) – requirements still met
Negligible (1)	No effect on effort

Table A23.8 Probability of Occurrence Example

Probability Range (%)	Description/Occurrence
1–10	Very unlikely
11–40	Unlikely
41–60	Occurs about half the time
61–90	Likely
91–99	Very likely

Instead, it uses the Borda voting scheme. The Borda voting scheme involves each voter ranking candidates rather than picking just one. For example, if there are five candidates, a voter will select their favorite, awarding it 5 points, their second favorite awarding it 4 points and so on. In this way, this method attempts to capture the consensus among those making decisions regarding risks. This method employs a modification of the Borda method involving a 2-factor points system:

■ Impact (of the risk)
■ Probability of occurrence

B23.5.4 Obtaining the Composite Score

Each firing event is assigned a composite score, ScoreT, where ScoreT = points for severity + probability of occurrence. In the case of a two-way tie, ScoreT = $(1/2)*(1 + Score1 + Score2)$ then Score1 and Score2 are replaced with the new ScoreT in the rankings.

Using our earlier example, we can form Table A23.9 using this method.

Applying our point assignment scheme, we get Table A23.10.

Table A23.9 Firing Events and Costs Example

Firing Event	Probability	Cost	Impact Rank
Server failure	0.0010	10,000	4
Power loss > 2 hours	0.0020	20,000	3
Weather prevents shift change	0.0100	5,000	5
Hacker/malware intrusion	0.0010	250,000	1
Change in law without prior notice	0.0001	100,000	2

Table A23.10   Example Point Assignment

Firing Event	Probability Points	Impact Points	Points Rank
Server failure	3.5	2	5.5
Power loss > 2 hours	4	3	7
Weather prevents shift change	5	1	6
Hacker/malware intrusion	3.5	5	8.5
Change in law without prior notice	1	4	5

Note how different a result we would have obtained if we considered the risk(s) based on impact or probability of occurrence alone. Also, agreement or disagreement with this method but at least it provides a consistent means of addressing risk.

References

[1] Peters, L.J., *Getting Results from Software Development Teams*, Microsoft Press Best Practices Series, May, 2008.

[2] Masticola, S., "A Simple Estimate of the Cost of Software Project Failures and the Break Even Effectiveness of Project Risk Management," *29th International Conference on Software Engineering Workshops*, 2007, Minneapolis, Minnesota.

[3] The Standish Group, *The CHAOS Report*, West Yarmouth, MA, 2004.

[4] Kamooshi, H. and Cioffi, D.F., "Program Risk Contingency Budget Planning," *IEEE Transactions on Engineering Management*, Vol. 56, No. 1, pp. 171–179, March, 2005.

[5] Ghazi, P., Moreno, M. and Peters, L.J., "Looking for the Holy Grail of Software Development," *IEEE Software*, Vol. 32, Jan/Feb 2014, pp. 92–96.

[6] Flyvberg, B., "From Nobel Prize to Project Management: Getting Risks Right," *Project Management Journal*, Vol. 37, No. 3, August 2006, pp. 5–15.

[7] Northrup Grumman Corporation, "Risk Management Plan for the H-60 Airborne Mine Countermeasures Integrated Product Team," Version 0.21, December, 1998.

[8] Straffin, P., *Topics in the Theory of Voting*, Birkhäuser, Boston, MA, 1980.

Appendix 24

Software Project Management Antipatterns

You may not be familiar with the term, antipattern. Although it is often spelled without an embedded hyphen (e.g. antipattern), there are many definitions which can be summarized as "an apparent solution to a problem which makes matters worse." In other words, an antipattern is an idea which seemed like a good one at the time but when it was tried it turned out to have a decidedly negative effect. It was, in reality, a bad idea. More than 90 of these bad ideas as they pertain to software project management have been catalogued and published [1]. But, as you might guess, the list of seemingly good solutions to software project management problems grows with each new project run by an untrained software project manager. The repeated scenario goes something like this. A problem occurs during the project, the software project manager (or a member of the development team) comes up with a creative solution for it and if the solution works, he or she is a hero otherwise a new antipattern is created. Notice that the solution creation cycle is extemporaneous. That is, it is not part of a process but is a response to an unanticipated situation. But there is hope for antipatterns. It is called, *refactoring*. Refactoring refers to the reengineering or revising of the antipattern so that it actually benefits the project and solves the problem the antipattern was intended to solve. At least one author [1] has proposed that to qualify as a true antipattern, it must be observed a minimum of three times. That should not be hard to do in software engineering. For example, software project managers still continue to add people to projects that are behind schedule with the expectation that this will help. As Brooks [2] pointed out, it makes matters worse. Also, the entire software engineering profession continues to pursue technological solutions to the problems encountered during software projects qualifying that approach as a high-level anti-pattern of sorts since the data do not indicate that it is effective at improving our ability to deliver projects [3]. As you may have guessed, there are many other antipatterns some of which we will discuss presently. One of the goals of this book is to provide you with the information you need to avoid antipatterns. An overwhelmingly popular assumption among software project managers is that technology will solve project problems. I propose that this presumption be classified as a "super anti-pattern" because the data do not support it and it is a pervasive belief. Here is why, a study by IBM of failed software projects [3] found that 53% failed due to "poor management while 3% failed due to "technical challenges." The implication here is that if we did a better job of managing software projects, we would be more successful. A few antipatterns are listed in Table A24.1 as examples of what has been documented in the referenced works. In reviewing the contents of Table A24.1, most of us will find

Table A24.1 Some Examples of Antipatterns

Name	Description	Reference
Absentee Manager	A manager who engages in avoidance behavior or is invisible for long periods	I-2
All You Have is a Hammer	One-dimensional management that uses the same techniques on all subordinates in all situations	I-2
Appointed Team	The false assumption that a management-selected group of people will immediately become a team	I-3
The Brawl	A project manager with no leadership or management experience	I-4
Detailitis Plan	Excessive planning leading to complex schedules with a high level of detail, giving the false perception that the project is fully under control	I-5
The Domino Effect	Moving critical resources between projects and blurring project boundaries	I-4
Dry Waterhole	Specifying stringent requirements for a job when this isn't really necessary, resulting in a limited pool of available talent	I-3
Fire Drill	Months of boredom followed by demands for immediate delivery	I-5
Glass Case Plan	Lack of tracking and updating of initial plans, assuming the plan is enough	I-5
Inflexible Plan	Lack of flexible plans and processes	I-4
Irrational Management	Irrational management decisions, habitual indecisiveness and other negative management practices	I-2, I-5
Leader Not Manager	A manager with a vision (leader) but no plan or management methodology	I-2
Micromanagement	Excessive management involvement in tasks beyond their responsibility	I-4
Mushroom Management	Isolating developers from users, under the mistaken assumption that the requirements are stable and well understood by both the software engineering team and end users at project inception	I-2, I-5
Myopic Delivery	Management insisting on the original delivery date even when there has been a reduction in staff or funding	I-4

(Continued)

Table A24.1 (Continued)   Some Examples of Antipatterns

Name	Description	Reference
Process Disintegration	Failing processes due to a decline in overall cooperation and morale	I-4
Project Mismanagement	Lack of proper software project monitoring and control	I-5
Proletariat Hero	The false assumption that coercion is an efficient way to increase productivity	I-2
Rising Upstart	Superstars who can't wait their time and want to skip learning phases	I-2
Road to Nowhere	Lack of planning	I-2
Size Isn't Everything	Assuming developers are interchangeable and that the number of people working on a problem is inversely proportional to the development time	I-5, I-4, I-2
Ultimate Weapon	Relying heavily on a superstar on the team	I-2

Adapted from [1].

some ill-advised practices that we have fallen prey to. If you didn't, remember there are many more not listed there that have been catalogued. Again, the point of all this is that there exist a plethora of software project management practices which, when first engaged in, seemed like a good idea but later proved themselves to be just the opposite.

In reviewing the preceding list of antipatterns, keep in mind that there are a lot more where those came from and the number is increasing all the time. The key to stemming the growth of this population is educating software engineers and software project managers so they will not have to make up solutions on their own.

Another goal of this book is to put the concept of software project success into perspective. In the early days of software engineering, bringing a project in on time, on budget and meeting requirements was the "gold" standard. Today, the complexities and risks of the user environment, rapidly changing requirements and system user preferences make achieving those early goals a necessary but not sufficient starting point. For a myriad of reasons, what may be seen as a successful project by one stakeholder may be seen as a failure by another [4–6]. So, success is something of an ethereal phenomenon in that it not only is subject to change from one venue to the next but changes during the project as well.

A24.1 Should We Be Concerned?

For years, university business schools have done studies regarding the role of project managers in all types of projects, including software. The bottom line from their findings is that without well-trained, competent software project managers, even the best-funded and adequately staffed software projects can fail. Similar studies done by others in our industry have come to the same conclusion.

How could this be? There are many reasons why an incompetent software project manager's actions may inadvertently sabotage a software project. Some of the more obvious ones include:

1. Not comprehending the level of complexity inherent in the software project.
2. Making commitments for the software engineering team without first consulting with the team and determining what they can commit to.
3. Chastising a member of the team in front of other team members.
4. Putting too much pressure on the team to perform at a higher level.
5. Using an ineffective reward system (Hint – money is an ineffective reward for knowledge workers).
6. Overruling the technical decisions the team has made.
7. Increasing team size, even from the start, believing that a larger team is more likely to be successful (the law of diminishing returns).
8. Conducting an individual's performance review in a way that reduces their productivity.

There are others but the point is that the software project manager's role is a vital one. Some of the actions of the software project manager may be a spur-of-the-moment reaction, taken without thinking, resulting in demotivating the team. Remember, a motivated team will likely outperform a demotivated one every time. To be clear, the role of the software project manager is not a dual role such as software developer and project manager. Why? Project management and software development involve two very different mindsets. The development role is focused on complying with the syntax and semantics of the programming language, satisfying functional and performance requirements and ensuring that interface conventions with other parts of the system are adhered to, complying with the build process and so forth. Conversely, the project management role is alternatively focused on the "big" picture (i.e. where the project is and where it should be with respect to cost, schedule, functionality, reliability, ease of use and so forth) and the "small" (i.e. identifying and alleviating factors that are causing the project to fall behind schedule and/or over budget). One, the development side, is tactical while the other, the management side, is strategic.

Over the years, the practice of software engineering has made tremendous strides on the tactical side. Analysis, design, programming, testing, user interfaces, code libraries, development methods, development environments and more have all contributed to our progress. But based on SWEBOK, IEEE Software Society publications, software conferences (most of these do not mention project management as a topical category for submission) and other resources for our profession, those who manage software projects are getting little or no help. For example, software project managers have assumed that money is the best motivator for software engineers. As will be discussed in more detail later in this text, it is not. In fact, it really is not a motivator for software engineers. What is the best is free – it is simply saying thank you.

References

[1] LaPlante, P.A., *Antipatterns: Identification, Refactoring and Management*, Auerbach Publications, New York, NY, 2005.
[2] Brooks, F.P. Jr., *The Mythical Man Month: Essays on Software Engineering*, Addison – Wesley, Reading, MA, 1995.
[3] Gulla, J., "Seven Reasons Why IT Projects Fail," *IBM Systems Magazine*, February, 2012.

[4] Portland Pattern Repository, "Management Anti Pattern Roadmap," 2014. http://c2.com/cgi/wiki? ManagementAntiPatternRoadMap

[5] Brown, W.J., McCormick, H.W. and Thomas, S.W., *Anti-patterns in Project Management*, John Wiley & Sons, Hoboken, New Jersey, 2000.

[6] Brown, W.J., McCormick, H.W. and Thomas, S.W., *AntiPatterns: Refactoring Software, Architecture, and Projects in Crisis*, John Wiley & Sons, Hoboken, New Jersey, 1998.

Appendix 25

Software Project Managers

Software project managers are largely untrained [1] for their new role prior to making the transition from software engineer to software project manager. Worse, they rarely know the nature of the activity they are embarking upon [2]. The differences between coding and management could not be more pronounced [2]. For example, in the software development domain, code either compiles error free or it doesn't, it passes a test or it doesn't and so forth. This "either or" world is often labeled as dealing with "hard" issues while management has been described as having to deal with "soft" issues such as developing a project plan, a communication plan, a business case and others [3, 4]. In the management domain, it is not known whether or not the software project manager and the development team got it "right" until it is too late to take corrective action. For example, using whatever means at your disposal, if you significantly underestimated the cost of the project, this may not become apparent until the project plan is being executed and the cost overruns and/or schedule delays become insurmountable. For example, there is ample evidence [5] that if your project is 15% complete and over budget or behind schedule, your chances of ending within budget or on schedule are nil. Because of the uniqueness of software projects, it is unlikely that one could know in advance what a similar project ended up costing and use that to gauge whether or not the estimate for this new project is within the realm of possibility. This leaves the software project manager on her/his own with respect to most of the "soft" issues. Of course, the business manager of the company developing the software might not agree that estimating is a "soft" issue since overruns on a fixed price contract will negatively impact the company's bottom line by reducing its profit.

References

[1] Garvin, David A. "How Google Sold Its Engineers on Management." *Harvard Business Review*, Vol. 91, No. 12, Dec. 2013, pp. 74–82.

[2] Ghazi, P., Moreno, A. and Peters, L.J., "Looking for the Holy Grail of Software Development," *IEEE Software*, Vol. 31, Jan/Feb 2014, pp. 92–96.

[3] Peters, L. and Moreno, "Enriching TraditionalSoftware Engineering Curricula with Software Project Management Knowledge," *International Conference on Software Engineering, Special Track on Software Engineering Education and Training (CSEET)*, May, 2016, Austin, Texas.

[4] LaPlante, P., *Antipatterns: Identification, Refactoring and Management*, Auerbach Publications, New York, NY, 2005.

[5] Fleming, Q.W. and Koppelman, J.M., *Earned Value Project Management*, 4th Edition, Project Management Institute, Newtown Square, Pennsylvania, 2010.

Appendix 26

Software Engineering Ethics

Why are we discussing ethics in a book on managing software projects? The simple answer is that in developing software, at nearly every turn, the software engineer is faced with ethical questions. Some of these questions are obvious while others are more subtle and those questions impact productivity. For example, software engineers often use the term "hack" in referring to software that works but was thrown together quickly and is not likely to survive use by others unless revised and/or replaced. It is just something thrown together quickly to check out a problem or for some other reason, but it is definitely not intended to be released as part of a working product. Unfortunately, sometimes in the rush to release a product, some of these "hacks" make it through testing and unknowingly end up in a released product with serious negative consequences. Depending on the company and the software project manager, some of these hacks are knowingly released in order to meet a deadline. The question that seems to have eluded some people is, "Is this the right thing to do?" Why does this make any difference? It is important because everyone wants to be associated with quality results because they reflect on the person's self-image, their self-esteem and so forth. Hacking out a piece of a product is a definite productivity killer because the software we produce is an extension of ourselves and if it is flawed, we are flawed [1]. Fortunately, a set of ethical principles was set forth for the software engineering profession some decades ago [2]. These are the canons that comprise software engineering ethics (Table A26.1).

The preceding is a compact or abbreviated version of the software engineering code of ethics. The latest full version is available from the IEEE at http://computer.org/tab/swecc/code.htm#full. The preceding may sound like a list of commandments and in some ways it is. Like principles in religion, abiding by them can only have a positive effect on your team and its performance. Try reflecting on them and how they were or were not followed in your current or most recent project – it might just be revealing. Software engineers have been exposed to a practice called technical debt. In it, the conscious decision is made by management to defer employing a technically superior approach in favor of an inferior one, and documenting the decision usually with the intent of returning to this issue at a later date and using the superior method. The problem with this scheme is it is a productivity killer [4] because people want to be associated with quality results [1]. Being forced to knowingly employ substandard techniques reduces productivity and, worst of all, sends the wrong message to the team. That wrong message is "our number priority is to deliver something even if it is not of the highest quality." Besides, there is no economic incentive for the company to go back at a later date and institute the deferred changes.

Table A26.1   A Short Version of the Software Engineering Code of Ethics Principles [3]

Principle Title	Abbreviated Description
Public	Software engineers shall act consistently with the public interest
Client and Employer	Software engineers shall act in a manner that is in the best interests of their client and employer consistent with the public interest
Product	Software engineers shall ensure that their products and related modifications meet the highest professional standards possible
Judgment	Software engineers shall maintain integrity and independence in their professional judgment
Management	Software engineering managers and leaders shall subscribe to and promote an ethical approach to the management of software development and maintenance
Profession	Software engineers shall advance the integrity and reputation of the profession consistent with the public interest
Colleagues	Software engineers shall be fair to and supportive of their colleagues
Self	Software engineers shall participate in lifelong learning regarding the practice of their profession and shall promote an ethical approach to the practice of the profession

A26.1 Teaching Software Engineering Ethics

While the principles of software engineering ethics are important, almost as important is how they may be taught. This is because ethics and values systems are not the usual concerns at the forefront of the software engineer's thinking during development. Teaching ethical principles and their applications has been researched and refined [5, 6]. They defined three goals that students must understand:

1. "The power of ethics in creating products and interventions."
2. "That value choices are not automatic, they are linked to decisions made by designers."
3. "That ethical decision making is not abstract, but is incorporated into each design step and algorithm."

The training has to start with the basics of what ethics are as well as why they are important. Remember, people naturally want to do what is good and they want to do it well. The reference [5] lays out what has been developed as well as how to apply it in the classroom and beyond. The bottom line here is that software should be designed and built on ethical principles.

References

[1] Weinberg, G., *The Psychology of Computer Programming*, Van Nostrand Reinhold, New York, NY, 1985.
[2] Gotterbarn, D., Miller, K., and Rogerson, S., "Software Engineering Code of Ethics," *Coomunications of the ACM*, Vol. 40, No. 11, November 1997, pp. 110–118.

[3] Gotterbarn, D., Miller, K., and Rogerson, S. "Software Engineering Code of Ethics," *Communications of the ACM*, Vol. 40, No. 11, November 1997, 110–118. DOI: 10.1145/265684.265699

[4] Peters, L., *Technical Debt – The Ultimate Antipattern*, Managing Technical Debt Workshop, Victoria, BC, Canada, September 2014.

[5] Gotterbarn, D., "How the New Software Engineering Code of Ethics Affects You," *IEEE Software*, November/December 1999, Vol. 16, No. 6, pp. 58–64.

[6] Haliburton, L., Heimerl, A., Bohme, S., Andre, E. and Schmidt, A., "Teaching Ethics as a Creative Subject: Ideas From an Interdisciplinary Workshop," *IEEE Computing Edge*, Vol. 20, No. 3, August 2023, pp. 52–55.

Appendix 27

Technical Debt – The Ultimate Productivity Killer

The concept of technical debt was first proposed by Ward Cunningham in 1992 [1]. The concept seems innocent enough. It often happens that a better way to implement some part of the system is discovered well into the development schedule but implementing it late in the project would involve rework costing us flow time and money. It is a difficult decision but it is decided that the best solution would be a compromise. We note this improved approach but keep the one we already have in place with the intention of returning to this issue at a later date and implementing it. Perhaps, it could be part of an update to the product. Even with the best of intentions, because of a poor business case or other constraints, that return and implementation is unlikely to happen. The practice of technical debt is, in part, an attempt to remedy the usual budget and schedule overruns so common in software projects. It recognizes that software projects often involve making decisions that are expedient in that they may not select the best way to resolve an issue or architect the code but, even though we know there is a better way, there is just not enough flow time or labor resource to do it. What makes it problematic is that employing it demonstrates a failure to understand the nature of work in general and the nature of software engineers and software engineering in particular. Let's take a look at both issues as they relate to technical debt.

The first step in exploring the hidden effects of engaging in technical debt is to understand its impact on software engineers. This closely relates to people's motivation to work. For several decades, psychologists have been trying to figure out just why people work. The obvious answer is that people work in order to make money so they can acquire the stuff they need to survive. But it goes much deeper than that. In the 1954 movie "On the Waterfront," Marlon Brando's character is having an argument with his brother about having been forced to intentionally lose a boxing match. His brother Charley reminds him he received a lot of money to which Brando's character replies, "it's not about money, Charley, I could have been somebody." That quote summarizes one of the most powerful driving forces behind work-self-fulfillment. Three models about why people work have been developed and accepted by the larger psychology community. The three most widely accepted are listed below by author:

- Herzberg [2] proposed a "Two Factor Theory" to explain why people work. These were "hygiene" defined as being survival related having to do with pay, working conditions, respect and job stability. The other factor "Relationship to the job" involves advancement, promotion, fair treatment and potential for higher rewards.

- Maslow [3] proposed that people have a hierarchy of needs and working satisfies the hierarchy. Starting at the top, these are psychological needs, safety and security, social needs, esteem needs and self-actualization.
- McClelland [4] proposed that people work to satisfy three needs – achievement (to do something important), power (to have control over others and/or their own actions) and affiliation (friendly relationships).

While all three models involve some issue(s) related to self-esteem in one way or another, Herzberg's model may be the most widely accepted model of the three. Software project managers who rely on these factors (i.e. pay rate, working conditions and so forth) to control and motivate software engineers have high turnover rates [5], and turnover increases development costs by as much as 60% [6]. Since no one wants to be associated with a failed project or poor quality, taking shortcuts reduces productivity. In addition, more recent work [5] has shown that technology workers have a common value system which places a high priority on producing work that they can be proud of, that their colleagues will be impressed by and is at or near the state of the art. Producing work that incurs technical debt violates these goals. These goals can be extremely strong in some software engineers. For example, a software engineer who I managed was part of a team on a very aggressive schedule. Some of the work involved fixing bugs in what might be most kindly described as "spaghetti code." He informed me that since his name was going to be associated with this stuff, he would go beyond just fixing the latest bug and reconstruct and retest the routines assigned to him. Even though he voluntarily worked quite late some nights, he still met the schedule and, due to some requirements changes, actually saved himself and his successor a great deal of time to respond to these changes. His colleagues who simply did the minimum were not so fortunate. An environment in which doing the work less than the "correct" way reduces productivity making it more expensive in several ways than doing it right in the first place. The ways in which these "hidden" expenses are incurred include:

- Loss of Productivity – When a person knows that what they are being asked to do is in conflict with what they know they should be doing, they are working at their lowest productivity level [5]. The phenomenon is called cognitive dissonance [7]. Cognitive dissonance reduces productivity. In the case of software development, productivity is often equated to the production of source code. But source code production has only increased by less than one line of source code per programmer per month per year in the period from 1960 to 2000 [8]. This increase has been linear even though dozens of programming, analysis, design, testing and other methods were developed and engaged in over that period [9]. Cognitive dissonance means that even though the coding practices being used are seen as justified because they will foreshorten development flow time, they may, in fact, increase it making this practice something of a self-fulfilling prophecy. Management may be inclined to speculate that even though shortcuts were taken, we still had trouble meeting the schedule. When people are able to fulfill their perception of being productive with work that reflects positively on them, they become highly motivated and are more productive. Therefore, technical debt may actually increase, not decrease, development time.
- Reduced commitment to quality practices – Cutting corners and/or abandoning our standard development process simply sends the wrong messages to the software engineering team. These negative messages all reduce productivity and motivation, while undermining the self-confidence of the development team. They include:
  - The development process you so diligently spent time developing and refining is OK when things are going smoothly but must be abandoned when we get behind.

- We are committed to quality only when it is convenient.
- Management does not believe we can do it right and finish on time, within budget.

■ Reduced use of collective team experience – Most project managers try to compose development teams in such a way that each member possesses skills and experience that complement the skills and experience of the other team members. In this way, the team as a whole possesses the skills and experience needed to be successful. Schedule pressure may be the key driver behind engaging in technical debt [10]. But to overcome possible resistance to engaging in technical debt, a lot of pressure will have to be brought to bear on the team. We now know that if enough pressure is put on a team, they cease to work together as a team and revert back to working as a group of disconnected individuals [11]. Meaning that the collective knowledge and experience within the team is lost.

■ Increased cost – We know that in most job markets, software engineers can experience a high degree of mobility. If they do not like working at one firm, there is often another one seeking to hire or, in the case of larger firms, they can transfer to another organization. Experiencing cognitive dissonance, pressure to cut corners and so forth can increase turnover. As stated earlier, we now know that turnover can account for as much as 60% of the cost of a software project [6]. So we have a paradox, the very practice engaged in to reduce flow time and costs (technical debt) may actually increase both due to lower productivity via reduced motivation and increased turnover.

■ Putting off correcting/paying technical debt can be really expensive. We have known for decades that the later in a software system's life cycle we correct a problem the more it costs and that these costs increase exponentially [12]. Taking shortcuts now with the intent of correcting the problems they cause until later practically guarantees increased total system life costs. Besides, software engineers prefer to be creating new code, not cleaning up somebody else's mess.

■ Undermining a culture of professionalism by setting a tone of just getting the code out when, in fact, people want to be associated with a culture in which getting quality results is the norm. We know the long-term benefits of generating quality code in terms of maintenance [12] but the short-term benefits in terms of improved productivity have only more recently been identified [5]. Five factors were identified that effected the motivation of high technology professionals [13, 14] (Table A27.1).

Looking at Table A27.1 we can see that engaging in technical debt is the antithesis of several of the factors that enhance motivation thereby reducing productivity.

Table A27.1   Motivating Factors in Software Tasks [13, 14]

Factor	Description
Skill Variety	The task requires the use of multiple skills
Task Identity	The task is something the software engineer would like doing
Task Significance	The task is seen as important
Autonomy	The software engineer can accomplish the task as they see fit
Feedback	Management provides feedback on how well the task has been done

A27.1 Summary

As a minimum, the subject of technical debt has brought with it discussions regarding what software development practices are advisable and which should be avoided. Missing from these discussions is the subject of the human toll involved due to cognitive dissonance, personnel turnover and the potential for an attitude in the organization that doing things the "right" way only occurs when the project is on schedule and within budget. As we have seen, the intended effect of engaging in technical debt is illusory. That is, in some cases it may appear to have helped the software project manager's cause but closer inspection reveals it has likely made matters worse – frequently in hidden ways. Hopefully, this will not become a *de facto* standard practice within software project management.

References

[1] Cunningham, W., "The WyCash Portfolio Management System," *OOPSLA' 92 Experience Report*, Vancouver, BC, Canada, 1992.

[2] Herzberg, F., *Work and the Nature of Man*, The World Publishing Company, Cleveland, OH, 1966.

[3] Maslow, A.H., *The Farther Reaches of Human Nature*, The Viking Press, New York, NY, 1971.

[4] McClelland, D.C., *The Achieving Society*, Van Nostrand Rheinhold, Princeton, NJ, 1971.

[5] Katz, R., "Motivating Technical Professionals Today," *IEEE Engineering Management Review*, Vol. 41, No. 1, March 2013, pp. 28–38.

[6] Cone, E., "Managing That Churning Sensation," *Information Week*, May, 1998, No. 680, pp. 50–67.

[7] Weinberg, G.M. *The Psychology of Computer Programming*, Van Nostrand Rheinhold, New York, NY, 1971.

[8] Jensen, R.W., "Don't Forget about Good Management," *CrossTalk*, August, 2000, p. 30.

[9] Rico, D.F., "Short History of Software Methods," downloaded from web, August, 2010 – referenced with author's permission.

[10] Kruchten, P., Nord, R.L. and Ozkaya, I., "Technical Debt: From Metaphor to Theory and Practice," *IEEE Software*, November/December 2012, Vol. 29, No. 6, pp. 18–21.

[11] Gardner, H.K., "Performance Pressure as a Double Edged Sword: Enhancing Team Motivation While Undermining the Use of Team Knowledge," Working Paper 09-126, Harvard Business School, January 2012.

[12] Boehm, B., *Software Engineering Economics*, Prentice-Hall, Englewood Cliffs, NJ, 1981.

[13] Peters, L. "Motivating Software Professionals," *The Software Practitioner*, May, 2013.

[14] Peters, L., "Technical Debt – The Ultimate Antipattern," Managing Technical Debt Workshop, Victoria, BC, Canada, September 2014.

Appendix 28

Transitioning from Software Engineer to Software Project Manager

Some software engineers will eventually decide to become software project managers. Their motivations may vary but as we have discussed, if their primary motivation is increased salary, they are unlikely to be successful in their new role. Due to a lack of training, most software engineers do not know what software project managers do. To complicate matters, most companies do not have a clear path from software engineer to software project manager [4]. Compared to managing a software project, actually writing the software is relatively straightforward in that there are requirements to be met, programming language syntax and semantics to be observed, tests to pass and so forth. Throughout the development effort, the activities of the software engineer are, in a sense, guided or dictated by the stages the software development effort passes through and the software development environment. Software project management activity, except for legal and corporate restrictions, does not have those clear lines of demarcation. Making the transition from the coding environment to the management environment can be unsettling for some. The management environment is viewed by many as a "soft" one in that there are few hard and fast rules analogous to the syntax and semantics of the programming language and other issues. It is also viewed as being "soft" partly because there is no objective measure of whether or not the project manager got anything right usually until it is too late. The remainder of the softness has to do with what most software project managers consider the most difficult and frustrating aspect of their job – personnel issues [1]. Unlike the software engineering role, software project managers are rarely properly prepared for working in this alternative role [2, 3]. Unlike code development, at this point in time, there is no definitive test that reveals whether or not a candidate for a software project manager job is qualified. This is the result of two factors:

- Software project management is not a well-defined discipline. The role, activities and expectations of the software project manager vary from one popular methodology to the next, project to project and company to company and in most companies, the path from software engineer to software project manager is not clearly spelled out [4]. That may be one of the reasons for the general lack of training in project management among software project managers [2, 4]. Another possible explanation is the widespread lack of knowledge regarding just what it is that software project managers do. For example, advertisements for software

195

project managers often require that the person in this position will be required to contribute to the programming effort. Using the professional sports analogy, it is rare that the manager of a sports team is also a player on that team and the team is successful. Management involves focusing on the five basic functions of project management – Planning, Scheduling, Controlling, Staffing and Motivating [4, 5]. How these are done is an open question in most companies since various authors propose a variety of schemes to achieve success in one or more of these areas.

■ Training in project management is optional in most graduate and undergraduate software engineering degree programs [6]. Worldwide, there are more than 400 software engineering programs at the graduate and undergraduate level. Of these, less than 10% list software project management as a required course in order to obtain a degree in software engineering while approximately a third do not even offer a course in software project management. This may explain why there is so little understanding among software engineers as to just what software project managers do or should be doing resulting in a broad range of views regarding the value software project managers bring to software projects. Google's experience stands as an impressive, highly successful exception. When the company was founded, the perception on the part of its founders was that managers inhibit innovation, so the company started without any managers. Within a short time, the founders realized that management was needed if they were to achieve their goals. They instituted a process for vetting prospective managers, training, performance evaluations and a structure that helped ensure project managers would not micromanage [2].

But the fact remains that throughout their career, software engineers are going to be asked management-related questions such as how long an effort will take, what will it cost, how many people may be required and so forth. Without even minimal training in management, they may be predisposed to failure by relying on what seems reasonable to them with no basis in fact. An example of this may be found in a study of thousands of advertisements worldwide for project managers. Significantly, the only category of project managers that required competence in communications and managing project finances was in the area of software project management [7]. It is significant because project managers in other disciplines are assumed to have had the training needed to communicate well and control costs. Not training software project managers leaves them at a disadvantage with respect to these topics and more [8].

A28.1 A Change in Attitude

There is an adage that "we learn from our mistakes." If that were true, over the last 50 years, software projects should have gotten more and more successful with respect to better cost and schedule predictions, on-time within-budget results and quality of deliverables. There have been improvements but not to the extent one would expect through more than a half century of learning. As children and young adults, we recognize that taking an action that results in some form of failure (e.g. not studying for a test) should cause that action or inaction to be called into question and altered. This happens largely because we conclude we are responsible for what happened. But in software project management, a project which fails due to running over budget, delivered late and/or of poor quality can be attributed to many factors (e.g. the schedule was too short, we had to use the Waterfall life cycle, the requirements kept changing and the client was difficult to work with) which enable us to shirk responsibility for failure thereby avoiding learning from the experience [8]. By reviewing the pre-project checklist presented in Appendix 20, the software project manager and those developing the code get a preview of the kinds of impediments to success that will have to be overcome. The commitment at that point to go forward with the project means that the team is essentially negating the possibility of shirking responsibility for failure because they knew what they were getting into but went ahead with the project anyway.

A28.2 Why Is Needed Training Missing?

The software engineering community appears to treat software project management as a "soft" subject as opposed to writing code as a "hard" topic. Perhaps as a result, there has been a lack of training in software project management resulting in software project managers being ill-equipped to perform satisfactorily. This has resulted in software project managers who do not see the need to review whether or not the needed elements for a project to be successful are in place prior to project initiation. The pilot analogy comes to mind in that pilots are trained to consider the operational status of all key systems of the aircraft prior to taking flight via a checklist which is executed with the copilot prior to takeoff. The strategic goal [9] of employing such a list is to prevent obvious problems or oversights (e.g. not having the flaps in the takeoff position before beginning their takeoff roll) and to ensure that an unsafe status is not found for a flight critical system. Some of the more obvious undesirable situations that the software project manager should be concerned about include having the development team believe that the project will not be successful, not having the support of senior management [10, 11], having the client prefer a different project manager to conduct this project and others. The point here is that the software project manager is focused on having the project be successful which can result in overlooking one or more important issues which may jeopardize project success.

References

[1] Tarim, T., "Making a Transition from Technical Professional to …," *IEEE Engineering Management Review*, Vol. 10, No. 3, September 2012, pp. 3–4.

[2] Garvin, D.A., "How Google Sold Its Engineers on Management," *Harvard Business Review*, December, 2013.

[3] Myers, C.G., Staats, B.R. and Gino, F., "My Bad! How Internal Attribution and Ambiguity of Responsibility Affect Learning from Failure," Harvard Business School Working Paper 14-104, April 18, 2014.

[4] Katz, R., "Motivating Technical Professionals Today," *IEEE Engineering Management Review*, Vol. 41, No. 1, March 2013, pp. 28–37.

[5] Dyba, T., Kitchenham, B.A. and Jorgensen, M., "Evidenced Based Software Engineering for Practitioners," *IEEE Software*, Vol. 22, No. 1, Jan-Feb 2005, pp. 58–65.

[6] unpublished Google searches 2016-2019 done by L. Peters.

[7] Chipulu, M., Neoh, J.G., Udechukwu, O. and Williams, T., "A Multidimensional Analysis of Project Manager Competencies," *IEEE Transactions on Engineering Management*, Vol. 60, No. 3, August 2013, pp. 496–505.

[8] Ghazi, P., Moreno, A.M. and Peters, L.J., "Looking for the Holy Grail of Software Development," *IEEE Software*, Vol. 31, No. 1, 2014, pp. 92–96.

[9] Kaplan, R.S. and Norton, D.P., "Linking the Balanced Scorecard to Strategy," *California Management Review*, Vol. 39, No. 1, pp. 53–79, Fall 1996.

[10] Busch, J., "Senior Management Support: What Is It and Why You Need It," *Spend Matters website*, July 29, 2009.

[11] Thamhain, H., "Team Leadership Effectiveness in Technology-Based Project Environments," *IEEE Engineering Management Review*, Vol. 36, No. 1, 2008, pp. 165–180. College, Cambridge, UK.

Appendix 29

Why Smart People Make Dumb Decisions

Nearly every day, we learn of some person in a leadership role who has made a dumb decision. Closer to home in the software engineering field, a similar phenomenon happens whereby a project manager or senior manager makes a decision many of us question because it is seen as seriously in error. In many cases, these people are unusually bright but yet, often ignoring the data, they go ahead and decide to take "the wrong path." Often, we have wondered how did this happen? Fortunately, some researchers at the Harvard Business School have found the answer. What they found was that when people are at the lower echelons of the power structure in an organization, they base their decisions on facts and data. As they are promoted and progress through the ranks, they acquire more power and influence and begin to rely on their intuition more and more. The higher they go in the power structure, the less they rely on facts and data until their decision-making is totally based on intuition. Sometimes, this turns out well but that may be a comparatively rare occurrence. The message here for software project managers is to be aware of this phenomenon and to pay attention to the facts and data in order to avoid what may be a serious mistake. But do they? The problem here lies with our brains and society. We tend to think, "If I am smart enough to have achieved being promoted to this position, do I need to pay attention to contrary opinions from those less accomplished than me and data contrary to my judgement?" That leads us down a potentially dangerous line of thought leading to a decision which may be based on inaccurate information or intuition alone. Either way, input from an opposing view could have prevented a disaster.

One researcher [1] identified six reasons why people in leadership positions make "really dumb decisions:"

1. Loss Avoidance – This reason relates to the desire of people to prefer to avoid a loss than to acquire a gain. Research by psychologist David Kahneman [2] showed that losses are twice as powerful as gains. This seems reasonable since a loss is giving up something you already have whereas a gain is potentially acquiring something you as yet do not have. The difficulty with loss avoidance is that it usually means that the decision-maker defaults to the *status quo*. The way to overcome this bias is to put the potential loss in perspective. That is, to consider whether or not the potential loss is as valuable or is less valuable than the potential gain. Alternatively, consider that you can recover from the potential loss but can you recover from not achieving the potential gain?

2. Recall Bias – This is often referred to as the "availability heuristic." It is based upon the underlying psychological presumption that if I can remember it, it must be important or at least as important as something I do not recall. This results in our giving heavier weight to recently acquired information as opposed to previous, older information. This biases our decision-making toward recently acquired information. One problem with this phenomenon is that the more spectacular the event, the more likely we are to remember it. What "Recall Bias" is saying is, I recall it so it must be true. The way to put this bias into a proper perspective is to do additional research to ensure the data the decision is based on isn't just recent but is, in fact, pointing the decision in the best direction.

3. Survivor Bias – This bias focuses on events or people that "survived" from among those who didn't. For example, we hear a lot about people who pursued a career as a professional golfer right out of college but very little about those who, though skilled, failed to make the grade in the Professional Golfers Association qualifying school. The real problem with this bias is that the scheme used by the singular exception is unlikely to work for others. Spending 8 hours a day at the driving range is unlikely to make you as good a golfer as Tiger Woods, dropping out of college to pursue a career in software engineering is unlikely to produce the results Bill Gates has seen and so forth. The advisory here is to base your strategy on *your* strengths and avoid *your* weaknesses.

4. Anchor Bias – This bias refers to the basics of negotiation. In negotiation, the final value of an offer is highly influenced by the first relevant number (referred to as the anchor) that begins the negotiation process. It is well known that this initial value is very influential in the remainder of the negotiation process. The influence of the anchor value is hard to overcome. So whether negotiating a salary or other value, have in mind a value you believe is the value you are willing to pay or settle for *before* negotiations begin.

5. Confirmation Bias – This bias is based on our desire to confirm how smart we are – so smart that we want to show others how smart. This causes us to filter the information presented to us. For example, course evaluations for a class I teach will contain both positive and negative comments about the class and my delivery of the information it contained. Confirmation bias causes me to favor the positive comments and place little value on the negative ones because the negative ones tend to refute my underlying belief embraced by this bias. The problem this creates whether teaching a class or managing a software engineering team is that the negative comments may contain valuable information that could help to improve our teaching or our management skills which this bias may cause us to ignore.

6. Idea Origination Bias – This bias is often referred to as the "Not Invented Here" syndrome. The premise for this bias is that if we didn't think of this, it cannot be of much value. It actually may go deeper than that and be based on a tribal or club-like viewpoint. The key to overcoming this bias is to ignore the source and focus on the idea or suggestion itself. An example of overcoming this bias occurred many years ago during the design and development of Boeing 747. Engineers were working to reduce the weight of the aircraft any way they safely could. A technician overheard a discussion about this and suggested they remove the vertical part of each step leading to the upper deck and strengthen the horizontal portion as necessary. Under other circumstances, the engineers might have ignored this idea but they were desperate and it helped to enable them to bring that portion of the cabin within the weight budget. They focused on the validity of the idea, not its source. Obviously, we can get so entrenched in the way we currently view things, we might fail to see valuable alternatives.

Some additional advisories that may be useful include:

1. Don't Restrict your search to the software industry – Often, methods developed in other industries prove quite useful when adopted by software engineering. After all software engineering is not so unique that only methods developed within this field are applicable.
2. Be open to suggestions from anyone in your group – Some members of your team may have some great ideas. Just because you are in charge doesn't mean you are the only one with great ideas. Besides, this may open up the floodgates to other ideas from everyone.
3. Be open but reasonable – While suggestions are fine, given your experience with the team in previous situations, you may want to restrict suggestions to schemes the team has seen work elsewhere on similar projects.

Remember, the goal here is to be an equal opportunity idea channel by finding what works no matter where it comes from. Finally, the pattern which has been studied [3, 4] is that the more success and influence one has, the more they rely on their own intuition and the less on facts and data. Finally, when they have reached what amounts to the pinnacle of success within the firm, they rely totally on their own intuition which can and does lead to some puzzling, stupid decisions.

References

[1] Haden, J., "6 Reasons Really Smart People Make Really Dumb Decisions, According to Science," *INC. newsletters*, December, 2017.
[2] Kahneman, D., *Thinking Fast and Slow*, Farrar, Straus and Giroux, New York, NY, October, 2011.
[3] Bonabeau, E., "Don't Trust Your Gut," *Harvard Business Review*, May, 2003.
[4] Locke, C.C., "When It's Safe to Rely on Intuition (and When It's Not)," *Harvard Business Review*, April 30, 2015.

Appendix 30

Why Software Engineering Teams Should Be Kept Intact

"Success in Software Engineering is the result of a <u>system</u> – not a secret."

–L. Peters

Every senior manager is pleased with software engineering teams that are successful. This has led many senior managers to conclude that to increase the number of teams that are successful within the company, the members of these successful teams should be distributed throughout the software engineering department so that their knowledge and experience can be shared resulting in an overall improvement in the department's performance. This is another example of an anecdotal presumption that has no factual basis [1, 2]. It turns out that data indicate keeping successful teams together (i.e. intact) is advised and breaking them up is counterproductive. Much like sports teams, simply acquiring a highly talented player won't necessarily cause a poorly performing team to become a championship contender. This is because members of the successful software engineering team are familiar with each other to the extent that they know the knowledge strengths and weaknesses of each member and can rely on them for help with specific problems in the topics they are proficient in. They also learn what other team members' propensity for certain kinds of errors and help them to avoid them. If senior managers want to improve matters on a department-wide scale, what they should do is identify what it is the software project manager of the successful team does that contributed to their success and encourage other software project managers to adopt similar behaviors. Once again, what seems reasonable without supporting data ends up being an antipattern, where an antipattern is an action that is thought to be beneficial but has the opposite effect.

References

[1] Huckman, R. and Staats, B., "The Hidden Benefits of Keeping Teams Intact," *Harvard Business Review*, December, 2013.
[2] Staats, B. and Upton, D., "Lean at WIPRO Technologies," *Harvard Business Review*, October 16, 2006.

Appendix 31

Why We Don't Learn from Success

In comparison to learning from success, learning from failure is relatively straightforward. We try some new approach or engage in a type of software development we had never tried before and the project fails. In many cases, we have an easily identifiable culprit. Sometimes it is not so obvious but a postmortem of the failed project should be successful at identifying the cause of the failure. However, success presents us with a much more complex cause-and-effect scenario. In fact, success can breed failure by hindering learning at both the individual and organizational levels, in inter-related ways:

1. When we succeed, we tend to give too much credit to our talents, our method or strategy and too little to external factors including luck.
2. The common belief among software project managers is that we learn from failure. If that belief was true, software project management would be a relatively easy task with all we have learned from all the failed software projects that have occurred over the years. Obviously, that is not the case. But what is the situation when we are successful? Work has been done to study the effects of success on learning and management [1]. The results may surprise some people. Success can change an organization's perspective. When they are successful, they attribute their success to their superior talent at doing whatever it is they do. They tend to rule out the possibility their success is due to luck and or circumstances beyond their control. Given the assumption that they have superior skills, it implies that they do not need to change anything; after all, they are successful. This is consistent with the adage "If it ain't broke, don't fix it!" The problem with that adage is it results in a static approach to managing when a dynamic approach is needed [2]. That dynamic approach means we will constantly seek to improve regardless of our success rate. In interviews with successful sports coaches after a victory, it is common to hear them comment that the team played well but they have a few things to work on. Why should they work on other things – they won didn't they? The successful coach realizes that some of the deficiencies the team displayed were not preyed upon by their opponent that day but some other, better coached team could take advantage of them resulting in a loss.

Many of us have been there – the department meeting during which some software team is honored for having brought a project in on time and within budget or finishing a project that was universally considered impossible. Senior management sees this as an opportunity for all software engineering teams to adopt the same techniques and methods that were used in anticipation of more successful projects in the future. Of course, senior management is ignoring the fact that this may be a one-of-a-kind event since not all software engineering teams are the same and not all software projects are the same. This ignores what successful projects can teach us. As a matter of company policy, everything about the successful project is treated as company proprietary information and not to be published to the industry. Senior management should learn the error of their ways when other software engineering teams fail to achieve the success the original team had but they often do not. Why? Is there something special about this team that enabled them to achieve these feats? Actually, their success is not due to a relatively small number of factors but something much larger. Senior managers and just about all of the management team are seeking to be successful. When a software team is deemed to have been successful based on the success criteria in vogue in that organization, others want to emulate the practices they embraced in the hope that they too will be successful. But this rarely happens. One of the reasons for this is fear of change. But there are other factors in play here as well. These include the fact that many people in the organization thought there was little chance this project would succeed. That is actually an important asset. This leaves the development team free to be innovative perhaps trying something new. They have nothing to lose because trying something new and unconventional is likely to be overlooked if it fails since it was expected to fail. If it succeeds, others will want to emulate the methods that overcame near-certain disaster. Let's look at what a software development team in that situation is focused on. They are trying something new so they focus on learning how to use the new method or making one up on their own. They are not nearly as focused on successfully bringing the project in on time and budget. There is an important principle involved here that is often overlooked by management [1]. The experience of the Ducati Corse Motorcycle Company may help shed some light on how we can learn from success [1]. The company is based in Bologna, Italy. In 2003, they entered the MotoGP for the first time with low expectations. They viewed this first season as a learning experience. They fitted their bikes with sensors to measure every variable they could. To their surprise, they finished in the top three in nine races and were ranked second overall with the fastest bike overall. At that point, the team began to focus on winning rather than on learning why they did so well. They noted that "You look at the data when you are losing, not when you are winning." At that point, things started to go badly for their team. The next season they went with a bike with 60% of the 915 bike components new. They finished third which was considered a failure causing a reexamination of the team's approach to developing motorcycles. They began the development of their next bike much earlier than ever before, tested and measured everything. They improved in 2005 and 2006 and then took the title in 2007. Researchers have found a similar pattern in many industries including software – that is, success–failure–success (if the company survived). The advisory here is it is dangerous to not determine what it is that makes your team successful. Incorrectly attributing our success to the following can be also dangerous:

- Only to our expertise and our own insights.
- Ignoring factors beyond our control that resulted in the success.
- Taking credit for the team's positive numbers when this could just be due to luck.

Psychologists have proved the preceding are normal but normal or not, the problem remains. How we respond to success can also present us with what seems to be a rational approach but which will get us into trouble. The approach is to let our experience outside of software engineering dictate that in the next project, we do everything the same way as on this successful project. To quote one study, if we do that, the whole exercise is a failure [1]. Why a failure? Even if the next project is very similar to the successful one, the people have (hopefully) learned something and are different. So what should we do? Remembering Heraclitus' [Greek philosopher in Ephesus (present-day Turkey) ~535–475 B.C.] admonition that change is the only constant, look at how we could have done even better than we did. Try to determine what the major contributors to our success were and continue to promote a learning environment. Again, we need to attempt to avoid attributing our success to our (assumed) superior skills. Tinkering with success in this way may cause us to do a little less well but we will be more consistent and at least we will know which project elements should not be fooled with.

References

[1] Gino, F. and Pisano, G., "Why Leaders Don't Learn from Success," *Harvard Business Review*, April 2011.
[2] Weick, K., "Organizational Culture as a Source of High Reliability," *California Management Review*, Vol. 29, No. 2, Winter 1987, pp. 112–127.

Appendix 32

Stoplight Charts

An important part of successfully managing a software project is to know the status of each part of the project continuously. For a number of reasons, verbal statements can be unreliable. Conversely, some software engineers are reluctant to put a status in writing if the status is a negative one. So the first step in obtaining and maintaining project status is to establish an environment within which open, honest communications are encouraged regardless of whether or not they are negative about status or other matters. This approach was popularized by Allan Mulally at the Boeing Company and later at the Ford Corporation. It is commonly referred to as "Stoplight Charts" or "Four Square Statūs Charts." In his acceptance speech on being inducted into the Automotive Hall of Fame in 2006, Mulally related the part these charts played when he first started in his role as Chief Executive Officer (CEO) at Ford. He held a meeting with the heads of all the various project and product efforts. Each manager was to present the status of their effort on a stoplight chart. The status was communicated via one of three colors:

1. Green – Indicating that everything is OK, on plan and so forth.
2. Yellow – There is a problem (s) but we have a solution we are implementing.
3. Red – There is a serious problem(s) for which we have no solution(s) at this time. We could use some help.

After a few presentations, Mulally stopped the proceedings. He noted that all the charts were green and that Ford was projected to lose $17 billion that fiscal year and could potentially be forced into bankruptcy. The attendees were instructed to revise their charts to reflect reality and meet again the next day. The environment at Ford prior to Mulally's arrival was that to report the equivalent of a red status was the first step to losing your job or being demoted. In that second meeting, one of the first presenters was a manager who reported a red status. It had to do with the tailgate on a particular Ford model. The concept was that the driver could push a button and the tailgate would open or close but there was a problem. It wasn't working and the people working on it could not figure out why. Another manager indicated his team had something like that happen in the past and maybe he could send a couple of engineers who had worked on it over to help out. The problem stayed red for a short time, then yellow and finally green. What happened was what Mulally had been espousing, "One Ford." That is everyone working together for the good of the company. This environment of honesty without repercussions helped turn Ford around making them profitable within two years. The preceding experience description has helped confirm my standard operating policy of telling every software engineering team I have managed that if there is a problem, I want to be the first, not the last to know about it. There will be no repercussions to the messenger. This is because my job is to solve problems and help others on the team solve theirs. That is why I believe the patron "saint" of all software project managers should be Ganesha – the Hindu god who is the remover of obstacles. Four square charts are one effective means of getting that early warning that there is a problem and something needs to be done about it before it sabotages the project.

Four square charts have four sections:

1. Goals – A high level summary of the project; it does not change unless the project charter changes.
2. Current Issues – These are the problems currently facing the project – these should change at each review as old ones are resolved and new ones occur.
3. Schedule – A high-level view of the schedule. This may not change much unless a slide in schedule is occurring which should have been mentioned in "Current Issues."
4. Planned Actions – This is a high-level description of what the project team will be doing until the next review – early in the list are actions directed at resolving the listed issues.

A32.1 Example of a Four-Square Chart

This chart (Figure A32.1) is related to developing some property.

As it turned out, the fire department ruling killed the project. They required a 70-foot diameter circle to turn an engine around which left the remaining too small for the needed building sites. In looking at Figure A32.1, we see there is more than a status being documented but the actions, schedules and goals of this part of the effort as well. This simple summary conveys the basics of the task for all to see while inviting possible suggestions for help.

Goals	Current Issues
> Develop half acre property by building a single story home	> Wetlands determination means redesign of site
	> Bids for topographical and survey
> Sell existing home	coming in at double earlier bids

Schedule as of 01 Sep 2023	Planned Actions
Get permits & bids X--------X	> Have vendors re-bid effort
Constructed home X---------X	> Revise site plan
Sell current home X-----X	> Petition city for variance
Final Insp./Move-in X—X	> Appeal fire department ruling

Figure A32.1   Example of a four-square chart.

Appendix 33

The Theory of Constraints

There are many definitions of this theory. The one we will use is based on a seemingly harsh statement:

> In every system (e.g. software engineering team) there are one or more resources which constrain the system to producing less than it could – to maximize productivity (or at least improve it) find that "bottleneck" and neutralize it.

That certainly sounds simple enough but it can yield some surprising results [1, 2]. Let's look at an example. You are running a seaport which has five piers and five teams to unload cargo container ships. It takes five days for one team to unload one ship. If five ships arrive at the same time, the conventional approach would be to assign one team to each ship. But the theory of constraints suggests we put all five teams to work on one ship at a time because our "bottleneck" is the number of teams we have. Is this any better? Table A33.1 compares the conventional approach with the theory of constraints.

When explained verbally, applying constraint theory to this problem produces an unexpected, counterintuitive even surprising result. But like other topics in this book, the data proves otherwise.

Table A33.1   Comparing Theory of Constraints with Conventional Approach Example

Ship Number	Days in Port using Conventional Approach	Days in Port using Constraint Theory Scheme
1	25	5
2	25	10
3	25	15
4	25	20
5	25	25
Totals	125	75

References

[1] Orouji, M., *Theory of Constraints: A State of Art Review*, Growing Science Ltd., 2016.
[2] Goldratt, E.M., *Theory of Constraints*, Croton-on-Hudson, North River, NY, 1990.

Appendix 34

Documenting the Undocumented

Worldwide, there must be billions of lines of source code that are either undocumented, poorly documented or whose documentation has been lost or so out of date as to be of no value. However, this code continues to be used. It is often maintained by one or more of its original authors. Given that in the United States alone, 10,000 people a week are turning 65 years of age which is the most common retirement age, many of these original authors of much of this code are retiring or otherwise becoming unavailable. Many companies are facing the prospect of transferring the maintenance of code that may be a vital part of their business to one or more software engineers with little or no documentation to guide their actions. In one of my consulting engagements, the company was faced with this situation. The last originator of a vital part of their operation who was a lifelong cigarette smoker had to retire due to failing health. The company's concern was that over the years, he had been so busy with legally mandated changes and upgrades that he had not been able to adequately instruct one or more colleagues on how that system was structured, details of why it was organized the way it was and many other important details needed to adequately maintain that code. The company felt obligated to comply with the employee's (we will call him Fred-not his real name) wishes as he had stayed on at the firm well beyond when he had originally intended to retire. Fred's deteriorating health made creating a solution in a timely manner even more urgent. What we did was to make use of some very simple tools which with the cooperation of Fred we were able to create a documentation of the system in a survivable form that could be used by others familiar with the programming language involved. What we did was to video Fred walking us through the various parts of the system. But we did not just video it, we put together a process focused on creating a video that captured the very essence of the system, its idiosyncrasies, how it had evolved, the various programming methods that had been used over the years and more. Here is what we did:

First, we put together a group consisting of a few senior software engineers most of whom were not familiar with the system we were trying to document and the one software engineer who knew the undocumented system well and had been maintaining it for decades. It was decided to reduce cost that we would use in-house personnel to put together the production which included operating a video camera, assisting with flip charts and so forth. We met and decided on some guidelines:

- The system was too large to convey an understanding of it all in one sitting.
- There would be five video sessions corresponding to an overview followed by four separate videos corresponding to the four major parts of the system.

- Fred would be in front of the camera doing the explaining to a few software engineers who would be permitted to ask questions in real time, on-camera about any item in the explanations they needed clarified.
- There would be a 2 foot by 4 foot list of points on a large flip chart off-camera that Fred could use during the video to ensure that important points were incorporated.
- If there were a lot of questions about some portion, it would be reshot with a revised script directed at the clarifications.
- A printout of the code would be provided to each attendee at each of the sessions to enable them to make notes on the source code listing to refer to later.
- There would be a few practice sessions to get Fred comfortable with being videoed and test out the process.

Since the code and videos contained company proprietary information, a restricted list of software engineers would have access via a personal password. The results were validated by having software engineers explain to Fred how the various parts of the system worked and what changes were likely. Fred then advised as to what they omitted or got wrong and the reference video(s) and comments in the source file were changed, as necessary.

Appendix 35

Making Documentation Transparent

The problem with documenting source code after it has been written is that what we document is what the code does, not necessarily why. The "why" is certainly difficult to capture but even the "what" often seems beyond our reach. Besides, documenting out-of-date or legacy code is a long-term investment which is difficult to develop a compelling business case for. I ran into this very problem some years ago. I was engaged as a software project manager to manage a project whose goal was to replace an existing system which had been written 20 years earlier using a proprietary programming language. The company that wrote the code was engaged every year to make changes for which they charged exorbitant fees. The contracting firm sought to replace the system with one written in an available programming language and maintain it themselves. Obviously, this would not only save them money but any needed changes could be made in a timely manner. One stipulation the firm made to me was that the replacement system be well documented. I was well aware of how hard it is to get software engineers to document their code. In addition, I knew that all too often, the documentation only tells me what the code does – not why it was decided to do it that way. To add to the challenge, they were short of staff and the staff they did have had little (less than a year) or no experience developing software in an industrial setting. As I saw it, whatever approach I did come up with had to satisfy four requirements:

1. It had to be an inherent part of the development process – By this, I mean that documentation should not be seen as a separate task but an integral part of the design and development effort.
2. It should be easy to use and keep up-to-date – Documentation is practically worthless if it is so difficult to update that it quickly becomes outdated.
3. It supports the development of test cases – All too often test cases are based on what the code does, not what it was intended to do. If the documentation is in a form that was usable by the subcontracting team tasked with testing the code, it would reduce project flow time. Of course, the key here is the code must correlate to the documentation or we will have created a real mess.
4. The documentation is in a form that is meaningful to software engineers – From experience with textual documentation, it does not communicate well with software engineers. What is needed is something between the stark logic of source code and a textual portrayal of the source code.

In addition to working to meet the preceding requirements, we developed some coding practices and standards, instituted a development process that incorporated walkthroughs so that more than one person was familiar with various parts of the code besides the portion they had volunteered to do and more. At that time, the target language did not support structured programming constructs like IF-THEN-ELSE, DO WHILE, UNTIL DO and others. Working with the development team, we came up with the following scheme:

1. We developed a pseudocode that supported all the structured programming constructs. It was not our intention that this actually execute.
2. We instituted a process in which each functional section of the code was walked through with the rest of the team for approval, interface verification and improvement.
3. Once approved by the team, the pseudocode would become comments for the source code which would be developed by the owner of that portion of the system.
4. The source code would also be walked through by the team to ensure correctness, compliance with our coding standards, ownership documentation, change history and other required information was present as development progressed.
5. Test cases were developed by another team based on the pseudocode. This saved flow time as described in Chapter 2, section 2.8.

Overall, this scheme worked providing embedded documentation together with a learning experience for the team. The most serious problem we had to overcome was that one team member challenged any critique or suggestion to the coding while viciously attacking everyone else's results. The team came to me and announced they would resign from the project unless this person was fired or reassigned off the project. Fortunately, we found an independent research position for this person elsewhere in the firm which they agreed to. Overall, this approach worked by providing in situ documentation, learning for the team members and, most importantly, the team took ownership of this development system at least partly because they participated in its creation rather than having it thrust upon them. This is an important point in that all too often a software project manager will read about some new method that promises high quality and increased source code production and try to impose it on the software engineering team only to meet strong resistance. Encouraging the team rather than demanding they use a predefined development system will reduce resistance to change(s).

Appendix 36

Capability Maturity Model (CMM)

The Capability Maturity Model (1) was originally published 30 years ago by the Software Engineering Institute (SEI) and has been refined several times since. It is based on an ISO concept that is more than 30 years old. ISO's contention is that if you wish to improve the quality of your product(s), you should carefully document the processes used to produce them. That way, if a product is released which has a defect, you can track down where the defect occurred through analysis of the process(s), alter the process to prevent the defect and try again. What the SEI research team found during the development and refinement of CMM was that most software development took place in environments which could most kindly be described as chaotic. That is, there was little or no documentation of the software production process making repeatability and correction of the software production effort impossible. SEI defined five levels ranging from Level 1 – Chaos to Level 5 – Systematic, repeatable and controlled development. The details and the intermediate levels and their characteristics are described in [1].

On the surface, managing a software project sounds relatively simple. Working with your team, you put together a plan and schedule, estimate the cost, get agreement from the client and execute the plan consistent with the schedule. But delve a bit deeper or better yet, talk to someone who has actually managed a software project, and you will discover it is not nearly that simple. Things happen that are totally unpredictable – both positive and negative events. For example, the following happened during some software projects I managed or consulted on:

- A key member of our team was married with two children, had a wife who was working and they barely made ends meet. He inherited a small fortune and moved himself and his family to another part of the country.
- A divorce caused a member of our team to leave the area in order to avoid being reminded of this failed past relationship.
- The woman a team member was engaged to ran off with someone else causing his productivity to plummet.
- A truly brilliant member of our team got hooked on drugs and went in and out of rehabilitation making their present and future contributions problematic.
- The client resolved some budgetary and logistic issues giving us additional funding and flow time to complete the project.

- Due to a sudden, unforeseen negative change in their business, the client canceled the project without notice at about the halfway mark in the schedule.
- A technology breakthrough by another firm who then marketed what we were building marketed it as off-the-shelf software causing our effort to be cancelled.
- Technical breakthroughs enabled us to replan and recost the project reducing the project schedule and cost.

Some of you may have experienced one or more of the above but the point here is that software projects are generally anything but smooth running and under control. This is why the term chaos appears in the title of this book. What we are attempting to do is control what is controllable and adapt as best we can to those events which occur beyond our control. This ability to adapt to the ever-changing landscape of a software project is what really determines success [2]. Some may think that this is unique to software projects but other projects experience the same phenomenon. For example, I assisted the project engineer on a kindergarten through high school construction project for nearly a year. Literally, we had to replan parts of the effort every week. The causes for replanning varied but included weather delays (under certain conditions you cannot pour and finish concrete), subcontractors finishing their work late or early, materials being delivered late due to labor strife, changes in building layout due to lack of compliance with safety regulations, school board directed changes that occurred after construction was underway, delays in getting inspections done and approved and others. This nearly constant state of change may be seen by some as chaotic but the project did finish well but with about a 10–12% budget overrun.

A36.1 How Much CMM Is Enough?

This question is a serious one and it relates to the return on investment made to advance from one CMM level to the next. Based on a survey of 50 companies, the return on investment seems to be the highest early on [2]. That is, making the transition from CMM level 1 to level 2 as shown in Figure A36.1. This seems reasonable since the organization is moving from a poor use of human resources (CMM level 1 – Chaos) to a more efficient one (CMM level 2 – some degree of organization and accountability). It turns out that there is nothing "magic" about any CMM but there is something very powerful. It is that as a team, we examine how we do things and ask,

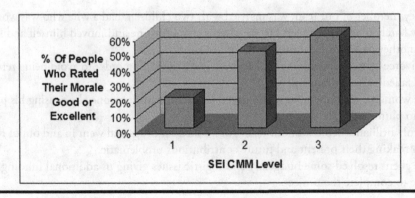

Figure A36.1 CMM transition level with highest return on investment [3].

"Is there a better way?" That encourages participation by everyone almost guaranteeing that they will support the resulting changes. Obviously, this stands a better chance of success than having the changes dictated by management.

References

[1] Paulk, M., Curtis, B., Chrissis, M. and Weber, "Capability Maturity Model for Software, Version 1.1." Technical Report CMU/SEI-93-TR-024, ESC-TR-93-177, Software Engineering Institute, Carnegie Mellon University, Pittsburgh, PA, February, 1993.

[2] Thomas, J. and Mengel, T., "Preparing Project Managers to Deal with Complexity – Advanced Project Management Education," *International Journal of Project Management*, Vol. 26, 2008, pp. 304–315.

[3] McConnell, S., *10 Myths of Rapid Development*, Lecture Presented at Construx, Inc., Bellevue, WA, January, 2003.

Appendix 37

Motivation Basics

Anecdotally, many software project managers have observed that software engineers who are motivated are more productive in terms of volume and quality of source code than software engineers who are not motivated. The term "motivation" has been used in many ways reflecting many different viewpoints. To help focus our discussion, we will use the following definition.

Motivation is the willingness to get the job done by starting rather than procrastinating, persisting in the face of distractions and investing enough mental effort to succeed [1].

It is estimated that motivation accounts for 40% of the success in team efforts [1]. So, if we want to improve our chances of success in software projects, we need to figure out how to motivate our team or at least not demotivate them. Fortunately, demotivators have been organized into four primary categories:

1. Values Mismatch – When a task does not align with what a worker sees as valuable, they are unlikely to be motivated to do it. In the case of software engineers, their value system favors tasks involving the state of the art and/or something they can point out to their colleagues as being important [2]. The way to cope with this is to point out the value of the task and its positive impact on the project.
2. Lack of Self-Efficacy – If a task is such that a worker sees it as being beyond their capability, this reduces their motivation to attempt it [2]. The remedy for this is to assure the software engineer that help will be provided plus working on this will expand their skill set and value to the firm or even other firms.
3. Disruptive Emotions – Software engineers are people and as such can be affected by what is going on in their lives. The remedy for this is to provide a listening resource to reassure them that things will work out. Scheduling a time to meet, providing some time off and other supportive measures can help. The key point here is that the person needs to feel their situation has been understood and their manager is willing to work with them to get through this stressful time.
4. Attribution Errors – This one may be the most common among software engineers. The engineer has worked out how to get this code working but it keeps failing. This calls into question their self-image of competency which drives them to avoid dealing with it. To help remedy this, try working with the individual going through the steps they have taken and offer the assistance of other team members.

The specifics of the preceding categories of motivation inhibitors will vary but the keys to overcoming them mostly involve observing what is going on and performing in the role of servant leader by removing obstacles to high performance by team members.

References

[1] Clark, R. and Saxberg, B., "4 Reasons Good Employees Lose Their Motivation," *Harvard Business Review*, March 13, 2019.
[2] Katz, R., "Motivating Technical Professionals Today," *IEEE Engineering Management Review*, Vol. 41, No. 1, March 2013, pp. 28–37.

Closing Comments

Throughout this book, I have stressed the importance of software project management as well as the need for software project managers to adapt their approach(s) to software project management to the specifics of the project and the people they are managing rather than applying a "one size fits all" formula. That is why a broad spectrum of methods and techniques have been incorporated into this book. When deciding if and when to use one of these methods, it is advisable to ignore its source and focus on whether or not it is likely to help you solve some problem that prompted you to select one or more of these methods in the first place. If you are new to software project management or are already a software project manager, remember, in order to make a change, you must want to change. As Heraclitus was quoted as saying, "Change is the only constant."

I wish you the best of luck in life and your software project management career.

Lawrence J. Peters

Chapter Questions and Suggested Answers

Chapter 1 Review Questions/Answers

1. Is the subject and practice of software project management, and its development actively supported by the IEEE Software Engineering Society? Explain your answer.

   Suggested Answer: The IEEE Software Engineering Society is almost exclusively focused on the technology involved in creating software. Software project management has yet to play a major role in IEEE Software Engineering Society publications and annual conferences.

2. In what way does one's viewpoint in moving from being a software engineer to a software project manager?

   Suggested Answer: Software engineering involves following a relatively well-defined path from concept to working code. The viewpoint is the code, the syntax and semantics and the desired functionality. The software project manager's viewpoint is somewhat analogous to that of the conductor of an orchestra in the focus is on synchronizing and coordinating the activities of the members of the software engineering team in order to arrive at a successful outcome. The path to achieve this varies from project to project and software engineering team to team. Another way to see this is the software project manager is focused on the project-wide picture, not the details of the source code.

3. When Barry Boehm developed COCOMO and later its successor, he assumed he did not have to consider software project management because he assumed a cadre of competent software project managers existed. What did a later analysis of COCOMO variables show?

   Suggested Answer: It showed that the variables that made up COCOMO were actually management related. So much so that they outnumbered members of all other categories combined.

4. How could the transition from software engineer to software project manager be best conveyed?

   Suggested Answer: Software project management is not a profession one can acquire skills in through "on the job" learning. That is where we are today with managers picking up tips from other self-taught managers leading to more and more antipatterns. The best way to prevent this would be training classes to convey the basic principles of successful software project management.

5. What is the most effective leadership style and how does it work?

   Suggested Answer: Studies have shown that the "servant-leader" style is the most effective. That leadership style involves the manager being a servant of sorts in that the manager's role is to work to remove any obstacles that are preventing individuals or the team from performing at their highest level.

6. Do software project managers need to be trained for their leadership role?

   Suggested Answer: Software project managers are not born, they are trained. That training would cover the five basic functions of software project management – Planning, Scheduling, Controlling, Staffing and Motivating.

7. What keeps teams from learning if they have been successful?

   Suggested Answer: The adage "We learn from failure" implies that we don't learn from success. Why don't some teams learn from success? Studies have shown that a major part of the reason why we don't learn from success is that we give too much credit to our own skills and downplay the fact that our success may just be due to luck. This includes attributing part of our success to the use of some new software tool or method.

8. In what way can software development and its management be characterized as "wicked?"

   Suggested Answer: Software projects do not, generally, have right or wrong answers to decisions. As a problem set, they change with time and they have multiple facets which are all linked together.

9. Name two personality characteristics that make software engineers unique among professionals and a challenge to manage?

   Suggested Answer: The characteristics are: (1) High Growth Needs Strength (the need to solve challenging problems) and (2) Low Social Needs Strength (the preference to solve problems by themselves).

10. What was unique about the experience at Google? What can we learn from it?

    Suggested Answer: They started without managers and later they discovered they needed them. They have instituted a system which has a clear path to become a manager – training and evaluation.

11. Name the five primary functions of software project management.

    Suggested Answer: The primary functions of software project management are planning, scheduling (including costing), controlling, staffing and motivating.

Chapter 2 Review Questions/Answers

1. What did General Dwight Eisenhower mean by "Plans are nothing, planning is everything?"

   Suggested Answer: He certainly did not mean we should not plan. What he was advising us was that planning is a continuous, ongoing activity because unforeseen, unplanned events will happen which will require us to replan the effort and this will happen throughout the course of the project.

2. Has it ever been documented and verified that the life cycle of a software project used caused the project to fail?

   Suggested Answer: To the best of my knowledge and many varied Google searches, the life cycle used has not been found to have caused a software project to fail.

3. What is the overwhelming cause of software project failure?

   Suggested Answer: Based on a study of failed software projects by IBM, the overwhelming cause for software project failure (53%) has been "poor management."

4. Approximately how many different software development life cycles are there?

   Suggested Answer: That number is likely unknown because the life cycle declared for a project is often an altered, perhaps unique life cycle tailored to that software project.

5. List at least four stages in a software project life cycle.

   Suggested Answer: Any four of the following software project life cycle stages will do:

   Planning

   Scheduling (and Costing)

   Designing

   Implementing

   Testing

   Deploying

   And over the long term, support and maintenance.

6. What is the planning fallacy? Explain.

   Suggested Answer: Some project managers believe that starting with a software engineering team larger than what is actually needed will serve to prevent the project from overrunning its allocated schedule. This is a fallacy because studies have shown that when it comes to the size of a development team, there is a law of diminishing returns. That is the effect of each person added beyond what is reasonably seen as what is needed provides less and less positive effect.

7. List the two primary reasons why humans can't estimate accurately.

   Suggested Answer: A 20-year study resulting in a Nobel prize found that the two factors are: 1) Overestimation of our skills and 2) seeing the benefits of the project to be so great as to cause us to miss the risks involved.

8. What was the primary goal of the Gantt chart?

   Suggested Answer: Gantt sought to visually combine flow time for the project and its tasks with costs.

9. Is the Agile life cycle unique? If yes, how? If not, why?

   Suggested Answer: The underlying principle of Agile actually dates back to the early 1980s and is not unique.

10. Name two concerns about using and managing Agile. Explain/describe each.

    Suggested Answer: Although Agile represents an advance of the state of the art, it comes with a couple of issues. One is that it needs to be employed by a disciplined team of software engineers or it could result in runaway coding. The other is that our clients still need to know at the outset what the estimated cost of the project will be and Agile does not solve this problem. Teams using Agile are still left to their own devices to estimate the project's total cost at the start.

11. What are "gates" in the stage-gate life cycle? Detail/describe.

    Suggested Answer: In the manufacture of large systems (e.g. aircraft), subsystems such as the wings are created only after all of the required preceding engineering, parts, personnel and tools are in place to do the job. Once that is the case, the manufacturer can proceed through that "gate" to the next stage. Similarly, in software, the confirmation that all is in place to move forward in a coordinated manner is a stage-gate scheme. The goal and desired effect are to prevent runaway development and ensure software subsystems are developed in a synchronized manner.

12. List and describe the pros and cons of three ways to shorten a software project's flow time.

    Suggested Answer:

    - Where possible have more tasks occur in parallel – This takes careful attention to detail so that we do not have some tasks occur earlier or later than they should.
    - Eliminate or delay features, particularly the ones most likely to run late and/or require the most labor – However, this can be demotivating to the team members who worked to design and build the feature(s) being eliminated or delayed.
    - Reduce the scope of the effort.

13. What is the Design Structure Matrix? What is it used for?

    Suggested Answer: The design structure matrix is a means of documenting the relationships between/among system elements. It has been used to optimize flow times and optimize the order in which tasks are performed in a broad range of applications.

14. What is a work breakdown structure?

    Suggested Answer: It is a graphic decomposition of a project into tasks, subtasks and sub-subtasks down to a subtask requiring eight hours or more but not broken down into smaller pieces upon the advice of the project management society in the PMBOK.

15. What are the primary causes of a communication gap between software engineers and software project managers?

    Suggested Answer: The primary causes are differences in the value systems between the two groups.

16. Why should we develop a communication plan to foster communication between our team and our client?

    Suggested Answer: Not all clients have the same communication preferences. Putting a communication plan together ensures we have developed a model of how the client wants to be communicated with rather than applying a "one size fits all" approach.

Chapter 3 Review Questions/Answers

1. What is the difference between planning and scheduling?

    Suggested Answer: A plan is, in simplest terms, a list of tasks to be performed whereas a schedule details when they will be performed and in what order.

2. What is the problem with using a "generic" software engineer as the basis for estimating?

    Suggested Answer: As Brooks pointed out, even though we may be stating that a competent software engineer should be able to do this task in the estimated flow time, we are actually thinking of a specific individual. Naming the person who will do this task avoids this. Also, the estimating activity can be a learning experience if we ask the individual what their estimate is.

3. What is the business case?

    Suggested Answer: The business case is the justification for the project. It describes the purpose, cost, risks and potential revenue associated with the project. If it is being proposed as a community service, the profit issue is not addressed.

4. What is the role of the business case in the development of a software project?

    Suggested Answer: The business case not only justifies the project but defines its scope, concept, costs, risks and (if it is to be a commercial venture) potential sales and profit.

5. Name the four viewpoints of the Balanced Scorecard?

    The four dimensions of the balanced scorecard are:

    - Customer – How it will affect the people who use it?
    - Financial – The profit/loss tradeoff involved once this system is released.
    - Organizational – The structural or other changes that must be made to implement this system.
    - Educational – The amount of training our team will need to implement as well (potentially) as training of the users of the system.

6. What is meant by the term "Burdened Cost?"

Suggested Answer: The "burdened" cost of an item or service represents what it actually costs the company consisting of the direct cost, general and administrative cost and, where applicable, the overhead plus profit.

7. What is the purpose of using the Burdened Cost when estimating a software project?

Suggested Answer: If we only estimated using direct costs, we would, in effect, be subsidizing our client since we would not be recovering our operating expenses via our pricing structure.

8. Why aren't there any accurate software project estimating methods?

Suggested Answer: Although some estimating methods are more accurate than others, as shown via a Nobel Prize study in 2002, human beings are not capable of estimating accurately. However, there is a way to correct for this.

9. Why do we base software project cost estimates based on lines of code?

Suggested Answer: This has been the convention used for decades but has some serious shortcomings. When asked about coding changes or new efforts, most software engineers give estimates in flow time, not lines of source code.

10. What is the difference between Direct and Indirect costs?

Suggested Answer: Direct cost is what we actually pay for an item or service. Indirect cost is the cost incurred in order to make that payment.

11. What is the difference between Overhead (OH) and General and Administrative (G&A) costs?

Suggested Answer: G&A is the cost we incur whether we have any business (contracts) or not. It is the cost of just keeping the doors of our business open. We incur OH when we have a business (e.g. a contract) to perform on.

12. When outsourcing, what are some of the forms of "Due Diligence" that are needed?

Suggested Answer: An alternate way to view due diligence is to see it as what we need to check out before agreeing to a legally binding contract. The potential issues that should be resolved in advance include:

   - Has the firm you will use done this type of software development before? Who did they do it for? Can we contact that client to see if they were satisfied with the results?
   - If there is a dispute requiring legal proceedings, will they be conducted in your country, near your location?
   - Do they agree to an escrow arrangement?

There are others as well.

Chapter 4 Review Questions/Answers

1. In Earned Value Management (EVM), what is the concept of "value?"

Suggested Answer: The entire concept of EVM is based on ratios of what was planned or expected to what actually occurred. The notion of value stems from the ratio or percent obtained versus a value representing 100%. For example, if we spent $100 in one store to purchase an item which we could have purchased in another store for $80, which store represented a better value – obviously the second store.

2. What information is needed to use EVM?

Suggested Answer: We need to have a project plan complete with costs, schedule and status of tasks to date. The various EVM parameters can be computed for use if we are using one of the project management software products such as Primavera, Microsoft Project or others.

3. In Earned Value Management (EVM), what is the concept of "value?"

   Suggested Answer: In a sense, EVM is all about ratios. The notion of value mathematically is about the ratio of what we planned versus what we actually got. For example, if we purchase a product at one store for $100 which we could have gotten at another for $80, we received only an 80% value. In a project analogy, if we expected a task to take 80 hours and it took 100 hours, again we achieved less than our expected full efficiency – it was only 80%.

4. If a project is 15% complete and over budget and/or behind schedule, without changing budget, schedule or requirements, what are its chances of eventually getting back on schedule and/or within budget?

   Suggested Answer: A study of more than 700 projects ranging from high technology to low technology found its chances of recovering are nil. That is right, it has not been recorded as ever having happened.

5. What underlying assumptions comprise EVM?

   Suggested Answer: The major underlying assumption within EVM is that our project plan (i.e. costs, flowtime task completions, etc.) is makeable.

Chapter 5 Review Questions/Answers

1. Name the three attributes common to successful high-technology project teams.

   Suggested Answer: These traits were found to be common:
   - Each member of the team had some knowledge of the technology involved. None of them were considered to be "experts" in that technical area.
   - Members had experience working on a team, not necessarily with each other.
   - The members had compatible personalities as measured with the Myers–Briggs Type Indicator (MBTI) or some other personality type and compatibility measurement system.

2. What does psychological compatibility mean?

   Suggested Answer: Regardless of which personality profiling model is used, there will be some personalities which do not work well with others and other personalities which work well together. This is compatibility and it can help or hinder the performance of the software engineering team.

3. What should you do if you have one or more team members who are incompatible with each other or other team members?

   Suggested Answer: It is not always possible to have a team of people whose personality profiles are compatible. In some cases, group counseling will help soothe the effects of the incompatibilities while in others a change in work assignments may be indicated if counseling does not work.

4. What role should the compatibility index play in the hiring process?

   Suggested Answer: The personality profile is only one element involved in the hiring decision and should not be the primary one. Some brilliant people are hard to work with but can contribute significantly to an effort if managed carefully.

5. In making team member task assignments, what role should the MBTI or other profiles you may be using play?

   Suggested Answer: A software engineer's personality profile has been shown to be a significant factor in one's performance because there are some tasks which their personality causes them to prefer and others that they do not desire. Working on what they prefer results in better performance. Since it may not always be possible to provide work an individual would prefer, mitigating the undesirable assignment in some way (e.g. making it temporary) would be an alternative action.

Chapter 6 Review Questions/Answers

1. What is the least effective form of motivation for software engineers?

   Suggested answer: Though the common belief among software project managers is to the contrary, the least effective motivating action is to reward with money. Studies have shown money is an effective motivator only in repetitive work like factory work and developing software is anything but repetitive.

2. What is the most effective form of motivation for software engineers?

   Suggested answer: Surprisingly to some, studies have shown the most effective motivator to be to thank the software engineer(s) for their efforts. Though it is free, it means more to the software engineers probably because it comes from the software project manager personally. The contrarian notion is that since we are paying the engineers to do the work, we don't have to thank is out of step with reality.

3. What do software engineers really want to work on?

   Suggested answer: Software engineers want to work on state-of-the-art technical systems – ones they can brag about to their colleagues. The challenge for the software project manager is that not all projects are going to be pushing the state of the art forward.

4. Why do software project managers continue to rely on money as a motivator?

   Suggested answer: The value system of the software project manager places money as the highest priority. That combined with a lack of knowledge of what the studies regarding motivating software engineers tell us predetermines many software project managers to continue to rely on money to motivate.

5. What are three practices that demotivate software engineers?

   Suggested answer: Any three of these will do

   - Technically high-risk requirements
   - High-risk schedule
   - Inadequate staffing
   - Inadequate resources
   - Software quality (lacking)
   - Reduction of features

6. Why do test teams need special attention to be motivated?

   Suggested answer: The people who test software are often viewed negatively by software engineers. This is because the test team is finding their mistakes and no one really likes to have their mistakes pointed out. To provide the test team with support, we need to educate the development team and management as to the fact that the test team is actually saving the company large amounts of money since fixing software after it has been released has been shown to be very expensive.

7. What is the motivation paradox?

   Suggested answer: The motivation paradox states that the most expensive means often used to motivate software engineers (money) is the least effective (saying thank you) and is the most effective.

8. Why do people work?

   Suggested answer: People work for more than just survival. They work for self-esteem, self-fulfillment and other factors related to how they see themselves in relation to the world.

9. Why should we keep software engineering teams together?

Suggested answer: When software engineers work together, they learn what knowledge areas each person is strongest in and conversely. What happens is, in a manner of speaking the team becomes something akin to a super software engineer. If we break up the team, we lose that knowledge and its benefits resulting in members of the team becoming individual contributors with their unique strengths and weaknesses.

10. Do all generations work the same way and have the same value systems?

Suggested answer: The simple answer is no. The more accurate answer is that each generation views the employee–employer relationship differently as reflected in their value systems and their relationship with management and their response to management directives.

11. How likely is it that you will be managing software engineers from different generations?

Suggested answer: No matter what country you are working in, it is highly likely you will be managing a team composed of software engineers from different cultures. Therefore, it is vital that we become familiar with the idiosyncrasies of each culture involved in order to improve our chances of success.

12. How does the physical environment the software engineers are working in impact productivity?

Suggested answer: Developing software often requires intense mental focus on the task at hand. Noise, interruptions, cramped space and other physical factors can inhibit the software engineer from performing at the highest level they are capable of.

13. Name some aspects of outsourcing often overlooked.

Suggested answer: Software engineering is being taught in colleges and universities all around the world. While the relative quality of the instruction varies, the goal of outsourcing is often to reduce cost. However, more recent experiences with outsourcing has shown there are many factors often overlooked which complicate the relationship. These include:

 – Geopolitical issues that may make dealing with the country involved impossible or illegal.
 – Time differences between your location and the outsourced firm's.
 – Costs and requirements for escrowing.
 – The reliability of the outsourced firm as well as their viability.
 – The strength of the protection(s) for intellectual property in both countries.
 – Where legal disputes will be pursued.

14. How can you prevent creating a team just like yourself?

Suggested answer: When selecting team members, there is a tendency to select people who are similar to ourselves. This creates a dilemma since we need a team composed of complementary skills with different strengths and weaknesses personnel hiring firms can be engaged to help with this.

Index

Pages in *italics* refer to figures and pages in **bold** refer to tables.

Printed in the United States
by Baker & Taylor Publisher Services